THE CINEMA OF
EXTRACTIONS

FILM AND CULTURE

FILM AND CULTURE

A SERIES OF COLUMBIA UNIVERSITY PRESS
Edited by John Belton

George Cukor's People: Acting for a Master Director, by Joseph McBride

Death by Laughter: Female Hysteria and Early Cinema, by Maggie Hennefeld

The Rebirth of Suspense: Slowness and Atmosphere in Cinema, by Rick Warner

Hollis Frampton: Navigating the Infinite Cinema, by Michael Zryd

Perplexing Plots: Popular Storytelling and the Poetics of Murder, by David Bordwell

Horror Film and Otherness, by Adam Lowenstein

Hollywood's Embassies: How Movie Theaters Projected American Power Around the World, by Ross Melnick

Music in Cinema, by Michel Chion

Bombay Hustle: Making Movies in a Colonial City, by Debashree Mukherjee

Absence in Cinema: The Art of Showing Nothing, by Justin Remes

Hollywood's Artists: The Directors Guild of America and the Construction of Authorship, by Virginia Wright Wexman

Film Studies, second edition, by Ed Sikov

Anxious Cinephilia: Pleasure and Peril at the Movies, by Sarah Keller

For a complete list of books in the series,
please see the Columbia University Press website.

THE CINEMA OF EXTRACTIONS

**FILM MATERIALS
AND THEIR FORMS**

BRIAN JACOBSON

Columbia University Press   *New York*

Columbia University Press
Publishers Since 1893
New York   Chichester, West Sussex

Copyright © 2025 Columbia University Press
All rights reserved

Library of Congress Cataloging-in-Publication Data
Names: Jacobson, Brian R., author.
Title: The cinema of extractions : film materials and their forms / Brian Jacobson.
Description: New York : Columbia University Press, 2025. | Series: Film and culture. | Includes bibliographical references and index.
Identifiers: LCCN 2024035430 | ISBN 9780231213585 (hardback) | ISBN 9780231213592 (trade paperback) | ISBN 9780231559928 (ebook)
Subjects: LCSH: Motion pictures—Production and direction. | Mineral industries in motion pictures. | Industrial films.
Classification: LCC PN1995.9.P7 J2125 2025 | DDC 791.4302/32—dc23/eng/20240828
LC record available at https://lccn.loc.gov/2024035430

Cover design: Elliott S. Cairns

CONTENTS

Acknowledgments vii

Introduction: Extractive and Extracted Media   1

1 Early Cinemas of Extraction   28

2 From Extractions to Resource Integration   49

3 Mining Media, or, Elemental Energy for Motion Pictures   77

4 Industrial Film's Spectacular and Prosaic Poetics   107

Conclusion: Counter-Cinemas of Extraction   139

Notes 161
Bibliography 197
Index 215

ACKNOWLEDGMENTS

Acknowledgments tend to emphasize one definition of the verb *acknowledge* ("to own or recognize with gratitude, or as an obligation"), and I, too, have much gratitude (and a few obligations) to express. But to acknowledge is also to "accept or admit the existence or truth of"—or in other words, tracking back to the Latin *confitērī* ("acknowledge"), to confess. So let me begin with a confession: I didn't mean to write this book. I was—still am—writing a longer one about the visual culture that developed in and around the French oil and gas industry after World War II. That book's more capacious engagement with visual materials and methods pushed me to reflect on how cinema and media studies has approached extraction and materiality, and this book is the product of that reflection and a companion to the now-delayed book to come.

Because it emerged out of a longer-term project, this book's debts quickly outpaced its size. First and foremost, I want to thank those who read every word. Vanessa Schwartz—lodestar, superego, and somehow both the angel and the devil on my shoulder—always pushes me harder than anyone to make the work better. I am an ever-grateful beneficiary of her vast knowledge, demanding rigor, and penetrating skepticism. Jennifer Fay's work has been an important model and inspiration, and her readings of the manuscript provided encouragement while also pushing me in just the right directions.

John Belton was the first person to read the book and helped steer it at every stage with sage guidance and valuable connections. I am also grateful to two anonymous readers for their support and for pushing back on key points. To Reader #2, let us indeed "rise to the challenges of the fucked-up world we live in."

The editorial team at Columbia has once again been a delight to work with. Philip Leventhal quickly saw this project's potential, and our years of conversation have shaped all my work. Philip and John Belton made the Film and Culture Series this book's best home.

For assistance with image reproductions, I thank Sandra Loupe and Laurent Mannoni at the Cinémathèque française, Heather Todd at the Eastern California Museum, the staff of the Celeste Bartos International Film Study Center at the Museum of Modern Art, New York, and Sanaz Sohrabi.

The book began as a speculative proposal for the New Perspectives on Early Cinema History conference held at Ghent University in November 2018. I am grateful to Mario Slugan and Daniël Biltereyst for sparking the idea and to them and all the conference attendees, especially Martin Johnson and Charlie Keil, for early conversations. An opportune trip to Frankfurt and to the Histories of Film History conference at the University of Marburg the following month helped me begin to connect the dots between early cinema and extraction, industrial/corporate film, and broader questions about film historical method. Deepest thanks to Vinzenz Hediger for hosting me in Frankfurt and for many years of influential conversations going back to the Films That Work Harder conference and to Malte Hagener, Yvonne Zimmermann, and Alena Strohmaier for their generous hospitality in Marburg.

Much of the research for the book was completed during my time at the University of Toronto in the Cinema Studies Institute (CSI) and History Department. I owe special thanks to CSI directors Charlie Keil and Corinn Columpar for facilitating my work and to the Connaught Fund and the Social Science and Humanities

Research Council for material support. My Toronto colleagues and graduate students, especially Meghan Romano, who read parts of the manuscript in progress, created a rich environment for the project's development. I miss you all dearly.

I wrote the book at the California Institute of Technology and thank successive Humanities and Social Sciences chairs Jean-Laurent Rosenthal and Tracy Dennison for their support. I am tremendously grateful to my new colleagues, especially Dehn Gilmore (colleague extraordinaire), Jennifer Jahner, Cathy Jurca, Nicolás Wey-Gómez, Hillary Mushkin, Jed Buchwald, and Diana Kormos-Buchwald for welcoming me so warmly into this formidable intellectual community. Thanks also to Ross Melnick, J. D. Connor, and J. V. Decemvirale for helping me see how Pasadena could be a new intellectual home.

Important parts of the book also came together during fellowship visits to the University of Cambridge, and I am grateful to Cambridge Visual Culture and its directors, Donal Cooper, Caroline Vout, and Amy Tobin, for the opportunity. John David Rhodes was a most welcoming and gracious host and an important intellectual interlocutor. Xin Peng gave me a valuable opportunity to test out ideas with graduate students, and I also thank Jules O'Dwyer, Damien Pollard, Kareem Estefan, Georgina Evans, Laura McMahon, and Olga Smith for helpful conversations during my visits. Alex Gushurst-Moore masterfully coordinated everything.

The graduate students in Vanessa Schwartz's VISS501 seminar at the University of Southern California gave me confidence that I was doing something right, as did the attendees in Bristol at Film Studios: Histories, Evolution, Innovation, Futures, where I especially benefited from conversations with Weihong Bao and the inimitable Noa Steimatsky. Special thanks to Sarah Street, Richard Farmer, Carla Mereu Keating, and the rest of the Studiotec team. Chapter 3 was substantially enriched by Paul Rayton, who kindly shared his memories of the ins and outs of working with carbons as chief projectionist at the Egyptian Theatre in Los Angeles. Chapter 4 benefited from feedback at the Media and/as Infrastructure conference organized by Tanya Goldman, Joni Hayward Marcum, and Meghan Romano and at World Picture 2022, especially including an important conversation with Scott Richmond. A discussion with Brian Larkin late in the revision process helped me clarify part of the introduction.

This (academic) life has been made indelibly better by Brian Price, true friend and confrère. Laura Kalba and Nadya Bair inspire me to work harder and be better. James Cahill—Derrida to my Deleuze—has been with me since the early days as a friend, colleague, and now a fellow member of the collective of incredible colleagues with whom I have been fortunate to think deeply about environmental film and media: Weihong Bao, Jennifer Fay, Yuri Furuhata, Katerina Korola, Debashree Mukherjee, and Jennifer Lynn Peterson. For enduring friendship and support, I also want to thank Anne Aghion, Grazia Ingravalle, Jeff Menne, Joshua Neves, Justus Nieland, Tom Rice, Wilfrid Rouff, Eric Smoodin, Tim Vermeulen, and Jennifer Wild.

To my parents, who would see me more if I wrote less, thank you for being there. To Catherine, always my favorite, *le voyage continue*. This book is for Wilfrid—let's go everywhere.

THE CINEMA OF EXTRACTIONS

INTRODUCTION
Extractive and Extracted Media

Looking back on the early days of Hollywood in his 1959 film *The Chaplin Revue*, the eponymous Tramp offered viewers a sarcastically nostalgic account of California in 1915, "with its sun-kissed oranges and lemon groves, before it was visited by the three horsemen of the apocalypse: oil, movies, and aeronautics, who strode the earth uprooting the orange and the lemon trees, and in their stead built factories and motion picture studios." Offering as evidence his own studio (figure 0.1), which rises like magic from a citrus grove quickly cleared by explosions, Charlie Chaplin proudly confesses: "I was one of the offenders."[1] The studio's accelerated appearance underscores Chaplin's insistence on the immediacy of film's (and oil's and aeronautics') arrival in Los Angeles, a city quickly defined by factories and motion picture studios—or factories that *were* studios, as they soon became popularly known in that lasting metaphor: the "dream factory."

Linking oil, movies, and aeronautics, Chaplin cannily recognized with critical hindsight that cinema's industrialization in southern California should not—and could not—be separated from the concurrent industrial transformation of the region. This transformation would go on to make it a hub in the twentieth-century remaking of Los Angeles—and the world more broadly—in the image and

FIGURE 0.1 *The Chaplin Revue* (dir. Charlie Chaplin, 1959), footage from *How to Make Movies* (1918).

infrastructure of oil, movies, and aeronautics. That configuration has had long staying power and continues to shape mediated experience in our time. As Vanessa Schwartz argues in *Jet Age Aesthetic*, the virtual networked experience that defines twenty-first-century life has roots in the midcentury expansion of aeronautics, which drew on and gave new life to the virtual mobility offered by the movies—all underpinned by oil.[2] Wizened by years of working at their intersection, Chaplin was particularly well positioned to recognize that the jet age's new aesthetics and experiences of real and virtual mobility had emerged from that earlier triangulation of movies, oil, and airplanes that shaped his career's origins.

This book is about how we think about and read movies, resources such as oil, and industries such as aeronautics together. It explores this way of thinking and reading under the more general rubric of "extractions," a term that has gained increasing importance in the humanities in recent years as scholars have made the material and environmental origins and consequences of culture—including its intersections and entanglements with various extractive industries, especially petroleum but also coal and other mined materials (as well as labor, data, and more conceptual resources)—key areas of inquiry.[3] Focusing on cinema and media studies, *The Cinema of Extractions* synthesizes and extends, by way of reading across and between, recent developments that have made materiality, infrastructure, and industrial and corporate media important but largely distinct areas of research that have also moved the field away from the analysis of moving-image texts.[4] The book has two broad goals: first, to unite these subfields by emphasizing cinema's role, in both its industrial and popular theatrical modes, as a literal, virtual, and conceptual world-making system and, second, to extend work on materiality, infrastructure, and industrial and corporate film by reconnecting it to feature fiction films and the broader field's longstanding strength in analyses of textual forms.

The unifying rubric—the cinema of extractions—names the historical conditions from which cinema emerged and through which it has continued to operate in its industrial forms. Building on the insight of the early film historians who so persuasively positioned cinema's origins in the industrial, commercial, intellectual, social, and cultural contexts of modernity, it narrows in on a specific structuring element of that modernity's industrial mass culture and its forms of technologically mediated experience.[5] Extraction fueled modernity and shaped its culture. In turn, modern culture, especially including cinema, a "specific art of the machine," as Lewis Mumford wrote, helped shape and extend extractive industries' image for a blossoming twentieth-century visual culture.[6] The cinema of extractions thus also names a category of film (with early, feature fiction, documentary, and industrial iterations) that expressed, promoted, probed, criticized, or otherwise explored that condition, sometimes reflexively, other times unconsciously, and whose significance is clarified when read historically, materially, formally, and allegorically. By outlining this condition and category, I intend this book to be a tool for research and teaching as well as a provocation for further work in three areas:

industrial film, a subfield that would benefit from a formalist turn; neoformalist film studies, in which feature films dominate and history and politics have at times been marginalized; and analyses of extraction (or what I will also describe as "raw materialism"), which have often tended, much like film ecocriticism in its early iterations, to focus only on representations or, when attentive to materiality, to produce ontological or neopositivist claims without connecting them to moving-image media texts.

Recent work in cinema and media studies has fruitfully pursued a well-established materialist approach to new ends, including research on environmental media and sustainability as well as architecture, infrastructure, and production studies' and media industry studies' attention to the conditions of film and media creation. The parallel emergence of the subfield devoted to industrial and corporate media has similarly used studies of industrial context to show that the work of film and media—or their "usefulness"—extends much further than popular media or documentary scholarship once recognized. These subfields share an attention to the political economy and material and social underpinnings that make visual media an essential component of modern economic exchange that we miss if we study only popular film industries and their products or deploy only the methods of textual analysis.[7] Put another way, scholars focused on materials, technologies, and the work behind the scenes have made clear that formal analysis of films alone has limits and those focused on nonfilm industries have underscored the importance of film's role beyond the film business.

These developments are not new. Cinema and media studies has long been shaped by a productive tension between, on the one hand, text-focused, often theoretical—and at times ahistorical—interests in film representations and their forms and, on the other, materialist and historical materialist emphases on machines, modes of production, and conditions of reception that have at times strategically downplayed texts and their analysis in the interest of focusing on historical context (including intellectual and theoretical contexts). During the 1980s, the balance in cinema studies shifted toward a method that shared with new historicism and the social history of art an increased attentiveness to a contextualized text, greater awareness of the importance of reception, and a differentiated view of the spectator. This work included new attention to film's technical histories that expanded—especially as the field began to grapple with its relationship to media studies—to situate cinema in more broadly conceived histories of technology, industry, and infrastructure.[8] When understood as part of this lineage of histories that have emphasized cinema's technological ontology (or essence as a media system), studying extraction marks not so much new ground as one endpoint of methods that have divided and subdivided this medium into its most basic underlying technical—and now raw material—units.[9]

At its limit, this turn to raw materials represents the logical outcome of the long move away from textual interpretation. As Thomas Elsaesser already recognized in his 1986 description of the "New Film History," for cinema studies, a field at the time arguably overinvested in the text, shifting the focus to context risked overcorrecting to the point that the text may have disappeared altogether.[10] The parallel emergence of media studies, especially the German tradition often associated with Friedrich Kittler, gave the now-converging fields—cinema *and* media studies—additional conceptual motivation to turn away from text-centered analysis. By defining media in terms of their hardware and categories such as inscription, storage, and transmission, Kittler forged a critical materialist path away from hermeneutic traditions of interpretation.[11] No longer the primary site where meaning was negotiated, the text could fade into the background of technical and discursive analyses focused instead on media technologies' "underlying discursive operations and materialities."[12]

One outcome of this anti- or more-than-textual turn has been the valuable growth of histories that look "past the screen," including those that offer another way of approaching what Karen Redrobe has well described as "the way cinema's high and hybrid technology binds it inextricably, if complexly, to capitalism's industrial system."[13] But it has also heightened longstanding methodological tensions and expanded the increasing gap between textual and contextual approaches, especially in cinema and media studies' more text-agnostic subfields and in certain calls for a return to ahistorical formalism. Working in that growing—and sometimes seemingly irreconcilable—space, in this book, I propose a framework for formal analysis informed (rather than sidelined) by new kinds of material and technical knowledge. This includes, especially, what we might term a "raw materialism" focused on the furthest ends of cinema and media's industrial supply chains.

The Cinema of Extractions returns, in particular, to the insight of the social history of art and the work of visual studies scholars who long ago articulated a method for reading visual texts as what Michael Baxandall, writing about fifteenth-century paintings, has described as "the deposit of a social relationship" or through what Svetlana Alpers summarizes as a method for "gain[ing] access to images through a consideration of their place, role, and presence in the broader culture."[14] The reading method pioneered by Baxandall, Alpers, and other art historians emphasized the complex relationships among artists, their patrons or clients, and the knowledge and expectations viewers brought to visual objects. Learning about the social, economic, and political contexts in which art was made and seen—and not just the history and aesthetic lineages of art—offered an important method for analyzing art's formal features, even those forms furthest removed from our own social and cultural context and visual lexicon. It also showed not just how art came to have meaning but also how, through its visual forms, art did work in the world—insight perhaps especially valuable today for a cinema and media studies ever more invested in "useful" cinema and "films that work."

Visual form, as these scholars demonstrate, had its roots in the relative scarcity and value (real or perceived) of the materials artists used (stone, canvas, pigments, and dyes) and in the social, economic, scientific, and political forms their works expressed, historical knowledge of which made them differently legible. As Baxandall emphasized, the reverse was also possible: "the forms and styles of painting," he argues, "may sharpen our perception of the society."[15] In many ways, these insights became the internalized, unspoken basis for subsequent generations of materialist visual analysis.[16] But as some scholars in art history and cinema and media studies have turned their attention more to the raw materials than the visual texts of art and media, some of that method's insights about visual form have faded into the background of a renewed emphasis on material context severed from its textual implications. The upshot may be greater knowledge about those contexts, but we should not miss the opportunity to put this new knowledge into that interpretive circuit, recognized by Baxandall, between the social and material realities of art production and reception, the forms and styles of the art, and back again.

At stake in this book, then, is an opportunity to reconsider how cinema and media scholars navigate the productive methodological space between text and context and what directions may be opened by new knowledge about cinema and media technologies and industries' debt to raw materials and the industries that extract them. More specifically, by focusing on those materials, the book seeks a better way of understanding how extractive industries simultaneously became the structuring basis for cultural technologies such as film and television; used those technologies to promote their work and conceal it behind spectacle; and became visible and knowable not just in their own audiovisual texts but also in the textual products of the cultural industries they make possible.

Priya Jaikumar and Lee Grieveson have emphasized that "the goal [of studying extraction] is not to neglect the aesthetic and experiential dimensions of cinematic images or digital screens but to also heed to the geological and material histories that bring them to us."[17] The result of this often-productive methodological shift—which, I should emphasize, has driven much of my own research—has nevertheless been to draw attention away from films, emphasizing context over text. This book argues that we should return, always better informed, to the question of form and formal analysis and that one of the unfulfilled promises of scholars' expanding insights about materiality and industry is to bring them to bear on the field's foundational roots in the close analysis of moving-image forms.

The Cinema of Extractions thus calls for a return to formalism, although it does so without intending to create unnecessary dichotomies between formalism and historicism, form and politics, or history and theory. Rather, it seeks a formalism formed in dialogue with historical, materialist, and historical materialist methods—a formalism grounded in what Vanessa Schwartz and Jeannene Przyblyski have described as "the conviction that media have no essence outside the contexts of their production and consumption, and that these contexts define and give shape and meaning to the formal conventions of each medium at particular moments in time."[18] This approach draws on but also diverges from film studies' poetic tradition and the more recent, context- and politics-resistant "radical" formalism proposed by Eugenie Brinkema. I share with Brinkema the conviction that reading *from* (and not simply *about*) form can "activate and launch the speculative potential of texts" and that reading for form need not be done simply for the purpose of using "form's strategic utility to make other [e.g., political or social] claims." I do not, however, find the same value in "displac[ing] contextualist readings." On the contrary, I will argue that reading context, particularly when we do so *from form* (and with textual forms), need not foreclose speculation or the unexpected, nor does it assume that films "immediately render the world."[19] Film forms render the world in an unpredictable and unsettled exchange with contextual forms. Let us read the forms of that exchange.

The approach to form I am advocating follows Roland Barthes's famous dictum that "a little formalism turns one away from History, but . . . a lot brings one back to it."[20] Or, as applied to cinema and media studies in recent years, we might equally say that a little history may turn one away from form, but a lot should bring one back to it. The formal method pursued here has four primary features: first, it reaffirms the value of reading texts in context; second, it extends, in dialogue with neoformalist literary criticism, the site of analysis to context, opening a reflexive con/textual dialogue; third, it shifts, in dialogue with histories of media materialism, the analytic lens opened by our new knowledge about media materials back to their textual products, again creating a dialogue between media texts and their material contexts; and fourth, it applies this approach to industrial and corporate media as well as feature films, all of which, I argue, should be read together.

In part, in this book, I suggest that film and media students and scholars reapply formal analysis to the industrial and corporate films (films, most often shorts, made by or for nonfilm corporations, a category of films also studied under the rubrics of "useful" and "nontheatrical" cinema) that have been treated, with some important exceptions, in largely form-agnostic ways.[21] But the method proposed here has equal application in analyses of feature films, documentary, television, and newer forms of media. Moreover, by connecting these various types of texts with cinema and media studies' related interest in materials, infrastructure, and production, I want to show how textual methods can be extended and enhanced when put into conversation with a text more broadly conceived and situated.

Neoformalist literary criticism, with its call for formal analysis of the worlds that appear within literary texts, points one way to this approach. Many ways of reading literary form have been proposed and fiercely debated in recent years, but I most closely follow Caroline Levine, whose 2015 book, *Forms: Whole, Rhythm, Hierarchy, Network*, argues for a mode of analysis in which historical context should be read using the formal modes with which we normally read texts.[22] Extending this model, I also treat form as a question of *formation*—the formation, that is, of the proto-cinematic spaces, technologies, infrastructures, and working practices—the domains of materialist film history, production studies, and media industry studies—that form on-screen form.[23]

In addition to these art historical, literary, and cinema studies models, I draw, finally, on the media studies tradition that has been more attentive to the materials and infrastructure that subtend media texts, an approach often associated with Kittler's work and well summed up by the title of Hans Ulrich Gumbrecht and Karl Ludwig Pfeiffer's 1988 volume *Materialität der kommunikation* or, as parts of it appeared in translation in 1994, *Materialities of Communication*.[24] As Pfeiffer puts it in the opening essay, the volume understands communication not simply as the exchange of meaning or signs but as it is "enframed into hardwares, guided by rules and styles, and 'crowned' by signified effects that, once sufficiently routinized, can appear as realms of their own."[25] Kittler, who praised Gumbrecht and Pfeiffer for having "granted literature its origin and its end," left seemingly little room for textual interpretation in a method that insisted that the more important work of media happened at the level of hardware and technical systems.[26] To study cinema, one needed to analyze not films but rather "an entire history of the industry," an industry, as Kittler, echoing Baxandall, put it about painting, which is always shaped by "approximations, conventions, and the pure chance involved in the historical availability of raw materials."[27]

Kittler's challenge to hermeneutics, with its emphasis on how media "determine our situation" independent of the texts they inscribe, store, or transmit, may seem irreconcilable with the return to formal analysis proposed here.[28] But while acknowledging—indeed embracing—Kittler's emphasis on "underlying discursive operations and materialities," I also make a case for the value of putting those underlying conditions back in dialogue with the texts they support.[29] I do so, in part, by drawing on Kittler's own sometimes undervalued approach to texts. As John Durham Peters explains, Kittler was "generally friendly to hermeneutics as a practice of rigorous textual analysis since it is close to his own method."³⁰ In fact, he was a masterful analyst of texts ranging from the subject of his early training, German Romanticist literature, especially Goethe, to twentieth-century rock music. He simply "read" them differently. No plumbing the depths for meaning and no search for hidden ideology—for Kittler, as David Wellberry argues, texts were to be treated more literally: "Everything lies on the surface, precisely because this surface materiality of the texts themselves . . . is the site of their historical efficacy." Textual content, in this approach, is reducible to "information and noise."³¹ The medium is the message.

But this medium-focused "radical historicism" nevertheless left room for other ways of treating media texts.³² The "optical media" lectures, for example, draw on texts to illuminate what Kittler describes as "the cultural effects" of new media such as photography. "Mediocre poets," Kittler argues, become "media theorists," a reading that arises not from these poets' medium but rather from their poems' content.³³ Literature's action may ultimately have been in the discourse network, but Kittler had no need to comprehensively dispatch with the discourse found in texts. These textual "theorists," moreover, were part of the discursive world that generated new media. Kittler acknowledged that media took form in context, or as Geoffrey Winthrop-Young and Michael Wutz put it, "Media determine our situation, but . . . our situation, in turn, can do its share to determine our media."³⁴ Kittler was thus no simple technological determinist, but rather, as Peters emphasizes, he recognized "the role of historical, political, and economic contingency in the development of media," to which we may add the historical, political, economic, and *media* discourse generated in media texts.³⁵ Although Kittler may have stressed the power of the media more than their messages, those messages retained power, including the power to feed back into media development.

Finally, Kittler developed his own way of reading texts as evidence of—and not, importantly, reflexive *allegories* for—the discourse networks that ultimately superseded them in importance. Kittler the literary scholar began his career with an interest in texts that never entirely went away, even after his full turn to media theory. His description of the discourse network of 1800, for example, opens with a reading of Goethe, and Kittler was long invested in forms of interpretation that worked in tandem with his analyses of media.[36] He termed his reading method "implosion," an approach that does not lead to aesthetic, historical, political, or other traditional kinds of interpretation. Instead, as Winthrop-Young explains, it produces "a hermeneutic breakdown" in which "meaning is sucked out of a text and the latter collapses back onto the algorithms or systems of rules that govern its functioning in the first place."[37] In Kittler's reading, Goethe's poem "Wanderer's Nightsong" ("Wandrers Nachtlied," ca. 1780), for example, is not about nature or Romantic experience. Rather, it reveals the linguistic conditions that created it and that circumscribe its interpretation.[38] Similarly, Pink Floyd's "Brain Damage," from the 1973 LP *Dark Side of the Moon*, is not about drug use or schizophrenia but rather, in Kittler's reading, it is a performance of the technical history of its own creation.[39]

If "implosion" sounds like allegory, it may be because Kittler indeed had a "noticeable preference for texts . . . that themselves gesture toward the rules that govern their production as well as their effects."[40] But Kittler moves away from allegorical interpretation by insisting that such texts can no longer be imagined to refer to anything external to themselves and the media discursive systems that have programmed them. "Imploding" rather than interpreting texts thus takes textual interpretation seriously but quickly shifts the site of action back to the material conditions and discursive systems that define Kittler's posthermeneutic method. *The Cinema of Extractions* nevertheless recognizes "implosion" as a model, however idiosyncratic, for returning to media texts informed by new material knowledge.

When the "materialities" and infrastructure of communication appear within the text, as we find in certain feature fiction films (think of any Hollywood studio drama, from *Singin' in the Rain* [dir.

Gene Kelly and Stanley Donen, 1952] to *Hail, Caesar!* [dir. Ethan Coen and Joel Coen, 2016]) and often in industrial films, a form of reflexive synchronicity allows us to move analytically through and around the text and to read an encounter between text and context that may implode or may become allegorical. Another model for this analysis is thus one of cinema studies' versions of the methods developed in new historicism and the social history of art, *Allegories of Cinema* (1989), in which David James lucidly ties material conditions to textual forms by examining how every film allegorizes its own making. Echoing Hayden White's argument about allegory's function in historical narratives (which are always, as White puts it, "saying one thing and meaning another"), James's book shows that every film tells at least two stories: the one in its content, the other of its creation.[41] Like Baxandall and Alpers before him, James emphasizes that "the financial and technological resources employed and the social relations of a film's manufacture and consumption mark the limits of its formal possibilities."[42] "The financial and technological" that James described has become more refined in recent years by scholars with a more capacious view of the raw materials and infrastructures underpinning cinema's creation and distribution.[43] Reading allegorically, I will argue, should attend to those material contexts and the way they shape form or define its parameters—and it can do so most effectively by also taking account of those contexts' own richly dynamic forms.[44]

James applied this method to what he notably termed classical Hollywood's "industrial cinema," a name that may seem, on the one hand, perfectly natural but, on the other hand, given how it is used today in subfields defined explicitly against cinema and media studies' long emphasis on Hollywood and other commercial cinemas, feels methodologically mismatched. Taking this mismatch as an opportunity, I will return often in the chapters that follow to the historical and historiographic overlaps between types of cinema and areas of cinema studies whose division, I will argue, may have been methodologically advantageous but ultimately risks obscuring their deeper material and conceptual connections. At stake is how we understand the cinema of extractions as it developed from its origins with—and arguably *as*—cinema and then subsequently spanned out across various genres and formats, including "industrial cinema" in both its meanings.

WHAT IS A "CINEMA OF EXTRACTIONS"?

This book names a type of film that invites a richly layered, reflexive, allegorical, or "implosive" approach to analysis. Every film—whether analog or digital, fiction or documentary, Hollywood or homemade—relies to some degree on extraction. But not every film is a film *of* extractions. *The Cinema of Extractions* seeks a more specific definition—one rooted in cinema's technological origins, its early and enduring reliance on mined materials, and its conceptual debt to capitalist industries' defining ambitions for world creation and domination, including colonial domination and its associated racial and ethnic subjugation. Seen in its earliest form, the cinema of extractions defines a cinema that made extractive industries (coal, oil, and other mineral resources) and their industrial products and effects (trains and steamships, factories and manufacturing facilities, and industrialized mobility) frequent early film subjects. More conceptually, it names cinema's power not merely *to represent* but also *to participate in the creation of* a world remade in the vision of industrial and extractive forms of modernity—all grounded in what Schwartz and Przybylski have described as "the centrality of images to belief-systems."[45] Cinema helped achieve this goal by creating material and virtual worlds in studios and on editing tables, by immersing audiences in those worlds, and by "engineering consent" through its textual forms for these worlds and the work they required.[46]

The cinema of extractions emerged alongside the cinema of *a*ttractions, and indeed Tom Gunning and André Gaudreault's enduring heuristic for early film analysis has provided this book not just with its glancing title but also with a conceptual partner and foil. Where Gunning and Gaudreault emphasize reception and how audience expectations shaped early approaches to the film text, I join those scholars who have emphasized production, including how production shapes and defines reception.[47] Like the cinema of attractions, the cinema of extractions emerged in cinema's earliest years in films that foregrounded, at times consciously, at others simply conspicuously, cinema's extractive entanglements. Putting the mining, refining, and consumption of extracted materials on display, a cinema of material "monstration" made extraction a key iteration of early cinema's industrial attraction.[48] Similarly, just as the cinema of attractions steadily went "underground" during the years of narrative integration, fading into distant memory in the time of studio classicism, so too the cinema of extractions gave way in the 1910s to a "cinema of resource integration"—a cinema no longer driven by the explicit visual spectacle of extractive consumption but ever more reliant on its latent, largely unseen power.

But much as the cinema of attractions reemerged in avant-garde and experimental film and in fiction-feature films' moments of spectacle and wonder, so too the cinema of extractions found new life, especially in industrial films about extractive industries and also in documentaries and fiction films that have taken extraction as their subjects.[49] It also lives on today in new forms and sites such as oil and gas museums and themed exhibits "where a contemporary cinema of extractions," as Daryl Meador writes, "retains the excitement and stimulation of early cinematic spectatorship."[50] Put more schematically, with the emergence of commercial film industries in the 1910s and 1920s, the cinema of extractions split into three primary forms: first, the continuing on-screen depiction of extraction and a world made in the image of industrial productivity found in films made by nonfilm industries (typically referred to as "industrial," "corporate," "sponsored," or "useful" cinema); second, the subset of feature films and documentaries that take extractive industries as their subjects;

and, third, the cinema of "resource integration," in which extraction becomes a structuring absence that only occasionally appears on screen but may still be read in latent form.

READING FOR MATERIAL, INFRASTRUCTURE, INDUSTRY, AND FORM

Reading from cinema's origins, through this split in the 1910s, and into the mid-twentieth century, in this book, I examine films that make the extractive process and cinema's reliance on it reflexively visible, whether because those films are explicitly about extraction or because their subject necessarily requires an engagement with extractive content that impresses itself on their films' form. Reading in this way—from an extractive perspective—can be done with films that do not have the same reflexive qualities as extractions films, but reading extraction-themed films models a method for doing so. In this section, I go deeper into that method, first by surveying some recent work that already features certain aspects of this approach, and then by turning more briefly to the conceptual scaffolding behind it.

In writing this book, I have taken inspiration from the work of film and media scholars who have, in the past decade or so, developed sophisticated approaches to formal—and sometimes also historical and material—analysis. Brinkema's insightful readings, to cite some of the best-known examples, have sparked renewed interest in form-driven interpretation, but Brinkema is by no means alone. Rosalind Galt, for example, has consistently modeled an evocative reading practice based in the complex relay between global political contexts, (colonial) histories, and the politics of film form. Going back to her work on the "the pretty image," for instance, Galt makes clear why we "must situate film form and style within local economies of place, time, and culture." That book's formal analysis demonstrates film's capacity to make "visible the structuring forces of history," an approach, Galt emphasizes, that need not slip into ahistorical formalism.⁵¹ In *Queer Cinema in the World*, Galt and Karl Schoonover similarly analyze "cinema as a place where the politics of globalization are articulated and disarticulated," an action, they stress, that takes place "at the level of the individual films articulating the worldly in their form and style."⁵²

In *Spectacle of Property*, John David Rhodes further demonstrates how such an attentiveness to property can quickly connect formal and materialist analysis in ways I pursue in this book. Take, for example, his reading of the opening shots of Robert Mulligan's 1962 *To Kill a Mockingbird* adaptation. Moving between close attention to the images and situated knowledge of their production history, Rhodes generates an incisive argument about the "materiality out of which this diegetic world is constructed."⁵³ For all but the most knowledgeable viewers, that materiality would be difficult to decipher on screen but quickly comes into focus when informed by Rhodes's historical account of the "working class and largely Latino neighborhood" whose houses had to be removed to build the Los Angeles Dodgers' baseball stadium and ended up becoming part of a set on the Universal backlot. There they became the mise-en-scène for a cinematic retelling of racism in the U.S. South staged in the material space of Los Angeles's own race-driven politics of property. Understanding cinema as a set of property relations that shape how properties take form on screen, Rhodes offers an important way of thinking, more broadly, about the formal work of film historical context and the direct connections between material history and formal film analysis.⁵⁴

In her writing about filmed space, Priya Jaikumar, whose work about colonial cinema also has an important place in what follows, puts these material and formal connections more abstractly: "Cinema, with its referential powers . . . and representational apparatus . . . exemplifies and authorizes specific kinds of intersections between the material, social, and imagined spaces that constitute our world." Analyzing those intersections requires historical attention not just to where and how films are shot but also the numerous forces—and, as I will emphasize, those forces' *forms*—that place-focused analysis unlocks. The method, as Jaikumar sketches it most succinctly, involves "histories that radiate out" from a specific filmed place "to the other industrial, political, socioeconomic, and experiential sites that give it shape, form, and meaning."[55] The resulting form of what Jaikumar calls "place-images" can be read only in dialogue with the forms that form them.

What Jaikumar argues about the spatial and historiographic also applies to the social and political. In *Art Cinema and India's Forgotten Futures*, for example, Rochona Majumdar argues that "art films are intellectual histories" that do their historical and conceptual work not simply in "how society is reflected" but rather "through the figures and formal affordances specific to film."[56] Film becomes a site of spatial or political thinking, in other words, and it does so through specific forms, which are, for their part, also inspired and shaped by the available forms of their time.[57] Film as a form of social or political thinking thus takes shape in a complex formal exchange between context and text, both of which must be read.

Perhaps no corner of film studies has been as attentive to how film texts take form in relationship to the industrial contexts of their making as the one devoted to analyzing film and television as reflexive or allegorical forms of their industries' *business* thinking. Put most plainly by Jerome Christensen, "The Hollywood studio is a business that does its business right there on the screen as the projector rolls."[58] Going back at least to John Caldwell's analysis of the television industry's "self-interpretation" and to its "process of figuration and self-aestheticization," we find a strand of media scholarship deeply engaged with texts' propensity to reveal something about the contexts of their making, or what Jeff Menne, in his absorbing readings of post-Fordist Hollywood films describes as "the tendency among filmmakers to sensitize one's textual material to one's industrial situation."[59] Attempting to define what, precisely, that *something* is and how to describe its origins and motivations, these scholars have generated rich ways of interpreting texts that I take as exemplary models. Caldwell's attempts to synthesize ethnography and textual analysis highlights the upshot of what production studies and media industry studies have to offer to reading industry texts.[60] Building on Christensen's and Caldwell's respective insights, J. D. Connor has shown just how much is to be gained when we read "films as corporate and industrial allegories as deeply as we should," whether as "representations of experience" (of the makers), as "scenarios, strategies, suggestions, pleas, [and] business plans," or, more recently, as "the communicating channel between the material and the abstract; the pragmatic and the conceptual."[61]

Tracking back to cinema's laboratory, studio, and factory origins and through the early days of Hollywood's industrial integration, *The Cinema of Extractions* further historicizes these reflexive tendencies in an earlier period and often does so with a more specific interest in raw materials. Methodologically, it seeks a reading method that similarly moves between texts and their historical contexts, be they spatial, social, or political. Like this body of scholarship, it finds little value in ceding form to ahistorical formalism; by the same token, it also refuses to cede history to form-agnostic historicism. Because it emphasizes the value such an approach has for film and media histories of extraction and environment, it is particularly engaged with recent work in environmental (or "eco") cinema and media, particularly those works that suggest other methodological paths forward.[62]

In *Inhospitable World: Cinema in the Time of the Anthropocene*, Jennifer Fay highlights one critical argument for a text-oriented material approach to media environments through her important insight that "film enjoys a rather unique relationship to the material, elemental world." That relationship, rooted in cinema's foundation (or ontology) as a material, world-making form—an extractive form, as I will argue more fully in the next chapter—offers an unusual opportunity, Fay argues, to "appreciate both the artificiality of human world-making and the ambitions to design an artificial, unhomely planet." Building on this material connection and its underlying recognition that screen worlds only become worlds through material world-making, Fay generates a series of gripping analyses of film texts, including what she terms Buster Keaton's "weather comedy," with its simulated atmospheric effects, and a rereading of film noir as a didactic ecological genre about life (and death) in the "bleak landscapes" of soured social and natural environments.[63] At stake in Fay's approach is what cinema can offer to environmental and ecological ways of thinking as more than just a(nother) form of environmental representation. Film's specificity, as Fay demonstrates, and as I build on, is the connection between its material and screen worlds, its texts and contexts.[64]

Debashree Mukherjee takes a similar ecological approach to 1930s film production in *Bombay Hustle*, emphasizing the complex relations among machines, climates, and bodies (of both film workers and spectators) that make up "a dispersed, labor-intensive cine-ecology." In the book's exemplary chapter about energy, Mukherjee traces energetic transfers across this ecology, from broader historical discourses about the colonial body to film production practices and, most critically for this book's interests, into film genres and individual texts, where energetic discourses took screen form, both as allegory and as what Mukherjee describes as a potential "mimetic imperative to viewers."[65] More than just a question of mined materials and power-dependent machines, in other words, Mukherjee's approach to energy connects profilmic materials, machines, and bodies to screen texts and to reception. Although not formal in the sense I propose, this cine-ecology-spanning method demonstrates the richness of readings activated by more-than-material and not solely textual forms of analysis.

Finally, for media scholars, especially those working in the tradition of German media theory, with its emphasis on technology and cultural technique rather than just content, media and environment have increasingly moved into conceptual synchronicity.[66] Driven especially by John Durham Peters's important historical and theoretical arguments about media's conceptual connections to weather and mediation, this field has seen nearly everything potentially become a form of "media."[67] As a result, we now have much more sophisticated ways of understanding concepts such as medium, climate, atmosphere, and milieu as well as how media, understood materially and contextually, both reproduce and shape understandings of material environments.[68] Conversely, consistent with the antihermeneutical tradition discussed previously, this work has tended to downplay—and even, at times, explicitly dismiss—the utility of the text-oriented approaches associated with "ecocinema" or "ecomedia" studies.[69] While recognizing—and indeed extending and capitalizing on—the utility of that text-adjacent methodological turn, in this book, I seek to reconcile the parallel (sometimes competing) textual and contextual, content- and material-/technical-oriented approaches.

With these existing approaches in mind, let me turn now to the formal method deployed in the following chapters—the method of reading through the lens of extraction. My reading method proceeds from the underlying assumption that cinema embraced, enabled, and materially and conceptually embodied the world-making ambitions of capitalist industrial modernity. But moving beyond the often empirical and positivist approaches that have produced significant insights into film, photography, and other medias' debt to and reliance on extracted minerals and resources, I seek to extend those insights to their textual stakes. Doing so, I argue, requires a threefold turn to form, in which we must read, together, films' textual forms, the forms of their content, and the forms of the contexts from which they emerge. The result is a mode of reading defined by a circuit of feedback that moves among text, content, and context, all considered in an intermaterial/intertextual dialogue. This mode seeks, most broadly, to think at the intersection of what James Cahill, Weihong Bao, and I have described as "the many things involved in the configuration or dispositif we call 'media': images and texts; infrastructures and technologies; social experiences; psychology and affect; politics, policy, and ideology; and the ways media literally create climates . . . and both rely upon environments . . . and destroy them."[70]

To formalize this technique, I turn, following Christian Metz and, more recently, Hans Ulrich Gumbrecht, to the Danish linguist Louis Hjelmslev's expansion of Ferdinand de Saussure's signifier–signified model to two planes, *expression* (Saussure's signifier) and *content* (the signified), each with two features, *form* and *substance*. This expanded approach creates four categories for analysis: substance of content; form of content; substance of expression; and form of expression. Like Metz, I see in this schema an opportunity to develop a more nuanced approach to film's traditional distinction between content and form.[71] Drawing on Gumbrecht, who saw it as a way to map and challenge traditional forms of interpretation, I find that opportunity especially in a more capacious, materialist account of what Hjelmslev terms the "substance of expression." For Gumbrecht, this includes, for instance, art-making materials such as paint (before they take form in images) or the "computer as a technical array" (before it creates digital images)—that is, the stuff of media making.[72] The kind of text-agnostic materialist and environmentally oriented cinema and media studies research I extend here has had the important value of making it possible to think anew about the implications of reading for this "substance," which now includes the extracted materials upon which all film and media production relies. One key methodological extension I pursue is to read that substance, along with other aspects of the context of a film's material production and its content, formally.[73]

Hjelmslev's quadrangle provides a rubric for this approach. Applied to cinema and media, its four categories can be summed up most concisely as follows:

1. **Substance of content**: the raw material, including ideas and material things, available for film and media representation
2. **Form of content**: the forms that such raw material takes in the world independent of cinema and prior to filming
3. **Substance of expression**: film and media materials, techniques, technologies, and industries
4. **Form of expression**: audiovisual representations; elements of media language

This scheme offers a useful way to map various methods currently used in cinema and media studies and to imagine new paths forward. It tells us, for example, that standard forms of narrative-focused film analysis typically focus almost exclusively on how films thematize their *substance of content* (1); formalist approaches focus largely on *form of expression* (4); materialist media studies and production (or media industry) studies tend to focus on *substance of expression* (3); and the recent work of neoformalist literary critics such as Caroline Levine asks that we attend to *form of content* (2). To apply this to a canonical text, *The Classical Hollywood Cinema* largely combines *substance of expression* (3) and *form of expression* (4), with the former mostly concerned with technologies, techniques, and business/industry forms but not materials—not least including extracted materials—as we understand them now.[74] Similarly, the approaches associated with New Film History have expanded how we understand *substance of expression* (3) and *form of expression* (4) by contextualizing them in the broader material and social worlds that make up the *substance of content* (1). As Charles Musser has noted about studies of early cinema and modernity, this expansion has at times meant moving film to the margins of what essentially become cultural histories that are concerned much more with things we would analyze on the plane of content (1 + 2) than the plane of cinematic expression (3 + 4).[75]

In the chapters that follow, I propose how we can—and argue for why we should—bridge these four categories. In doing so, I give special attention to films that generate complex reflexive readings, for instance, when the *substance of content* (e.g., extracted materials such as coal or oil) can be put in dialogue with the *substance of expression* (the same extracted materials needed to make the film), or when the *form of content* (e.g., the routes of the pipelines that give form to the petroleum industry's distribution of its raw materials) shape the *form of expression* (the use of tracking shots that follow those same pipelines, synching, as I will argue in chapter 4, substance and form, content and expression). To be sure, reading across and between these categories generates better readings for some films than others—whether for textual reasons or because of what we do or do not know about the histories of their production or content. Part of what distinguishes the films I include in the cinema of extractions is precisely how their content or production lend themselves to reflexive formal and materialist reading strategies. Although the method may be more or less productive depending on the text, any reading, I believe, can be enriched by thinking formally across these categories.

This book develops its argument and reading method in two sections roughly divided according to the two definitions of "industrial" cinema previously described. Chapters 1 and 2 focus on the origins and early years of the industrial cinema David James associates with industries such as Hollywood. These chapters define the cinema of extractions and its division into the cinema of resource integration and subsequent industrial cinemas of extraction. They focus, historically, on early and silent cinema and engage primarily with histories of early film and early Hollywood. Sidestepping the aesthetic history told in the traditional cinema of attractions to narrative integration model, these chapters tell a material story about extractions and resource integration before tying materiality back to film texts and formal analysis. They do so by reading a combination of infrastructures—especially studio architectures and production technologies—and films—including early actualities, short fiction films [especially D. W. Griffith's *The Lonedale Operator* (1911)], and early features, including two films shot partly in Hollywood studios and partly in Los Angeles's oil fields: Lois Weber's *Sunshine Molly* (1915) and Joseph De Grasse's oil drama *Flowing Gold* (1924). Conceptually, the first two chapters emphasize cinema's shifting ontology as a set of world-making technologies and practices and track how those practices change with the move from early to industrial forms of film production.

The second half of the book continues this concern with world-making but shifts its textual focus to industrial cinema as it is more typically defined today—in industrial and sponsored films—and moves its historical focus to the period of that cinema's rapid expansion in the middle of the twentieth century. This second half begins by extending the first two chapters' material analyses of extraction from production studios to theater projection booths and two elemental materials—carbon and tungsten—used to light film projection. Focusing first on the carbon rods used for large parts of cinema's first half century in studio lights and theater projectors, I examine carbon as one of the most essential material and formal problems faced by theater owners and projectionists in their search for powerful and consistent forms of light. I then turn to tungsten, the element first used in lighting filaments in the early 1900s and quickly thereafter in everything from studio lights and projectors to radio, television, and computer vacuum tubes and today's mobile media.

From this material starting point, chapters 3 and 4 then shift to a series of close formal film analyses that model what I propose as an industrial film poetics. In chapter 3, I focus on *Tungsten: A Treasure of the Sierra Nevada*, a film produced by Union Carbide in the 1960s about its mining operations in California's Sierra Nevada mountains. By demonstrating how such films implicitly narrated their own conditions of existence, the chapter highlights a feedback loop that defines media–extraction relations. It ends by reading Union Carbide's vision of tungsten with and against John Huston's *The Treasure of the Sierra Madre* (1948), a midcentury Hollywood allegory about U.S. mining interests in Mexico that offers a formal lesson about industrial extraction that I read back onto Union Carbide's *Tungsten: A Treasure of the Sierra Nevada*.

Chapter 4 focuses on the formal language of the corporate oil films that played such a significant role in shaping public knowledge about oil extraction and distribution in the years of petroleum's rise to Western energy dominance after 1945. Although industrial film scholarship has tended to focus on content and production history—revealing the important fact that film was a significant part of corporate and industrial work—less attention has been devoted to the formal mechanisms through which films did this work. This shift away from form, I argue, is partly the result of the New Film History's synchronic devotion to context (e.g., corporate, industrial, or infrastructural contexts) that pulls us away from the film text, sometimes with the implicit promise of a rarely realized return with an eye better trained for analysis. But what, I ask, happens when we foreground form, both in its spectacular and even its most banal forms? Proposing a prosaic poetics of industrial film and applying it to the 1965 Shell Oil company-sponsored film *Shellarama*, I explore the forms that usefulness takes in industrial media. Using this primary example, I argue that we should read such films in the reflexive terms that define the cinema of extractions as a cinema that makes visible the correspondence, the interchange, and the feedback between cinematic forms and the forms of their extracted contents.

Although the early film or industrial media scholar may find particular interest in their respective half of the book, part of my point is that we should better recognize how these branches or aspects of cinema were cut from the same extractive cloth and can be read using many of the same techniques. Following these two sections, the book concludes in two parts. First, I outline the reading practice developed across the four chapters and emphasize its utility for nonextraction films. This summary aims to be useful—for instance, in film and media or environmental humanities courses—as a short *précis* on reading through the lens of extraction. I argue, in short, for a widely applicable practice based on reading around and across the interface of mediums and materials—that is, of images, the material conditions of their making, and the reflexive back-and-forth movement among the profilmic, diegetic, and textual that certain films invite, others allow, and only very few can refuse.

Second, I read two films—Margot Benacerraf's documentary about salt extraction in Venezuela, *Araya* (1959), and Sanaz Sohrabi's short feature *Scenes of Extraction* (2023)—as particularly redolent examples of films that challenge dominant extractive image forms and their archival legacies. These films are so evocative—and a fitting way to conclude—because they already treat extraction and images of it with the kind of attention to form and its intersection with materiality that animates this book's argument and reading method. They also offer the important reminder that, as historians know well, histories and their images—contexts and texts—are never fixed, never settled, but rather are always open to interpretation and reinterpretation. The task is to find interpretative routes. This book charts one.

1

EARLY CINEMAS OF EXTRACTION

Writing in 1986, wizened by the early film archive and the methods of the New Film History, and inspired by reading Eisenstein's "Montage of Attractions" and Fernand Léger's account of seeing an early version of Abel Gance's *La roue* (1923), Tom Gunning tried to define something of the radical possibilities of the historiography of early cinema. The potential of the new approach did not lie in "the mistaken path" of comparing film to the theater that preceded it or the classical cinema that followed. Early film history's power, achieved in part by reading more broadly in histories and theories of modernism and visual culture, was a "matter of making images seen" for what they were, not what earlier historians had thought they should have been. It is this harnessing of historical visibility with conceptual dexterity, this act of showing how—influenced by the methods of cultural and intellectual history—the early film image fit in modern Western cultures of spectacular display, consumerism, and new theorizations of perception and urban experience that early film historiography in the decade after 1986 displays most intensely. Its inspiration and value for the avant-garde historical methods of the early decades of this century needs to be reexplored.

Only the most perceptive reader will recognize, in the preceding lines, the language with which Tom Gunning opens his iconic essay

"The Cinema of Attractions."[1] But I reproduce them, with liberal variation, both to express a debt to that essay (and the broader historiography it often stands for) and to make a preliminary point about the argument that follows. Put simply, what Gunning recognized about early film history around 1906 we can now recognize about early film historiography around 1986. Both involved and can be fully recognized only in the context of the carving out of a new space for images and of new ways of seeing and presenting them. In Gunning's account, 1906 marked early cinema's successful emergence out of a broader field of cultural practices that helped shape cinema but from which filmmakers and those associated with the art and business of moving images had to separate themselves to succeed. Gunning's account similarly marked early cinema *history*'s successful emergence out of a broader field of disciplinary practices that helped shaped cinema *studies* but from which early cinema scholars had to distinguish themselves to create the subfield we know today.

This kind of resonance is of course not proper to early cinema or its history. Every history is a product of its time. I flag it, though, because in this chapter I also tell a story about our time (circa 2024) by returning to the medium's origins. The main components of the story that concern me include the power of technology and technology companies, the connection between such companies and new forms of art and media, the degree to which such technologies and corporations rely on natural resources and manufactured energy, and the various social forms they helped create and to which their art and media were forced to respond. Among the things that connect these various subjects is extraction, including the extraction of mineral and energy resources; land and property; and labor, wealth, and value. Within this story of art, technology, energy, and extraction lies a history of early cinema that is also, in different but connected ways, the story of our present.

Here, then, I begin to part ways with Gunning, not out of disagreement but rather because the argument I make in this chapter about the cinema of extractions is an argument, like Gunning's about attractions, of its time. But like Gunning's, this argument, too, might well begin with Léger. For Gunning, the key aspect of Léger's response to *La roue* was how, in Léger's estimation, Gance had shed cinema's debt to theater and in its place had created a new form of plastic visibility—a new way of seeing and showing the world of objects. Note, however, how Léger arrives at that point by arguing, perhaps more provocatively and with no less consequence for early cinema, that "it will be Abel Gance's honor that he has successfully presented an *actor object* to the public." Léger is referring to *La roue*'s train, which indeed takes on, in certain sections of the film, a dynamically prominent role—so much so, in Léger's estimation, that it even "crushes and eliminates the human object, reduces its interest, pulverizes it."[2] This apparent displacement of the human "object"—but perhaps we would say *subject*—will immediately evoke, for certain readers, a discourse not yet fully formed in the mid-1980s but that has since become common currency in the humanities, whether as object-oriented ontology, "vibrant materialism," or some other way of thinking about nonhuman natures and the lifeworld of things.[3]

Although Léger's claim about this "cinematographic event of considerable importance" may thus anticipate one of the theoretical concerns of our time, it offers more by transporting us back, once again, to the cinema that came before it. Readers familiar with early film may already be thinking about the many trains and other "actor objects" that preceded *La roue* and the human actors—foremost Douglas Fairbanks and Charlie Chaplin—who for Léger had, even for all their achievements, kept cinema tethered to the performative norms of theater.[4] These actor objects of early cinema point to a different account of cinema's emergence, one still attuned to cinematic presentation—or *monstration*, the act of showing, as André Gaudreault put it in 1987—but equally interested in the underlying material and technological supports that made early cinema possible and became, for a time, an important subject of early film.[5] After all, and with due respect to Gance and Léger, the world of early cinema that Fairbanks and Chaplin replaced had been replete with objects whose visual importance was easily on par with the human actors of cinema's early *attractions* and whose profilmic significance offers a starting point for making visible cinema's early form of *extractions*.[6]

In what follows, I briefly retell the history of early cinema, narrated from the perspective of our time in the so-called Anthropocene, as a history of resource extraction and an emerging conception of a world to be controlled by and for (certain) humans and to be reproduced in technological form.[7] In doing so, I underscore how the nontextual, materialist and elemental approach to film that has become increasingly important in cinema and media studies can once again help us rethink early cinema by steering away from early *films* and their aesthetic development to the specific material and environmental contexts of their making.[8] Just as important, however, I turn back to early film texts to examine how this conception of cinema—that is, the cinema of extractions—might change how we look at early films and their actor objects, which is but a first step in the larger project, continued in the following chapters, of illustrating the too-seldom considered formalist upshot of media materialist inquiry.

THE EARLY FILM ENVIRONMENT AND CINEMATIC WORLDING

In 1945, the Cinémathèque française director Henri Langlois, on a mission to preserve a unique artifact of early film history, traveled to the eastern Paris suburb of Montreuil-sous-bois. Langlois was famously obsessed with films as both texts and physical objects, but this was a decidedly nontextual mission. Photos taken at the time document Langlois's desired object as a dilapidated nineteenth-century greenhouse, its glass walls and roof shattered, its existence and what continued to exist within it suspended somewhere at those mediated limits that so fascinated Walter Benjamin, between interior and exterior, beginning and end, life and death, and nature and culture (figure 1.1). The industrial history of Montreuil made it both a long-time seat of French communist politics and the home to factory owners, such as one Jean-Louis Stanislas Méliès, on whose property this particular greenhouse was located. The name gives the rest away: this was no mere greenhouse but in fact the old studio of Georges Méliès, son of Jean-Louis, which had stood unused, at least in its intended sense, for three decades. During that time, it had, in another sense, remained what it always was: a hothouse sheltering a solar-powered environment. Peeking out from the broken planks of the studio's rotting stage, climbing old scaffolding and fading set pieces, and reaching up through iron frames left empty by shattered glass, a newly unruly "natural" environment had slowly replaced what had once been a site of rigorous artificial environmental control—with photochemistry having ceded its place back to photosynthesis.

The midcentury image of Méliès's plant-filled stages offers a critical lesson about cinema's origins in the nineteenth century. The controlled system of creation that filmmakers developed in cinema's earliest years built on and helped extend a broader ambition that remains as powerful as ever today: the ambition not simply to control nature for creation, as Méliès and many other early filmmakers did or as image-dependent scientists such as Etienne-Jules Marey and others had done before, but rather to replace what remains of nature with a manufactured world, ever more virtual and ever more reliant on destroying the very environment it seeks to recreate.

While Langlois was touring Méliès's lost studio, new cinematic environments with different but related connections to industry and technology were unfolding in forms similarly hidden behind the screen of text-oriented film histories. Consider, for instance, a seemingly different sort of studio set and what may at first seem like an unlikely coordinating point for a new phase in the same project that created early cinema and its first environments: Western capitalism's

FIGURE 1.1 Studio de Georges Méliès à Montreuil (ca. 1945).
© DR, coll. La Cinémathèque française.

FIGURE 1.2 *Station 307* (dir. Louis Malle, British Petroleum, 1955).

rapacious ambition to conquer space and to extract resources, all while recreating diverse ecologies in the image of instrumental productivity (figure 1.2). Here we are on the deck of Jacques-Yves Cousteau's *Calypso*, a British minesweeper turned research vessel but also a mobile film studio that made possible the spectacular undersea expansion of the cinematic environment around midcentury while also yielding a related kind of environmental expansion, one devoted to midcentury oil and gas exploration. A short film produced to promote the project, *Station 307* (1955), captured a scene in the Persian Gulf on behalf of British Petroleum, and similar scenes were replayed many times in many places by Cousteau among others.[9] Cousteau and crew, traveling with the young director Louis Malle, put cinema's epistemology—its capacity to expand environmental operability by extending vision—in the service of industry.

I want us to think of this as a worlding process—a process by which cinema helped not simply to document a world, not simply to represent or reproduce that world, but rather to create a new world in the form and image of extraction.[10] This world took form, on the one hand, in maps, photos, and films and, on the other, in the railcars, tanker ships, and pipelines that brought oil and gas from extraction zones to colonial and metropolitan markets. It was a project forged in lockstep with midcentury neocolonial oil powers, such as France and Britain, and their transnational corporations, including BP, Shell, and Total.

Cousteau's oil and gas work contributed to and looks ahead to rising seas and abundant greenhouse gases. But it also, when understood as studio work, looks back to nineteenth-century studio greenhouses like Méliès's and to cinema's origins in various forms and ideas of extraction, whether from the sun that illuminated cinema's earliest studios or from the coal-powered, tungsten-sourced electric lights, which always endeavored to burn brighter, eventually to supplant the sun along with what lighting companies referred to precisely as "artificial sun" or "daylight at its best" (figure 1.3). And it looks back to extraction from the lakes and rivers that companies such as Kodak exploited by the tens of thousands of gallons per day

FIGURE 1.3 "Super-Mazda Lamps," *International Photographer* (December 1929).

to make film stock or the lumber, the need for which was so great that it led companies such as Paramount to buy whole forests to build sets, much as John Rockefeller had done before them to build oil barrels when they were still made of wood (figure 1.4).[11] Let us also not forget the silver that named the "silver screen," sourced in mines from Canada and California to Mexico and other sites across the Global South. By the time Cousteau was prospecting for BP, this list had expanded to include, among other things, oil to make polyester and polyurethane for magnetic tape. This list would soon grow to include the heavy metals and other extracted materials in the computers, tablets, phones, and watches that dominate and define mediated experience today.

Equipped with this materialist knowledge, we can see that cinema emerged, in broad ontological terms, not simply as a set of textual forms but rather as a world-making system composed of a set of emergent technologies, resource economies, and industrial practices. Although film texts were one product of that system, they were not necessarily the primary or the most important product, and as such, they need not demarcate cinema's specificity as an object of study. Early cinema's primary product was a way of thinking about the world—a way that was not unique to cinema, although cinema may have been its quintessential form. I call this way of thinking the "cinema of extractions," a cinema that defined the world as manageable, usable, and manipulable. This cinema maintained, in its practices, and taught viewers, through its films, two lessons about world-making: first, that the material world was a resource—whether for energy, materials, or images—and, second, that this world could be remade, re-created, and simulated. The cinema of extractions insisted that by capturing and manipulating nonhuman worlds, humans could make artificial ones.

This argument extends one I have made by analyzing the history of early film studios. Previously, I argued that studios embodied a broader ambition, running through a deeper precinematic history

To the left—the forest primeval from which Paramount gets its lordly palaces and modest huts. Above—one of the big sets that use up a large amount of lumber.

From Forest to Film

SO much lumber is used by the Paramount and Artcraft companies working at the Lasky studio in Hollywood, that the company bought a big tract of timber land in Oregon, and conducts a complete lumber business to fill its own requirements, with a private sawmill and steamers to carry the material to San Pedro harbor. The carpenter shop, planing mill, and other equipment for making the timber into scenery are organized on a scientifically economical basis, so that not a splinter is wasted. Every stick is taken care of, after a set has been dismantled; sawdust and shavings are stored for various uses. And when a piece of wood has done its bit, it goes to the furnace room and serves its purpose even in death.

The scrap heap, where lumber goes when the scenic artists have no more use for it.

Scaffolding constructed from material salvaged from the scrap heap.

FIGURE 1.4 "From Forest to Film," *Photoplay* (April 1918).

of Western world-making, to control environments, resources, and bodies through technology. Studios were one scene, in other words, of a powerful anthropocentric orientation. Historians of technology have named the outcome of this process the "human-built world." Put in cinematic terms, we might call it the "studio-built world."[12] The resulting visual system promised world mastery—the world viewed and, thereby, to a degree—but only a degree—controlled.[13] Moreover, whatever degree of virtual control audiences experienced and imagined was achieved only through material forms of environmental mastery that remained hidden, working quietly in the background, almost always out of view.[14] Films were part of this world-making system; indeed, they represent an important end product that also offers a window into the broader world-making ambition of Western capitalism—something like what some now call the Anthropocene.

To take this claim further, I build, first, on the account of cinema's role in the capitalist world system developed in Lee Grieveson's *Cinema and the Wealth of Nations*. Grieveson argues most broadly that "films, and the institutions that produced and circulated them, were part of an expansive liberal praxis, driven by political and economic elites to establish new forms of subjective, economic, and political order fit for the new modality of mass production, consumption, and corporate and monopoly capital." For Grieveson, film's place and role in this "liberal praxis" was both textual and material. Film texts encoded and circulated liberal ideologies in the form of corporate public relations as well as classical Hollywood's star-driven narratives. In materialist terms, the film industry relied on capitalism's expanding circulation of extracted resources.[15] For nonfilm investors, often from extractive industries, the film industry also offered a site for further capital accumulation.[16]

Grieveson focuses on how this imbrication of media and extraction-based capital came into focus during the years between the world wars, but his work also offers both a model and key historical threads to trace its formation back to cinema's origins. Doing so has the upshot of further emphasizing how cinema was materially and conceptually produced by—and thus prepared, from the beginning, to become part of—the much older system, long predating cinema, as Grieveson describes. It also offers a new layer to our periodization of early cinema, with, I argue, a cinema of extractions giving way, with the consolidation of the studio system's industrial techniques and liberal capitalist modes, to what I analyze in chapter 2 as a cinema of "resource integration"—that is, a cinema in which film practice became fully yoked to a resource-dependent industrial economy. Before examining that transition as it can be read in both cinema's material conditions and its resulting film texts, we must first track back to cinema's first decade and the textual cinema of extractions that emerged out of the world-making ambitions of its material origins. The worlding process that created cinema, and that films, in turn, recreated and documented in their earliest years, defines that cinema's first reflexive mode.

THE EARLY CINEMA OF EXTRACTIONS

Early filmmakers shared with other artists a reflexive tendency to document the materials and conditions of their artistic production.[17] Among the first traces of the filmed image in the United States, for example, we find Edison assistant W. K. L. Dickson's early act of self-representation known as *Dickson Greeting* (1891), doffing his hat for the kinetograph in a test of his device's capacity to capture sufficient sunlight to render the world in legible form. In France, the Lumière brothers were inveterate self-presenters and promotors, making their local train station at La Ciotat and scenes of Lumière family domesticity, as in *Le repas de bébé* (1895) and *La pêche aux poissons rouges* (1895), icons of film's earliest years. Early photographs of studios and sets, or films such as *Alice Guy tourne une photoscène sur le théâtre de pose des Buttes-Chaumont* (1905), an interior panorama of the Gaumont studio during an early sound film production, similarly capture a powerful impulse to document and make known the film world and its capacity for world creation. Meanwhile, the self-presentation through which showmen, such as Georges Méliès and Segundo de Chomón, soon made themselves not just directors behind the camera but also recognizable stars of the screen embodied the mode of direct address that has come to define the early cinema of attractions.

But this act of showing and "making images seen," as Léger put it about *La roue*, did more than just capture viewers' attention and reproduce the successful models found in contemporaneous attractions and theater cultures. It also implicated viewers in particular kinds of scenes, forms of seeing, and ways of conceptualizing the world. Those ways included an instrumentalist worldview shaped by cinema's early and enduring use for advertising and promotion.[18] The resulting mode of turning cinema's reflexivity, self-presentation, and the work of attraction into a world-making force is part of what defines the early cinema of extractions.

Take, for example, another of the iconic early self-promotional films by Lumière, *La sortie de l'usine Lumière à Lyon*, which was the first film shot by Louis on March 19, 1895, and shown at the first private screening of the Cinématographe on March 22 and then as the first film on the program at the famed public screening on December 28 at the Grand Café. Much has been written about the film's multiple versions and the many remakes it has inspired, many of which highlight what such a scene—leaving the factory—may reveal about labor time and leisure time.[19] What, precisely, is being revealed has similarly been the subject of a debate that boils down to whether or not the workers are in fact simply leaving work or performing for the camera (and thus, in some respect, still working). That debate goes to the heart of a key question about the Lumière film corpus: to what degree did the Lumière *actualités* merely document or, in fact, shape the "actuality" of the early film world? Or put in the terms infamously established by Siegfried Kracauer, does a film such as *La sortie de l'usine Lumière à Lyon* represent a "realist" (as Kracauer would argue) or "formalist" tendency?[20]

From an extractive perspective, the answer is both. The film documents the Lumière world and its energetic resources even if—and in some ways *even more so* if—that world is being performed and thus *form*ed for the camera. The film makes visible the conditions of work and the extraction of human energy. Moreover, it revels in the conditions of its very possibility. In this respect, the fact that this should have been the first film screened both to scientific experts and the public makes perfect sense: without the scene this film documents, a screening would not exist in the first place. Put another way, the first film screened was a behind-the-scenes account of film's very origins, and not just in the sense that every film is a record of its own making but, more specifically, that the Lumière brothers made the place of film's production—and all its material and energy requirements—the place of film production.

The extractive perspective I want to consider was not always so directly reflexive, but we find, again and again in early cinema, similar forms of documentation of the extractive world upon which cinema and industries and technologies like it depended. Early nonfiction films are almost never, in this respect, mere documents of the world in which cinema emerged; rather, they were part of the constitution and propagation of modernity's world-making ambitions. If, as Leo Charney and Vanessa Schwartz have argued most forcefully, modernity was cinematic before the fact, making cinema's emergence to some degree a foregone conclusion, part of what modernity "needed" from cinema was a more powerful form of self-imaging and imagining.[21] Modernity needed "specific arts of the machine," as Lewis Mumford described photography and film in the 1930s, capable of giving form to its world-making and world-transforming imperatives.[22] Modern industrial corporations needed, as historian of technology David Nye has argued, to create and project "interpretations of the world."[23] For film corporations such as the Lumière company, or especially the more diversified Edison Manufacturing Company, these "construction[s] of reality" were often reflexive, and even when they were not, they still contributed, in the years before the mass expansion of industrial and corporate filmmaking described by Grieveson and Nye, to the broader work of world interpretation that modern industry required.

The cinema of extractions captured and propagated capitalist and imperial world-making imperatives in films about cars, trains, and ships; demolition, excavation, and construction; coal mines and oil derricks; technologies and techniques; and, again, factories such as the Lumière factory at Lyon and the labor of their workers. We see it already in the early arrival and departure films that put British audiences in touch with—and may have shored up their support for—British imperial domination.[24] And we see it in the early travel and ethnographic films whose framing of race often lent ideological weight to extractive empire.[25] Such films showed the world as it *was*, in all its "actuality," but also, more broadly, as it *may become*. They were the becoming actual of Western capitalism's gamble, the document of its ambition—to build, to move, and to control; to create, to destroy, and to create again.

The early Lumière catalog similarly holds endless examples. Some, including those arrival and departure films, are easy to pass over. *Les forgerons* (1895), for example, the fifth film on the Grand Café program, presents a simple scene of ironworking [reproducing Dickson's earlier *Blacksmithing Scene* (1893)], a banal scene of building destruction made magical when reversed to demonstrate film's power to virtually rebuild a world destroyed [much like the later Lumière film, *Demolition d'un mur* (1896)]. Even for all their simplicity, these films should be understood as the microscale vision of a world defined by labor, technology, and world creation—or as the evidentiary counterpoint to the modernity-defining expansion of pace and scale captured in so many other early "actuality" and nonfiction films.

Early films of New York made by the Edison Company and American Mutoscope and Biograph (AMB), for example, repeatedly capture scenes of the excavation and reconstruction that defined the city's fin de siècle "creative destruction."[26] More than just simple documents of the construction process that overhauled infrastructure and transformed the city from the tops of new skyscrapers to the subway depths below, such films took the building process or new forms of infrastructure as an opportunity to explore and express cinema's world-making potential.[27] *Demolishing and Building up the Star Theatre* (dir. Frederick S. Armitage, 1901), for example, uses an early instance of time-lapse special effects to emphasize the pace through which the urban world was being remade. Like *Demolition d'un mur*, it exploits the reversal technique to reflexively underscore film's worlding powers.

Films made about the early subway system similarly emphasize the new spaces and experience of an industrial world and its connected infrastructural and cinematic forms of world-making. In Edwin S. Porter's *City Hall to Harlem in 15 Seconds, via the Subway* (1904), for example, a familiar rube scenario—with a man who inadvertently blows himself up while setting off a bomb in a subway tunnel—mocks the city's creative destruction and its promise of rapid transport. In a different way, G. W. Bitzer's *Interior New York Subway* (1905) more earnestly syncs cinema's and the subway's respective worlding powers, mounting the camera on the front of a subway car to film the car ahead, which is illuminated by yet another car on a parallel track, giving viewers a virtual experience of the city's new subterranean world in perhaps the most haunting example of cinema's early phantom rides.

The directors and camera operators who took film around the world offered a more expansive vision of extraction and its worlding ambitions. Accounts of ecological, or eco-, cinema often begin with two Lumière-sponsored films of the Baku oilfields, shot by operator Alexandre Michon sometime between 1897 and 1899 (figure 1.5).[28]

FIGURE 1.5 *Puits de pétrole à Bakou. Vue de près* (dir. Alexandre Michon, ca. 1897–1899).

American producers made their own versions, from New Jersey, where Edison operators shot *Burning of the Standard Oil Co's tanks, Bayonne, N.J.* on July 5, 1900, to Los Angeles, where they shot *California Oil Wells in Operation* the following December. AMB shot its own version of California oil country in 1903 (figure 1.6), and similar films followed, especially as film producers relocated to the west coast. Already in 1910, Los Angeles's first three film companies, Selig Polyscope, Bison/New York Motion Picture Company (NYMP), and Biograph all released oil films. Selig's *Shooting an Oil Well* documented the extraction process, while Bison and Biograph created early examples of fiction films that soon made the oil industry a non-infrequent backdrop for narrative action (as I discuss in chapter 2). *Moving Picture World*'s capsule review of Bison's *Rivalry in the Oil Fields* (dir. Fred J. Balshofer, 1910) emphasizes that one of

FIGURE 1.6 American Mutoscope and Biograph oil extraction films (1903). Courtesy of The Museum of Modern Art Department of Film Special Collections, New York.

the film's "principal points of interest is the fact that it illustrates . . . scenes in the oil regions."[29] The marketing for Biograph's *A Rich Revenge* (dir. D.W. Griffith, 1910; starring Mary Pickford) similarly highlighted its setting: "A Comedy of the California Oil Fields."[30]

Such direct scenes of extractive industries may have been relatively rare, but the images of the world put in motion by their power dominate early film catalogs, especially those by Lumière, with their repetitive images of trains, steamships, and their arrivals and departures in cities and ports around the world. As Schwartz has argued, these "transport films" bore witness both to the global expansion of literal travel between the opening of the Suez Canal in 1869 and the Panama Canal in 1914 and to the presence of the camera operators whose new mobility offered viewers novel forms of virtual movement through cinema's worlding powers.[31] As Grieveson argues, the growth of transport infrastructure, notably including the Panama Canal, facilitated forms of capital expansion and the "fusion of economic, state, and geopolitical logics" in which "cinema was quickly made useful," for example, in the form of Edison's Spanish-American War films.[32]

As the example of the globe-trotting Lumière operators already suggests, the synchronicity between cinema and extractive and extraction-powered industries took concrete, mutually reinforcing forms. One need think only of the boards of directors of early film companies, such as Gaumont and Pathé, full of leaders from the electrical and mining industries, or of the connections between projects including ore drilling, batteries, cement, and the kinetoscope at the Edison laboratory, or of Edison rival George Westinghouse's support for another Edison rival, AMB. Such entanglements produced some of the most compelling scenes of early cinema. They include, for example, the series of twenty-one industrial films produced by AMB director G. W. Bitzer at the Westinghouse Works in 1904 for that year's Louisiana Purchase Exposition in Saint Louis. The panoramas Bitzer shot, both outside the works from a train, and inside, with the camera mounted on moving cranes, reframed the world from the perspective of industry and its associated technologies (figure 1.7) and modeled incredible forms of synchronicity between cinema and industrial machinery. Similarly, the numerous early rail films—some of cinema's first sponsored or "industrial" films—that companies such as Edison made as part of business agreements with the railroads in exchange for payment or free transport for their filmmakers facilitated North America's "documentation" in cinema's first decades and rested, like the Lumières' (or Pathé's) *tours du monde*, on the expanding networks and new speed of coal-powered transport (of both filmmakers and the films they made).[33]

In sum, early film texts frequently carry the mark, not just in their subjects but also in their conception and execution, of the same world of extractive industries and processes that defined cinema as a material

FIGURE 1.7 *Panorama exterior Westinghouse works* (dir. G. W. Bitzer, 1904).

and conceptual form. Not all early films, let me be clear, should be understood as "extractions" films, even if every early film was, in material and conceptual ways, made possible by extractive projects and an associated world-making and world-capturing ambition. But one lesson of cinema and media studies' recent emphasis on raw materials, when applied to early cinema, is that highlighting cinema's development out of the transformations of an extractive world offers a way to do more than just make what are essentially positivist claims about cinema's place in nonfilm stories about technologies, environments, and energy.[34] It also allows us to read those stories back onto films now seen from new materially oriented perspectives.

The cinema of extractions names film's revelatory power, especially in its earliest phase, to make the extractive work of industrial modernity more widely visible, often by syncing film's technological aesthetics with that work's industrial forms, and often to define the world as so many factories, railroads, and workers; mines, construction sites, and oil derricks; and consumer-end technical systems. When cinema's connections to extraction and the films align—as in films such as *La sortie de l'usine Lumière à Lyon* or the Westinghouse Works series—the cinema of *attractions* becomes an early cinema of *extractions* in its most explicit and reflexive form. But even when cinema's materiality is merely the *force behind*, not the *content of*, the filmed image, we again and again find cinema in the role of Mumford's specific art or Nye's industrial world interpretation—the role, that is, of fashioning a world in the image of extraction, its industries, and the industries whose work it made possible.

During the 1910s, this cinema of extractions split into two primary forms. In its explicit form, to which I turn in chapters 3 and 4, it became what we now know as the industrial, corporate, or sponsored film, which was developed earliest and most fully by companies such as Ford and soon by oil firms, industrial manufacturers, and government agencies as well as at the local level by municipal boosters invested in promoting cities and towns on their industries and infrastructure.[35] In its more implicit, less overtly visible form, it persisted in the classical Hollywood film industry that I describe, in chapter 2, as a cinema of resource integration. I want to emphasize, however, that this split is partly the legacy of the methodological division in cinema and media studies between a long-standing devotion to the feature film and its industry and the more recent recognition of parallel industrial film industries. Understood conceptually as different outgrowths of the early cinema of extractions described in this chapter, these two industries, though long—and mostly still—studied separately, have always been, even when seemingly most different, two sides of the same coin and two versions of the same modern ambition: to imagine, create, and control material and conceptual worlds.

2

FROM EXTRACTIONS TO RESOURCE INTEGRATION

As the cinema of attractions gave way in the late 1900s to a cinema of narrative integration and, by the end of the ensuing transitional era, to Hollywood's classical modes, so too did the cinema of extractions shift steadily into the backgrounds and margins of film texts. No longer the overt subject of an increasingly dominant film industry focused on studio-produced fiction, extractions nonetheless continued to animate the texts and worldviews spread by the growing domain of industrial and corporate film. But even in Hollywood's popular narrative films, the cinema of extractions remained important, both thematically and conceptually, to the emerging classical cinema. Tracing its continuation in this form, and not just in the industrial film world to which this book turns next, offers an arguably even more compelling way to demonstrate what materialist knowledge can do for textual interpretation in forms of cinema that concealed their progressively unconscious debt to extractive industries and worldviews. To see how this works, in this chapter, I track forward to the 1910s to read two examples from the transitional era—D. W. Griffith's *The Lonedale Operator* (1911) and Lois Weber's *Sunshine Molly* (1915)—as films that demonstrate the transition from extractions to resource integration by encoding, at times in reflexive ways, the enduring importance of cinema's extractive dependencies. The chapter concludes with a brief example of cinema's vertical resource integration.

As I trace this transition, I will also show how reading for extractions can help us think more expansively about early film form and its changes in the classical period—thinking, that is, beyond the form of films to the forms of the material world in which film emerged. Here I take my cues from neoformalist literary criticism, especially as articulated by Caroline Levine, who argues for a mode of analysis in which historical context should be read using the formal modes with which we normally read texts. Levine's work focuses largely on literature, but to take one of her moving-image examples, we should read, she argues, a television show such as *The Wire* formally in two interrelated ways: first, in the normal way, with attention to narrative structure, editing, cinematography, and so on, but also second, by reading its *content* as a series of *forms*—so for example, by reading the drug trade as a network with lines and nodes, street corners, and alleys; or the government as a hierarchical system of power relations; or the legal system as a binary between good and evil.[1] From Levine, I take the key point that we should read these forms—textual and historical alike—together; to investigate how the one puts pressure on the other; how telling a story about a historical phenomenon with its own formal features shapes or troubles the narrative or visual forms of the telling.

Adding to this method, I will also treat form as a question of *form*ation, or in other words with attention to the proto-cinematic work, spaces, and technologies that *form* on-screen form. These forms, which have become such a critical area of inquiry in recent years, include film and media materials and infrastructure (from studios and sets, cameras, and cables, to all of the mined and manufactured resources and materials used from production through to exhibition) as well as the people and processes illuminated by scholars in production studies and media industry studies.[2] Following Levine's neoformalist argument and adding this attention to the material conditions of production, I want to suggest that this method—in which textual, historical, and material forms collide and interact—offers a different and more dynamic way of analyzing early and transitional-era film than the one told in early cinema's enduring attractions-to-narrative historiography.

To make this more concrete, consider *The Lonedale Operator*, once (and sometimes still) "one of the warhorses," as Kristin Thompson has described it, "of introductory film history classes."[3] Put most succinctly, the film tells the story of a woman played by Blanche Sweet who takes over the telegraph at a remote rail station and the railroad engineer who comes to her rescue during an attempted robbery that she foils by fooling her would-be attackers with a wrench posed as a gun. Griffith narrates the drama using a system of crosscutting that was not entirely new but achieved a novel degree of intensity with an unusual number of shots, movement between three locations rather than two, and the rhythm of that movement. Owing to these traits and as what Tom Gunning sums up as the "perfect example of Griffith's Biograph style," the film has often been used to illustrate, in Raymond Bellour's words, "the systematicity at the heart of American high classicism."[4] As an exemplary case of the consolidation of narrative that anticipates, or, depending on your view, may have helped establish the Hollywood mode to come, the film might seem like an unlikely example for stressing the cinema of extractions' *nontextual* formal relations, but this makes it especially worth considering.

Having taught the film for many years, I am drawn to it now for how it brings special, although seldom and only partially considered, attention to early cinema's material reality. Unlike the early cinema of extractions, it does not do so by putting extraction literally on screen. Instead, it folds extraction into the narrative, as the structuring absence—like the infrastructure of cinema itself—for the film's action. This enfolding, through which film narrative subsumed extraction (just as it integrated attractions), defined the transition-era shift to a new cinema of resource integration that *The Lonedale Operator* makes unusually visible.

The primary clue comes in one of two handwritten cards, both transcriptions of telegraph messages, that appears around the seven-minute mark, just after Sweet's character has taken over the telegraph from her ailing father. The note reads, "Operator Lonedale Station: The money for Lonedale Mining Company will arrive train No. 6," signed "G. W. B." (figure 2.1). In this image, we find the collision of three formal systems: first, the form of film narration in which on-screen text like this note afforded filmmakers a means to explain actions and teach viewers to follow increasingly complex narratives. This formal system—part of the story of narrative integration—is well known, and indeed most formal analyses of the film, even the most sophisticated, have stopped there. But, second, this card also indexes

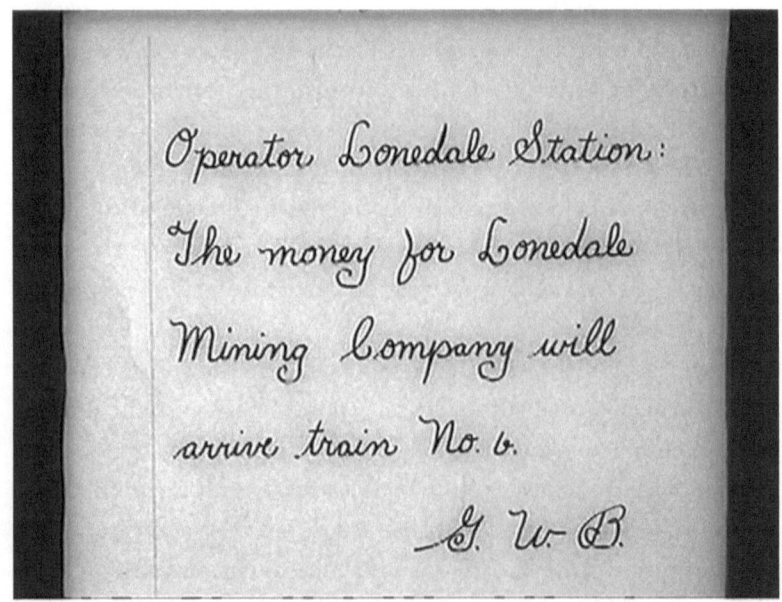

FIGURE 2.1 *The Lonedale Operator* (dir. D. W. Griffith, 1911).

a formal system of economic and material exchange: the movement of money and mined resources across time and space through formalized networks of creation, storage, delivery, security, and transfer. The *Biograph Bulletin* description of the film made this connection clear to potential exhibitors, noting that "Lonedale hardly belied its name, for it was the most isolated spot in the western country. The principal reason for its being on the railroad map as a stopping place was the fact that it is the location of a productive mine."[5] This formal system of mines and railroads—the form of the film's content, in the sense described by Levine—made extraction industries possible and profitable. Finally, third, the card points, in its encoded reference to the film's camera operator, Gottfried Wilhelm Bitzer (the note's signed "G. W. B."), to the form of cinematic production itself, the system of machines, the rhythm of working practices, and the conceptual development of the formal system of narration that gave this text its material and aesthetic forms.

Gunning has come the closest, to my knowledge, to the kind of reading we get if we pay attention to that second system, the form of the film's content. Highlighting aspects of the film such as the office scene in which the imperiled payroll money first changes hands before G. W. B.'s note appears, Gunning argues that "the systematic order of *The Lonedale Operator* extends beyond its narration and becomes part of its diegetic world." This is a world, Gunning writes, of "words, order, and routines" and of "modern systems of transportation [the railroad] and communication [the telegraph]." These worlds, he explains, "subtend the action of the film" that more typically define it—the criminals, the call for help, and the race to the rescue. And though he cautions against naively "claim[ing that] the styles(s) of early film were 'caused' by the demands of modern life," Gunning nonetheless argues precisely that "Griffith edits his film as if inspired by the telegraph, [and] constructs his dramaturgy as if mirroring the railway networks of interconnecting speed and urgency."[6]

This "as if" reading is what Levine would define as a form of epiphenomenal analysis that shows how form reflects or mimics context.[7] But it also approaches what Levine's neoformalist method defines as an analysis of the collision between two formal systems, one that need not, I want to emphasize, lead to the "naïve," as Gunning would have it, claim that the one system "caused" the other.[8] On the contextual side, we have a historical world of networks (with the rail stations and mines as nodes connected by lines), binaries (in a sense closer to Bellour's structuralist analysis of the film's treatment of gender, or of legality and criminality), and rhythms (especially the workday that separates the "sweethearts"). On the textual side, we have an emerging system of narrative form defined, in particular, by crosscutting, but also establishing shots, title cards, limited character development, dramatic tension, and resolution.

What makes *The Lonedale Operator* so successful is how the form of its content and the form of its aesthetics synchronize. Griffith's adoption of the formal strategy of crosscutting allowed him to tell stories about technological forms and systems of formal relations that similarly worked based on alternations across time and space. The railroad, with its lines and nodes—and even more so the telegraph with its binodal system of back-and-forth exchange—lent themselves to this kind of formal aesthetic system.[9] The mining industry, too, rests on a form of alterity between the site and time of extraction and the many sites and later times of use. Many of those sites and times appear prominently in Griffith's film, including the coal-burning locomotive that races ahead, tinted red, to the rescue, or the electrical light that Blanche Sweet turns off in one final effort to resist her attackers. That light also marks the endpoint of the fossil-fuel-powered system that in some ways completes the film's circuit from energy producer (mine) to consumer (light), connected by the money named in G. W. B.'s telegraph message. There is, in other words, a form of causation: the causation in which the formal system that Griffith uses as his film's raw material—the form of his film's content—necessarily encourages, if not quite demands (after all, there were other ways to narrate the same scenario), certain ways of recording it aesthetically.[10] But that causation also goes the other way in the sense that Griffith's adoption of crosscutting surely drove him to find stories—and, just as important, formal settings—through which to deploy his preferred cinematic form.

Finally, continuing to the third formal system, film's material underpinning, the collision of forms in the G. W. B. telegraph message tells us something more than we get from Gunning's analysis of the film's "words, order, and routines." It is not just that Griffith *seems*, as Gunning argues, to have mimicked or mirrored the telegraph and railroad, thereby generating a film form inspired by the forms of modern technological communication. It is also that these forms determine the film's very possibility. Without the Lonedale Mining Companies of the world, there could be no telegraph with its copper wires, no coal-powered locomotive rescue, and indeed no film itself. In this sense, the mining company's payroll delivery is more than just, as Gunning puts it, a "MacGuffin." Rather, it is a sign, encoded into the film image, of the formal relations subtending the film industry.

Although not, most likely, a conscious message, this sign nonetheless carries a political reading consistent with Griffith and Bitzer's political formalism. We know, thanks to analyses of other Biograph films of the time—most famously *A Corner in Wheat* (1909) but also *Song of the Shirt* (1908), *The Usurer* (1910), and *Gold Is Not All* (1910)—that Griffith and Bitzer recognized how contrasting editing could reveal political relations.[11] Such relations, as Charlie Kiel has demonstrated in his analysis of *The Musketeers of Pig Alley* (1912), could take a number of other forms too, including the relation between on- and off-screen space that, as Kiel puts it, "indicates the claims of another realm—of bureaucratic corruption."[12] The "claims of another realm" that appear in *The Lonedale Operator* signal, consciously or not, the other realm of extraction and film's dependence on it—a realm Griffith and Bitzer knew well from setting and shooting films in Los

Angeles's growing oil fields from the first moments of their arrival in 1910 (see chapter 1). Signed by Bitzer, the G. W. B. who doubly encodes himself into the film as a pivot both for the film's form of communication through title cards and of the exchange, fundamental to the film's formation, between the mines and the film industry, the telegraph message marks a reflexive acknowledgment of such formal collisions and their politics.

In sum, when taken in a multiformalist sense attentive to film form, the forms of its contents, and the material forms of its making, a film like *The Lonedale Operator* invites us to read—as on a mobius strip—between the three formal systems made simultaneously visible in G. W. B.'s reflexive telegraph message. It would be hard to imagine a better example than this message of what Grieveson describes when he writes: "the political economy of liberalism, in its corporate, globalizing, phase, was scratched into the surface of media like the images etched onto the photosensitive minerals and chemistry of celluloid."[13]

Just as they mark a key turning point in the transition from the cinema of attractions to narrative integration and on to feature film classicism, transition-era films, such as *The Lonedale Operator*, also mark a shift away from the early cinema of extractions forged in Lumière actualities and Edison nonfiction films to a "cinema of resource integration." In that cinema, to which I turn next, nonfilm industries subtended the film industry's expansion and the further integration of its resource dependence, especially with the expansion of studio backlots and the widespread adoption of artificial lighting in the studio factories that dominated U.S. production by the late 1910s.

Rethinking early cinema in materialist and neoformalist terms allows us to think beyond debates about style—especially including the charge that the so-called modernity thesis could not account for stylistic change—that helped drive early film historiography but now risk becoming a force for stagnation if they define the questions we ask. It also offers new ways to connect cinema's early conception and its textual forms to what came later. The "cinema of extractions"—understood as a way of thinking about, documenting, and imagining the world as a set of resources—initially worked in concert with the cinema of attractions, with its style and a mode of address—the cinema of *monstration*—that showed viewers an extractable world. The "cinema of resource integration"—understood as the film industry's integration of resource economies and its reliance on electrical power in all phases, from production with artificial lighting to theaters equipped with air-conditioning systems—both shaped and was supported by the ensuing process of narrative integration. The resulting development of film's growing industrial dependence often led to films that continued to define the world in extractive terms, even if extraction tended to become only a marginal element of on-screen action. As extraction retreated from view, however, in its place films offered more expansive views of extractive worlds and their broader social, cultural, economic, and political consequences.

THE CINEMA OF RESOURCE INTEGRATION

On March 15, 1915, Universal City officially opened for business, marking a starting point for the classical Hollywood studio system and the associated resource expenditure that has become a common subject of materialist film ecocriticism.[14] With its row of fifteen sets, Universal embodied the consolidation of a mode of efficient production fine-tuned for the system of classical narration that made the cinema of attractions a relic of a seemingly distant film past. With its vast infrastructure, storehouses of film technologies and production materials, and vast 230 acres of backlots, Universal also exemplified the cinema of "resource integration" that absorbed the early cinema of extractions into its basic constitution as a world-making system. This system was founded on capturing land and recreating worlds at ever-larger scales and with ever-greater powers of simulation.[15]

Much as attractions, in Gunning's account, persisted as the "primal power . . . running beneath the armature of narrative regulation," so too did extractions—in both the material and conceptual sense—continue to undergird classical cinema's armature of resource management.[16] In the aesthetic sense, extractions also took on a new role, no longer as the focus of film content but instead as the setting for narrative action or the event for attractions-like spectacle. Extractive processes and their material and conceptual products—their worldviews—thus remained visible in films that either took extraction as their subject or exposed, in their depiction of resources, cinema's material requirements. In this new iteration, the cinema of extractions revealed a complex negotiation between materials and visual forms that reflexively embodied the material-aesthetic relationship behind the creation of every film world.

Although this material-immaterial negotiation may be read in films with many subjects, I focus on two iterations of a recurring extractive trope that also well illustrates the connection between extraction and attraction that persisted long after early cinema: the spectacle of the burning oil well. This marvel of nearly uncontrollable fire has animated films of all types and genres, from the early Lumière actuality *Puits de pétrole à Bakou: Vue de près* (*Oil Wells of Baku: Close View*; dir. Alexandre Michon, 1897) to Henri-Georges Clouzot's drama of U.S. petro-colonialism, *Le salaire de la peur* (*The Wages of Fear*, 1953); Bernardo Bertolucci's Eni-sponsored industrial oil epic, *La via del petrolio* (1967); Werner Herzog's documentary, *Lektionen in Finsternis* (*Lessons of Darkness*, 1992); Sam Mendes's Gulf War film, *Jarhead* (2005); and P. T. Anderson's Upton Sinclair adaptation, *There Will be Blood* (2007).

From the many possible examples, I will focus on two of the earliest feature-film iterations: Lois Weber's *Sunshine Molly* (1915), a story set and shot in California oil country that was celebrated for its realistic portrayal of the oil industry and spectacular well fire, and, more briefly, the 1924 First National release *Flowing Gold* (dir. Joseph De Grasse). The latter film not only used Los Angeles's oil fields as the setting for melodrama and a studio-produced fiery spectacle but also shows, through its marketing and distribution, how the cinema of resource integration connected, as Hollywood became vertically integrated, with the interconnected systems of distribution and sales that shaped oil producers' integration with the downstream U.S. gasoline business. These films represent ongoing reflexive meditations on the material work of cinematic world-making examined in chapter 1. The need to source and control images of the oil industry and its fires while rendering them both legible and aesthetic becomes, I argue, an allegory for the tenuous balance of control and contingency, materiality and immateriality, that similarly makes cinematic worlds (profilmic and diegetic) and extractive worlds (like the oil fields) functional and most often mediated to the point of near invisibility.

SUNSHINE MOLLY AND THE HOLLYWOOD CINEMA OF RESOURCE INTEGRATION

Few films could better express extraction's material and formal integration in early Hollywood's narrative and industrial systems than Lois Weber's 1915 feature *Sunshine Molly*. Released three days after Universal's opening, the film was produced for the competing Bosworth company, which had built a production complex that, although soon overshadowed by Universal's, could still be described in two articles published that July as "one of the most complete studios of the west coast" and "one of the most efficiently equipped and up-to-date establishments in the country."[17] Like Universal, Bosworth's studio helped make cinema what Charlie Chaplin saw as one of those "horsemen of the apocalypse," with oil and aeronautics, that was transforming Los Angeles in the mid-1910s. Shot partly in the oil fields adjacent to Hollywood, *Sunshine Molly* made that transformation and the conditions for a cinema of resource integration remarkably visible.[18]

The film tells the story of the eponymous Molly, played by Weber, who takes a job at a boardinghouse for oil workers after, we later learn, a stint in prison for attacking a man who had raped her while she was working at a factory owned by the man's father. The eventual revelation about Molly's past casts a new light on the film's preceding drama, which turns largely on Molly's rejection of an oil worker named Bull who sexually harasses her from her first moments working at the boardinghouse. In a conclusion that is difficult to reconcile given his behavior, Bull nonetheless becomes Molly's husband after helping fight off her former rapist—although not before the latter sets fire to the oil fields in the film's visually spectacular denouement.

The film is thus primarily concerned, as Shelley Stamp has written, with "the issue of sexual harassment and sexual violence in the workplace," a theme that notably need not have unfolded in California oil country.[19] Although oil towns continue to report statistically higher rates of sexual violence, making the setting appropriate then and now, Weber might easily have found a different backdrop, as she did elsewhere, including in earlier films such as *Fine Feathers* (Rex, 1912).[20] There Weber plays Mira, a house cleaner who becomes the model for an artist who preys on her economic precarity, much like the customers who frequent the five-and-dime store in Weber's later classic, *Shoes* (Universal, 1916).

Weber always had a sharp eye for allegory, and *Fine Feathers* was just one of several films that used artistic settings to comment on the nature of women's experiences and the circulation of their images—all with clear implications for the film industry and a blossoming star system that relied on the commodification, objectification, and sexualization of women like Weber. As Stamp argues, *Fine Feathers* and Weber's next film, *A Japanese Idyll* (Rex, 1912), in which a woman is exoticized and exploited by a photographer, represented "self-conscious meditation[s] on the reproduction and commodification of the female image, on male and female desire, and on the use of voyeurism and exhibitionism to control diegetic space."[21]

Insofar as it did not parallel the forms of image exploitation seen in Weber's earlier films, the oil industry was not an obvious site for such a reflexive or allegorical commentary. But like *Fine Feathers*, *Sunshine Molly* has all the elements of an allegory about exploitation in Hollywood—a reflexivity built, this time, not on the similarity between artistic settings but instead on the material connections between the work of extraction and the emerging work of resource-dependent film production. When understood in *materialist* rather than *aesthetic* terms, in other words, the connections *Sunshine Molly* draws between the worlds of oil and cinema and their allegorical implications become clear. It is precisely the material nature of its allegory that makes *Sunshine Molly* such a powerful example of what the cinema of extractions became in the early era of resource integration. More than just a document of the early California oil industry and its proximity to early Hollywood, the film uniquely and reflexively opens onto the similarities and synchronicities between two industries founded on what soon became mutually reinforcing conditions of production. As I did with *The Lonedale Operator*, I will trace these connections by reading across and between three formal registers: the film's textual form, the forms of its content, and the material conditions of its formation, but this time in reverse order.

The story of the film's material formation on the Bosworth studio set and in nearby oil fields quickly reveals a fascinating web of land and resource interests that shaped Los Angeles in the film industry's early years. In part, the Bosworth team did exactly what one would expect of a studio in the emerging classical Hollywood system: it built a scaled-down model of an oil field on a studio stage (figure 2.2). Pictured in a brief article published in *Moving Picture World* three weeks before the film's release, the set demonstrates studio cinema's growing powers of simulation and its world-making aspirations. "Everything was there even to a clothesline and the string of oil cars," the article

FIGURE 2.2 *Moving Picture World* (February 20, 1915).

enthuses, underscoring both the emerging imperatives of studio realism and the material requirements such imperatives demanded. Whole industries and industrial worlds—the stuff of early actualities and attractions—could now simply be reproduced by set painters and pulled from the studios' growing supply closets, one of the key sites of resource integration that required companies such as Paramount to acquire whole forests.[22] Such abundance advanced studio simulation to a point that it even risked exceeding its ultimate aesthetic obligations. "The derricks looked too real," the article insists.[23]

Even accounting for boosterish rhetoric, it does at times become difficult to discern if certain scenes feature studio backdrops or the incredible location scenes that Weber combined in postproduction. The most spectacular of the latter shots include an opening panorama (figure 2.3) filmed as close as the film industry could possibly

FIGURE 2.3 Opening panorama of *Sunshine Molly* (dir. Lois Weber and Phillips Smalley, 1915).

get to its oil counterpart: the oil fields located just a few miles west of the Bosworth studio, south of present-day West Hollywood in a rough rectangle running east from La Brea Avenue to La Cienega, and south from Beverley Boulevard to Wilshire.[24] Panning across a murky stream and through fields with drilling sites as far as the eye can see, the shot ends with Molly, stepping off a dirt road, framed on either side by perfect lines of derricks stretching to the vanishing point behind her head. Molly stares forward, almost into the camera, back where the shot began in her new home, "Oilfield."

First explored by oil prospectors in 1902, that home, the Salt Lake Oil Field (figure 2.4), so named for the first company to drill there, had 326 wells at the beginning of 1912, with 280 in operation (and another 143 already abandoned) by June 1916. Production during these years ranged from 1.5 to 3 million barrels per year.[25] Companies operating

La Brea Lease; Salt Lake Oil Field, Los Angeles County.

FIGURE 2.4 Salt Lake Oil Field (Paul W. Prutzman, *Petroleum in Southern California*, 1913).

in the field notably included the Getty Oil Company (whose iconic museum now sits ten miles west of the first wells), Union Oil of California (Unocal, creator of the Union 76 brand of service stations), and the Clark & Sherman Land Company. The latter firm's coowners, E. P. Clark and Moses Hazeltine Sherman, were among the most significant figures in Los Angeles real estate and had a hand in the subjects of some of the city's best-known (film) stories, including the Pasadena and Pacific Railway, the demise of which drives *Who Framed Roger Rabbit?* (dir. Robert Zemeckis, 1988), and the Board of Water Commissioners that worked with William Mulholland to develop the Los Angeles Aqueduct loosely referenced in *Chinatown* (dir. Roman Polanski, 1974). Perhaps only Angelenos will recognize Sherman's name in the community of Sherman Oaks, but most everyone knows their more significant development, Hollywoodland, with its iconic sign, still a metonym for U.S. commercial cinema. Sherman and Clark founded the development with Los Angeles *Times* publisher Harry Chandler and developers Sydney Woodruff and Tracey Shoults in 1923.[26]

In sum, Weber's 1915 location shoot indexes a web of material relations that was defining the city's future in concert with—but often overshadowed by—the work of film companies such as Universal and Bosworth (which soon merged with Paramount). As the film industry became increasingly energy and land dependent, it relied, for example, on electricity, some of which was powered by oil flowing directly under Weber's tripods. Deals were cut with people, including Sherman and Clark, who owned the vast swaths of land and ranches that became studio backlots and communities for the growing population, and who contributed to the film industry's boosterism designed to support commercial opportunity.

As the two industries flourished, they also became financially entangled in other conspicuous ways. A May 1923 *Variety* cover story announced an "oil well craze" among film stars, with Jackie Coogan, Claire Windsor, Constance Talmadge, and Buster Keaton among the most notable actors with interests in the oil business. Even the derricks were given Hollywood celebrity sheen with names such as "The Buster Keaton" and "Coogan No. 1." Hollywood's elites were so enthralled with this new "fad," the article claimed, that "oil and real estate investments are discussed more frequently and with more fervor . . . than motion pictures."[27] By July, a *Photoplay Magazine* article went so far as to proclaim, "It's a poor star who hasn't an oil well to his credit!"[28] And while Keaton later lamented that he and Fatty Arbuckle had narrowly missed out on an oil treasure after being dissuaded by their cautious studio manager, press reports of the time noted that Keaton had struck a gusher near Long Beach in 1923 and sold out at 100 percent profit two years later.[29]

None of these relations readily appear on the surface of *Sunshine Molly*, but their significance becomes legible, I suggest, when read formally in conversation with the film's textual form and the forms of its contents. Consider the oil field as a formal system, with its rows of derricks, plumbing the depths for untapped resources and wealth; its prospectors, both wizened veterans and eager upstarts, all hoping to strike it rich in a "boom-or-bust" binary; and its gender, racial, and class hierarchies, with rich white male investors at the top (most often conspicuously absent from the field, connected only by tangents running to wealthy neighborhoods far removed from the dirty, dangerous work) and women, minorities, and laborers in supporting roles on the ground, dreaming of—and sometimes attaining—social mobility. Consider also its sprawling networks of financial investment and speculation, with nodes in oil fields, banks, land companies, such as Clark and Sherman, and reinvestment industries, such as cinema, as we find early with companies, including Gaumont, Pathé, Edison, and Biograph, and later in the classical Hollywood years.

As with *The Lonedale Operator*, these formal systems shape the form of *Sunshine Molly*. First, and most plainly, the oil industry structures the film's visual form, with its opening panorama of the field, high-angle shots taken from the tops of derricks (figure 2.5), and the

FIGURE 2.5 *Sunshine Molly*'s derrick's-eye view.

oil-powered conflagration that gives the film its spectacular conclusion (and a prime aspect of its marketing). The film's narrative structure and character development similarly, if less obviously, take their cues from oil industry forms. Part of the film's drama, for example, rests precisely on prospecting's boom or bust dynamic, which drives one of the narrative's turning points when young prospector Pat O'Brien strikes a "gusher." The resulting sudden wealth relocates Pat's family to the city and up the social hierarchy into a class that includes Molly's rapist, who follows O'Brien's sister Patricia back to Oilfield, setting up the film's dramatic conclusion. Similarly, an industry shaped by consolidated wealth and redistributed risk leaves unsuccessful prospectors like "Old Pete" without resources or care systems and thus dependent on the kindness of women like Molly. The resulting social formations drive the film's character and narrative development, not least including Molly's and Bull's ultimate union, which is shaped by Bull's willingness to help Molly with Pete's care.

When taken as a shaping force, and not merely the interchangeable backdrop for the film's narrative action, the context of the early Los Angeles oil industry becomes a striking allegory for its early film counterpart. In this reading, the prospectors, each with their drill and derrick, are analogs for Hollywood's producers and directors, each on their stage hoping to tap the metaphorical well of success. Salt Lake Field's rows of derricks are Universal's rows of sets. "Oilfield" is, in both a profilmic and a diegetic sense, a backlot. But consider especially Molly, the new arrival, searching for opportunity in the West. Her story of a woman in California oil country readily stands in for what Hilary Hallett describes as the boosterish claim of these years that the movies were the "gold rush business for ambitious, single, young white women on the make."[30] Molly, in other words, might just as well have landed on some producer's couch as in the Oilfield boardinghouse and with similar results. In sum, it was the oil industry's gendered forms, its backlot-like settings, its boom or bust dynamic—and its proximity and material connections to the movie industry—that made it, like the worlds of art and photography, a suitable, if less obvious, analog for Hollywood and a place to explore the experiences of women who came to Los Angeles looking for a new life in a new industry.

We can tie these intersecting formal relations together by looking more closely, finally, at how they shaped Weber's approach to visual form, and in particular how oil becomes present in *Sunshine Molly*, shifting in and out of focus, in part as the film moves between studio and location footage. The management of land, bodies, and resources that the film narrates—again, in an allegorical form that implicates the film industry—is particularly visible in how Weber directs the oil industry setting. Put simply, her approach illuminates how, in the new era of resource integration, the cinema of extractions moved to the margins of visibility, although still ready, as with attractions, to reappear spectacularly at any moment.

In its purest textual form, *Sunshine Molly* is a circle with a series of circular messages. This circularity appears visually in the opening panorama, which slowly traces its arc around Oilfield, carving out the primary field of action into which Weber and Molly arrive at the shot's conclusion. Molly's story follows a similar circular path. Having escaped her past life, she is nonetheless forced to face it again, circling back, unwillingly, to face her former rapist, whose own circular path brings him back to harm Molly again. That circle is finally broken in the conclusion when the oil men attack the rapist, enacting informal justice where it has otherwise been denied (what goes around comes around). But it also leads Molly back to Bull, a difficult to understand outcome that does make, however, a political argument, when read formally, about the challenge of breaking cycles of misogyny.

Just as interesting is the formal path oil takes. Following the Salt Lake Field's prominent appearance in the opening panorama that establishes the field of action, the oil fields shift, for much of the film, into the background of the narrative action. With that shift in emphasis comes a shift in form, with the Bosworth studio's oil set largely replacing the early location shots. Weber circles back to location footage, not least in moments of spectacle such as when Pat O'Brien's well strikes oil (figure 2.6). But often Weber opts—as one expects in the emerging classical mode of studio production—for the painted backdrop, which appears most frequently as characters enter and exit the boardinghouse's open door (figure 2.7). Prefiguring the iconic doorway shots that frame *The Searchers* (1956), with John Ford's camera tracking out of the domestic interior and into the "wild" west before tracking back inside as John Wayne departs at the conclusion, in *Sunshine Molly*, the door demarcates a powerful distinction, this

FIGURE 2.6 Location shot of Pat's "gusher" in *Sunshine Molly*.

FIGURE 2.7 Oil as literal and figurative backdrop for narrative action in *Sunshine Molly*.

time a material cinematic one. The location shots from Salt Lake Field tell us that the exteriors are oil land, and the painted backdrop preserves the illusion. But what we see when we look through the door, in both a literal and ultimately an allegorical sense, is the film industry and its powers of worlding illusion. Although the painted backdrop thus represents, in the most straightforward sense, the early Los Angeles oil industry it depicts, on a deeper level, it signifies cinema. This layering of meaning becomes meaningful when we appreciate the geographic and material relations between cinema and the oil it both references and requires.

Read in this way, *Sunshine Molly* shows us how, in the cinema of resource integration, the stuff of extraction becomes, at once, the film industry's structuring material and the film image's structuring absence. Oil was everywhere in early Hollywood, flowing around and beneath the studio backlots; supporting the industry's increasing dependency on lights; enriching its derrick-crazy stars; and fueling its growing reliance on the endless rows of cars that appear in studio publicity photos and throughout early Hollywood films.[31] *Sunshine Molly* not only puts this oil on display from its opening shot but also moves it into the literal and figurative background, where it remains the "primal power," as Gunning put it about attractions, "running beneath the armature" of both narrative and resource integration. That the oil cannot fully be suppressed, returning as it does in the film's fiery final act, which circles back to the film's material origins in the real oil fields, highlights the similarity between how extractions and attractions remained visible in early Hollywood and beyond. It also foreshadows how the industry's repressed primal energy would return, again and again in fiery form, as a constant reminder that making film, like pumping oil, comes with material costs that leave formal traces—a cycle that has yet to be broken.[32]

CONCLUSION: VERTICAL RESOURCE INTEGRATION

As Hollywood vertically integrated in the years after *Sunshine Molly*'s release, the importance of resource integration extended to the forms of distribution and exhibition that connected texts with viewers. Consider, in this respect, one final example: the 1924 Texas oil drama *Flowing Gold*. Long believed lost, the film was discovered in the National Film Archive of the Czech Republic and is, at the time of writing, being restored with funding from the National Film Preservation Foundation under the direction of the San Francisco Silent Film Festival. Although it is not possible to subject it fully to the kind of layered formal analysis this book advocates, the film nonetheless helpfully demonstrates, in its parallels with *Sunshine Molly*, both that Weber's film was not an isolated case and the course that the cinema of resource integration took as the classical period entered its prime.

Based on a novel by popular writer Rex Beach, the film takes place in post–Civil War Texas in the early days of the U.S. oil boom but was shot, like *Sunshine Molly*, in two sites: on location in an unidentified Los Angeles oil field and on the backlot of the United Studios complex adjacent to the Hollywood Cemetery.[33] As with *Sunshine Molly*, coverage in the trade press highlighted a combination of the film's realism (based, reportedly, on photographs and notes taken by producer Richard Walton Tully during a visit to Ranger, Texas), its use of the local oil fields (including a call for oil companies to donate wells to be burned), and the eventual staging of the dramatic well fire on the backlot (figure 2.8).[34] But the film's real interest lies, particularly in the absence of having the film to analyze, in how its marketing and distribution connected Hollywood's classical system to the integrated interests of the oil industry's growing systems of marketing and distribution.

The film in many ways embodies the studio system as it came into focus during the 1920s. It was produced by playwright Richard Walton Tully for First National Pictures, which originally was

FIGURE 2.8 Filming *Flowing Gold*'s burning well (*Exhibitors Trade Review*, March 22, 1924).

an association of independent theater owners that transformed into a distribution company. By early 1924, First National began moving into production, only to be bought out by Warner Brothers in 1928 as the latter sought to expand its theater holdings. The United Studios, where Tully shot the film's staged scenes, was a common destination for independent producers looking for more space, not least including Buster Keaton, who shot parts of *Our Hospitality* (1923) there the same year, and it too became part of the majors when Paramount acquired it in 1926.[35] In short, it would not be too much to say that *Flowing Gold* emerged from classical Hollywood ground zero.

As First National began marketing the film in early 1924 (figure 2.9), the oil industry connections that helped give the film form quickly also shaped the forms of its sales and distribution. As no reviewer failed to note in the months ahead, the company attempted to profit, in particular, from the Teapot Dome scandal that had plagued the Harding administration from 1921 until the president's death in 1923 and continued to make headlines as *Flowing Gold* reached screens in early 1924.[36] A bribery case involving Harding's secretary of the interior, the scandal took its name from a Wyoming oil field but also involved fields in Los Angeles and implicated Los Angeles oil man Edward L. Doheny, who had made a fortune in 1892 after tapping the first oil wells north of present-day downtown and played a critical role developing oil publicity in the 1920s.[37] As one reviewer counseled potential exhibitors, "play up the Government oil scandals in your exploitation."[38] A February 18, 1924, advertisement made the connection clearer: "Teapot Dome scandal is busting Washington wide open. Richard Walton Tully's presentation of Rex Beach's 'Flowing Gold' (also an oil problem) will bust open the box offices of the whole country."[39]

As the film reached exhibitors on the national distribution circuit, local forms of advertising also emerged to connect the film's theme to local oil concerns. In Peoria, Illinois, for example, the Madison Theatre partnered with the Eraco Oil Company to line the front of

FIGURE 2.9 *Picture-Play Magazine* (April 1924).

the theater with oil cans spelling out the film's title.[40] The Mainstreet Theatre in Kansas City similarly teamed up with the local White Rose gasoline stations, which "carried a 'Flowing Gold' line on their sign board in connection with the station's own boost for En-Ar-Co."[41] A more elaborate gimmick appeared at the Strand Theatre in Laredo, Texas, home to a recently discovered "5,000 barrel gusher," where owner Jack Rowley built a scaled-down derrick (Rowly No. 1) to frame the box office, leading, according to a booberish *Moving Picture World* article, to "results at the box office [that] were as good

FIGURE 2.10 *Flowing Gold* (dir. Joseph De Grasse, 1924) tie-in for the Rex Theatre (Eugene, Oregon).

as though he were pumping by the barrel."[42] In Eugene, Oregon, finally, the Rex Theatre borrowed the window display of a local oil firm featuring a painted backdrop and miniature derrick and a mechanical pump that endlessly raised and redeposited a splash of crude (figure 2.10).[43]

These kinds of publicity tie-ins were a common feature of Hollywood's classical distribution system and reveal the close ties vertically integrated production companies kept—by way of publicity managers and regional distribution hubs—with their theater circuits as well as the competitive theater environment that required local owners to find novel ways to capture the interests of audiences presented, week after week, with the similar fare churned out of Hollywood's studio factories.[44] This system's form mirrored the form of the nation's expanding gasoline distribution system, which integrated producers, distributors, and consumer-end sales points, all selling a standardized product differentiated by increasingly innovative forms of marketing: the oil industry's competing images. The latter soon included sponsored filmed images produced alongside and at times in coordination with the film industry. Such connections are the subject of the following chapters. But already films such as *Flowing Gold* show the shared, at times intersecting, practices of film and extractive industries that shaped cinema's resource integration in the 1910s and into the 1920s and became visible and occasionally reflexive markers of narrative films in both their textual and paratextual attractions.

It will have to be left to future viewers of a restored *Flowing Gold* to read these industrial forms and formations in dialogue with the film's textual forms and the forms of its content. As I have attempted to demonstrate in this chapter's analyses of *The Lonedale Operator* and *Sunshine Molly*, the upshot of a materially informed formal approach is both a more nuanced account of cinema's textual and contextual engagements with extractive industries than we get with either textual or material analysis alone *and* a way of tracing cinema's expansive world-making ambitions as they took form before, in, and beyond film's textual worlds. I turn next to the other side of the media-extraction equation to consider how extractive industries came at this engagement from a different perspective but ultimately with similar world-making ambitions. Thinking about early cinema and Hollywood classicism through the lens of extraction should remind us that these two industries—the Hollywood industry that David James named "industrial cinema" and the cinema of industry to which we apply that name now—were not parallel pursuits to be studied separately but rather two sides of the same coin that need to be read together.[45]

3

MINING MEDIA, OR, ELEMENTAL ENERGY FOR MOTION PICTURES

Powered by the publicity tie-ins that connected films such as *Flowing Gold* (dir. Joseph De Grasse, 1924) to U.S. gasoline sales, cinema's material and energetic requirements flowed across its distribution networks and spiked at their nodes, the theaters. Inside, pressing material and formal questions awaited, especially for the projectionists tasked with managing cinema's most essential element, light. Richly described by one technical guide as "energy for motion pictures," light defined film practice at every step, from production stages to processing darkrooms and on to projection cabins (figures 3.1 and 3.2).[1] The technologies and techniques for creating and controlling it offer another instance of cinema's broader debt to extractive industries and the new scientific knowledge and industrial processes needed to transform raw energetic and electrical conducting materials into manageable light sources. Setting aside cinema's obvious need for extracted energy to generate the electricity powering every film device after hand cranking, this chapter centers on two of the most important materials needed to give that electricity visible form: the carbon used in carbon rods for arc lamps and the tungsten used first in incandescent lighting filaments and then in everything from studio lamps and projector bulbs to radio, television, and computer vacuum tubes, smart phones, and watches. Extracted,

FIGURES 3.1–3.2 Using iconography that recalls early ads for the kinetoscope and cinematograph, carbon manufacturers sold their product and its managed light as the very essence of the film image. *Moving Picture World* (July 10, 1915, and November 23, 1912).

processed, and refined, these two elements shaped cinematic lighting for more than a century, and they also point to modern media's broader reliance on the various mined minerals commonly referred to as "rare earths."

Mastering these materials and their illuminating technologies was part and parcel of the cinema of resource integration, which involved similar forms of resource consolidation for exhibitors as it did for producers. Although film production has more often been the focus of materialist film ecocriticism, exhibition was similarly driven by enormous quantities of extracted energy and labor and generated significant waste and pollution.[2] During cinema's first two decades, its light came from various chemical and electrical sources, most of which was borrowed from broader industrial contexts, including street lighting and factory illumination.[3] By the 1910s, the arc lamp emerged as the most common light source, both for production and projection. Incandescent lights offered another option, and eventually, thanks to the development of brighter and more efficient tungsten filaments, they became the source of choice in sound production (in part because they were quieter). Arc lamps, however, remained the norm in projection for almost another half-century.

Cinema's need for light was no less important than—and inseparable from—the other material things, not least of which was celluloid, that made recording and playback possible. But managing light was also a formal concern that I approach in three ways. First, I consider how carbon and tungsten became cinematically useful forms as the carbons in arc lamp projectors and the raw materials for bulb filaments and vacuum tubes. Those forms were important film-industry trade secrets and the basis for patent disputes shaped, to a significant degree, by the question of whose processes made useful materials take form. Second, I highlight the role form played in these materials' practical deployment, with an emphasis on film projectionists' preoccupation with just how to position arc lamps' carbons. Technical guides and trade press columns featured frequent discussions about the proper arrangement of carbon rods, and the stakes were at once material, economic, and aesthetic. What the audience saw—and how much theater owners earned—remained, for many years, partly a question of formal choices made by the projectionists tasked with arranging two lines to create a perfect arc, the shape that named their projecting devices.

Finally, I use these material histories and the forms they reveal, along with the forms of the mining industries that extracted these minerals, to read the films mine companies made to promote them. If, as John Durham Peters and others have argued, media scholars must recognize the "elemental legacy of the media concept," we must do so not just by considering the elements that make the media but also how media make visible the elements.[4] Not surprisingly, useful film and media materials, such as carbon and tungsten, became the subject of "useful" films that I read as reflexive and literal media archaeologies forged in deep time and space. Such films' forms have too seldom been analyzed but merit attention both for how closely they followed the forms of their subjects and for what they reveal about the role aesthetics played in making them "useful." To illustrate this formal correspondence, in this chapter, I analyze one primary example, a 1960s film made by Union Carbide (seller of C, W, and related alloys). Here, and more fully in chapter 4, I pursue what I describe as industrial film's "prosaic poetics," the often banal but important formal system through which corporate-produced films sought to shape broad understandings and opinions about their work—or, to put it more boldly—to create the worlds, and formal systems, in which their products could succeed.[5]

CARBON CINEMA

During the summer of 1915, a looming material crisis threatened to disrupt the resource integration underwriting Hollywood's growing studios.[6] Trade press articles attempted to calm concerned readers, who feared shortages of raw materials, including cotton, wood, and gelatin, as well as chemicals, such as hydroquinone and metol, needed for film processing.[7] Many of these materials could be found in the United States, and even those largely imported from German chemical companies could, the articles assured, just as easily be produced closer to home. Still, the trade press reported runs on materials and soaring prices that sent shudders across the industry. The threat of resource scarcity had suddenly put resource integration—and with it, U.S. cinema's bright future—in doubt.

Arguably no product generated greater anxiety than the carbon rods found in the arc lamps used by studios and theaters to create that most essential cinematic element: light. Interviewed that August in the trade paper *Motion Picture News*, George Kiewert, vice president of the company producing "Bio" carbons, promised readers that the market in carbons would remain robust and that the company had even refused massive orders (up to ten thousand rods) from nervous clients. So long as the German supply chains held, he insisted, exhibitors had nothing to fear.[8] Kiewert's hopeful promise proved to be an ill-fated prophecy, but in the meantime, other U.S. industrialists had seen an opportunity in the emerging chaos and rushed to fill the gap. By September, readers of the same paper could take some solace in the coverage of a new endeavor: an American-born carbon rod ready to roll off new assembly lines in Saint Mary's, Pennsylvania.[9] Their producer, the Speer Carbon Company, specialized in making other carbon products, including brushes used in electrical machinery and automobile engines. Adding facilities for rods required capital investment and expanded infrastructure but little additional expertise in what the company later celebrated as its oil-powered "black magic" (figure 3.3).[10]

"Carbons," as they were commonly termed in the industry, were cylindrical rods, typically measuring 12 inches long and between 7/32 of an inch and 1 inch in diameter. Their composition varied and remained a trade secret, but in general, they included three primary

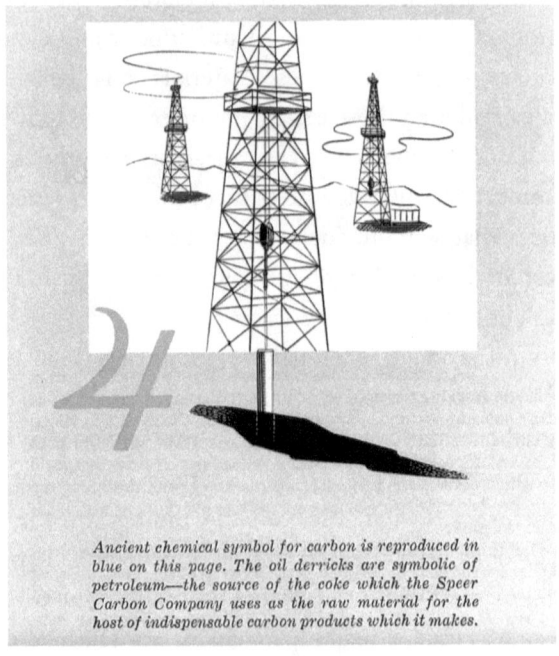

Ancient chemical symbol for carbon is reproduced in blue on this page. The oil derricks are symbolic of petroleum—the source of the coke which the Speer Carbon Company uses as the raw material for the host of indispensable carbon products which it makes.

FIGURE 3.3 Carbon's extracted origins, from the Speer Carbon Company's corporate history, *Black Magic* (1949).

materials: "lampblack," a powder of pure carbon collected from the soot residue left by combustion (first of wood, but by the twentieth century more often, as Speer noted, oil); tar, a by-product of another extractive process, coke production; and pitch, a by-product of dry distilling wood. This standard mixture formed the outer part of the rod, which was often cored and filled with an additional proprietary mixture of mined rare earth minerals that might include "cerium, lanthanum, neodymium and praseodymium."[11] Some rods were then coated in yet another critical mined media element: copper.[12] Once mixed, the carbon "dough" was pressed into molds, cored and filled, and, in a final energy-intensive process, baked at a low temperature for several weeks before trimming, pointing, coating, and packaging.

A carbon's relative success depended on the uniformity and intensity of the light it produced, which in turn depended on how precisely and uniformly it conducted electricity. Through managed conduction across two carbon rods placed in proximity, the arc lamp achieved its essential function: to make electricity visible. The light it produced came from one of two sources: one source was the eponymous arc of electricity leaping between the two carbons, and the other was the surface of the carbons and the combusted gas they produced as their core materials vaporized under heat approaching 3,500°C. This thermal transformation made the carbon rod a prototypical example of how, in Nicole Starosielski's words, "matter becomes media."[13] That heat was also just one of the reasons, in addition to highly flammable celluloid, that theater fires posed such a high risk and projection booths had to be built from or encased in fireproof materials. As F. H. Richardson's *Bluebook of Projection* put it, the resulting "luminosity produced is second only to that of the sun itself," a common comparison for studio lights that promised to reproduce nature's conditions in the film studio.[14] For the projectionist, producing proper cinematic light was similarly a question of nothing less than bringing something like the sun itself—"artificial daylight," as one carbon advertisement put it—into the theater.[15]

LUMINOUS CARBON FORMS

Even the most formally pure carbons did not, however, ensure a screening of uniform brilliance. Projectionists struggled throughout the arc lamp's early years to master a variable quality that depended on another formal question, that of proper carbon positioning. Week after week in Richardson's trade column and other similar articles, projectionists queried and debated the varying merits of alternating versus direct current, amperage settings, and especially how to position the two carbons (figure 3.4). Because so much depended on the arc created

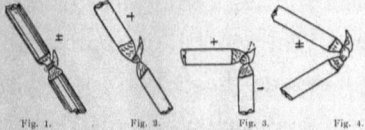

FIGURE 3.4 The art of carbon form, one of the essential "Problems of the Operating Room," *Motography* (May 1911).

at their interface, the carbons' relative distance and angle had a direct effect on the quantity of light produced and, ultimately, the quality of both that light and the projected image. Novice projectionists puzzled over potential angles (e.g., end-to-end, forty-five degrees, ninety degrees?) as well as the precise settings needed to avoid "penciling" or "needling," an undesirable burning and narrowing of the rod's tip that could result from poor carbon form. Even the most experienced operator could be forgiven for straining to discern the intricacies of ideal crater sizes and shapes (figure 3.5). Seeking to exploit projectionists' uncertainty and theater owners' demands for efficiency, companies sold positioning devices known as "clamps" or "jaws" with names like "the carbon saver" that promised to make carbon form an objective science rather than the skilled projectionists' art. Projectionists followed suit, fashioning their own devices and sharing the results in the trade press. Their designs multiplied to the point that, as one inventive operator put it, "everybody seems to have a jaw."[16]

MINING MEDIA, OR, ELEMENTAL ENERGY FOR MOTION PICTURES • 85

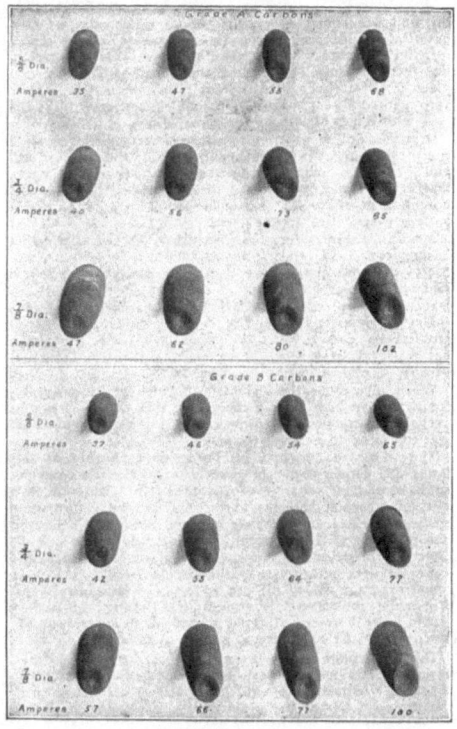

FIGURE 3.5 Variations in carbon crater shape and area based on amperage settings. F. H. Richardson, *Handbook of Projection for Theater Managers and Projectionists* (1922).

At stake was not only the projected image but also, as concerns about carbon shortages during World War I underscore, a resource problem that at times pitted projectionists against theater owners and managers. Carbons represented a consistent cost of doing business, and their use cut into any theater's bottom line. The good projectionist learned to burn carbons efficiently, which depended on the form and timing of their placement. Swapping carbons too soon would lead to inefficient waste. But doing so too late might result in a projectionist's nightmare—worse even than mistiming a reel change—when the lights, and, with them, cinema, would simply go out. Timing was everything, and Richardson recommended that projectionists do their own in-house tests to be sure.[17] To increase efficiency, carbon fragments could be used for short subjects, such as newsreels or cartoons. But more important, in the long run, was mastering carbon form: the right position at the right electrical settings would mean sun-like luminosity and a clear image at an acceptable cost. The wrong form could mean both a poor screening and a poorer theater owner.

MINING THE MEDIA OF MEDIA

By the 1920s, projectionists seeking perfect carbon-powered light faced a cascading range of labels and packages: Bio, Arco, Alterno, Excello, or Holo; Henrion, Electra, or Reflex; Columbia, Kinarko, or Victory. Advisers such as Richardson tended not to take sides, but there were profits to be made, and U.S. industrialists such as Speer leaped at the opportunity. Among the most notable corporations to enter the business during World War I was the Cleveland-based National Carbon Company (NCC). Like Speer, NCC had a background in carbon brush manufacturing, but its more significant and ultimately telling origins lay in the development of batteries and illumination. Before the war, NCC acquired the company that became Eveready and expanded into lighting technologies. Moving into the newly opened carbons market thus extended both the company's material expertise and its growing interest in selling light. To facilitate the move, the NCC hired projection expert and regular *Motion Picture News* contributor W. C. Kunzmann.[18] With fewer qualms than Richardson about promoting a specific product, Kunzmann used a combination of insider film industry knowledge and canny self-promotion to make the NCC a player in the carbon business, selling "White Flame" and "Silvertip" carbons on quality and patriotism (e.g., in ads featuring the Statue of Liberty, whose flaming torch was no doubt meant to be associated with carbon-sparked light).

In 1917, the NCC merged with a group of other chemical manufacturers to found Union Carbide, soon one of the most important U.S. material manufacturers, with an expanding global network of mines and factories specializing in everything from batteries, lights, and carbon products to liquid oxygen, calcium carbide, ethylene glycol, and, later, uranium. Union Carbide is well known today for the catastrophic breakdown of a pesticide factory in Bhopal, India, which killed at least 2,259 people (the official figure) and injured more than half a million more in December 1984. Other disasters preceded it, not to mention the harder-to-trace "slow violence" its practices frequently involved, all of which drove an industrial empire that supplied manufacturers—and film studios and theaters—with their products' most essential extracted ingredients.[19]

Those ingredients notably gave visual form to the company's famed regional headquarters, built in Chicago in 1929. One of the most famous buildings designed by the Chicago-based firm of architect Daniel Burnham, the thirty-seven-story art deco skyscraper evoked its corporate product in part through color, rendering carbon architecturally as polished black granite and dark green terra-cotta. Stylized organic motifs above the entrance further literalized carbon's distant origins in prehistoric plants, making the building tell a condensed story of carbon's movement from plant matter to raw material, refined form, and ultimately the corporate products displayed behind plate glass on the ground level and the associated profits embodied and represented by gold leaf accents above it.

Three decades later, a new Manhattan headquarters again expressed Union Carbide's material ambitions, this time in the international style, the abstract form of which suited the company's expanded role supplying the raw materials for glossy alloys that concealed their composite origins. Designed by Gordon Bunshaft and Natalie de Blois for Skidmore, Owings, and Merrill, the fifty-two-story skyscraper had none of the literal connections to carbon seen on the Chicago building's façade. But it again gestured to the company's founding source of wealth chromatically in the dark glass of its curtain wall.

By the time the New York headquarters reached the drawing boards, carbons were part of the equation, but they were just one component of Union Carbide's diverse material footprint, which notably encompassed another critical film—and increasingly media—material: tungsten. Promotional pamphlets from the 1950s have little to say about the NCC's film carbons, instead emphasizing the company's hand in visual media by way of another affiliate: the U.S. Vanadium Company, which was the manager of a mine in eastern California's Sierra Nevada mountains. Like carbons, tungsten functioned well at high temperature, making it useful in a range of processes and products. Mined in California and separated there from other mineral compounds, it was then transported to factories on the east coast to become an important part of the alloys used in steel and iron production, with significant applications in military and commercial aviation as well as the auto industry. From there, tungsten alloys quietly entered everyday life, losing, as one Union Carbide pamphlet emphasized, their very "identity once they are used."[20] That transformation made for a good story about material and corporate malleability—the promise that separated glossy consumer products from their gritty material origins.

Fifty years earlier, however, tungsten's identity—as an element, a mined material, and a useable form—had defined its early potential as an essential component of media technologies. Until the early twentieth century, tungsten had few applications in industry and was understood to be an unworkably brittle material with crystalline form that might be useful but only if it could somehow be made ductile (i.e., capable of being shaped into strong, useful forms). Scientists recognized tungsten's potential value and had used it in bulb filaments but only in composite forms devised using binding agents that still left it brittle, inefficient, and with a short lifespan. But in 1906, William D. Coolidge, a researcher at General Electric (G.E.), started a veritable media revolution when he developed a working tungsten filament that G.E. brought to market five years later in new incandescent bulbs.

Coolidge's solution involved a series of steps to process a compound of tungstic oxide (WO_3) into another, more workable state. His 1912 patent application laid claim not only to the filament but also to the process for making it, which was, he maintained, the process for making tungsten workable for any application.[21] U.S. courts later ruled that this workable state was nothing more than tungsten itself, even if the latter was rarely found in nature in pure form. But for more than a decade, Coolidge—and G.E., which held the license for his patent—had achieved one of the more evocative positions in the history of nature-culture relations, casting themselves as the creators and sole proprietors of nothing less than a naturally occurring chemical element. The stakes were high, for Coolidge's tungsten filament proved to be many times more efficient than those used previously. Under G.E.'s stewardship, tungsten also became an essential media material in lights and vacuum tube filaments. That stewardship ended in 1929, when the De Forest Radio Company successfully defended its use of tungsten for cathode filaments found in the vacuum tubes of its radios against a G.E. patent lawsuit. As the court's ruling explained, "what [Coolidge] discovered were natural qualities of pure tungsten. Manifestly he did not create pure tungsten, nor did he create its characteristics. These were created by nature."[22] Nothing could thus stop De Forest and others from making pure tungsten the elemental basis of modern media.

ELEMENTAL SCREEN FORMS

Propelled by Coolidge's innovations but free from G.E.'s monopolistic control, tungsten proliferated across new media forms. It became an essential element in incandescent lights and helped make possible the vacuum tube revolution that drove developments in radio, television, and eventually computer communication. Like other mined elements, tungsten became a reflexive media form as it crossed over from structuring material to screen subject. In the remainder of the chapter, I explore this reflexivity and its formal relations through one primary example, a film made sometime in the 1960s for Union Carbide about its affiliated tungsten mine in Pine Creek, California.[23] The film first attracted my attention because of its references to how the tungsten mined at Pine Creek became a key component of media display technologies—a reflexive gesture that recalls Dziga Vertov's and Ingmar Bergman's respective uses of carbon rods to illustrate the power at cinema's ontological core (figures 3.6–3.7). It ultimately merits close analysis, however, not simply for these reflexive references but more broadly for what it reveals about the formal correspondence between elemental extraction and its media forms.

Industrial films about extraction are almost always about more than simply illustrating extractive processes.[24] Rather, they involve a more complex formal relay between the infrastructure of mining, those mines' extracted minerals, those minerals' associated products and by-products, and, ultimately, their filmed images. This kind of industrial cinema kept extraction on screen during and beyond the years of Hollywood's resource integration, in which, as I argued in chapter 2, a parallel, extraction-dependent "industrial cinema" emerged that largely moved these extractive processes to the aesthetic margins, moments of spectacle (extraction's attractions), and the narrative backdrop. For all their differences, these two forms of industrial film shared a reflexive tendency to reveal cinema's material debt to extractive industries and its ontological connections to those industries' world-making ambitions.

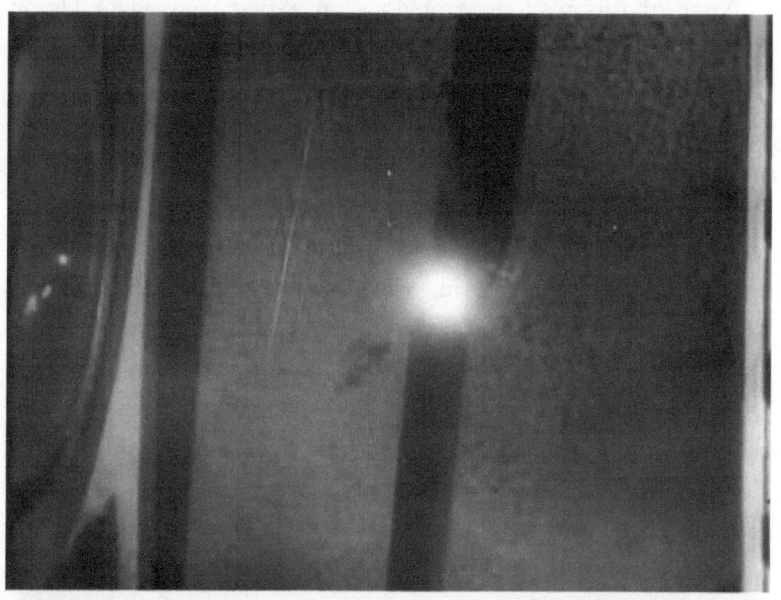
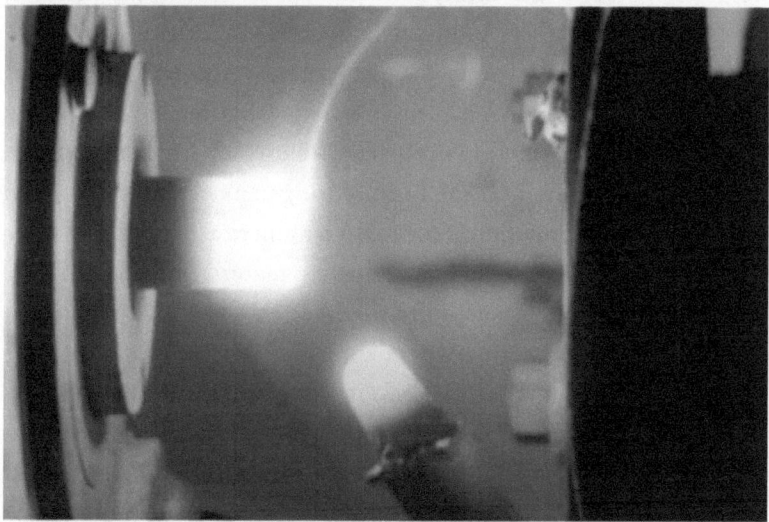

FIGURES 3.6-3.7 Carbon rods as reflexive media materials in *Man with a Movie Camera* (dir. Dziga Vertov, 1929) and *Persona* (dir. Ingmar Bergman, 1966).

None of this may seem obvious on a first viewing of Union Carbide's *Tungsten: A Treasure of the Sierra Nevada*. The film is, on the surface, an industrial film like any other. It tells a story about the extraction of an industrial resource, the people who do the work, and that resource's applications in everyday life. It offers a celebratory account of its sponsoring corporation, Union Carbide, and, like other industrial films of the 1960s and 1970s, it acknowledges environmental risk while assuring viewers that solutions have already been developed.[25] Aside from its reflexive nod to its subject's use in media technologies, *Tungsten* offers no special reason to be read more closely than any other film like it, but most industrial films can and should be analyzed with formal rigor and an eye for what else they may, under such scrutiny, reveal.

It would be easy to assume that an extraction-focused film like this would follow a straightforward processual logic, tracing tungsten from its source in the mine, through the extraction and refining process, and out to its eventual applications. Although the film does include some aspects of this process, especially a central account of tungsten's transformation from blasted boulders to a fine white powder, the film ultimately follows a more complex formal logic shaped by both the form of tungsten's extraction and the logic of its transformation into useful commercial products. Rather than moving in a straight line from raw material to end product, its path is more circuitous, spiraling in from two broad settings—the California mountains where tungsten is found and the element's various industrial and commercial applications—down to the specific location of its extraction at Pine Creek, into the mine, and then back out again to those same mountains. The film then retraces that same path a second time to describe the mine's managed threat to the local environment, and finally, it ends roughly where it started. Moving on something like a mobius strip, the film thus tells a story of extraction, retells it in inverted form, and finally arrives back at the center.

That center is tungsten, the stuff that names the film and must be explained, and which is also, in two reflexive senses, part of the film's condition of possibility. The first falls on the exhibition side. As the narrator explains early on, tungsten is in "the filament of your television tube" and "it's in the lamp of the projector that's showing you this film." Without tungsten, the film implies, you would not be watching it. On the production side, too, the film narrates its own creation, if less overtly. Because the mining industry's low-light worlds posed a significant challenge to cinematic visibility, early mining movies tended to focus on open-pit mines and surface-level operations, leaving the work in the depths to studio trompe l'oeil. Mitchell and Kenyon's 1904 short, *Black Diamonds: The Collier's Daily Life*, for example, features two shots documenting the mine's surface infrastructure and the processing of coal, but only after it has been dredged up from the unseen darkness below. Ferdinand Zecca's fictional *Au pays des mines* (1905), meanwhile, did take viewers on a tour of the subterranean depths but only by way of studio simulation.[26] Even the most famous early exception, Charles Urban's Kineto company documentary, *A Day in the Life of the Coal Miner* (1910), can offer only limited views of miners picking the coal face, instead focusing more on the miner's (and coal's) life up above.

Overcoming these lighting limitations relied in no small part on mining itself. The extraction of minerals, such as tungsten, produced the brighter lights that allowed filmmakers to enter the mines in increasing numbers from the 1930s to the 1950s, trading the illusionary dimensionality of studio backdrops for the literal depth of the depths. As *Tungsten* emphasizes, its title metal set itself apart for its hardness and heat resistance, which were ideal traits for making stronger drills that allowed miners to go ever deeper, the mined stuff thereby becoming the mine's self-reinforcing condition of possibility. The Pine Creek mine documented in *Tungsten* was the product of this very process, having been expanded in the 1950s

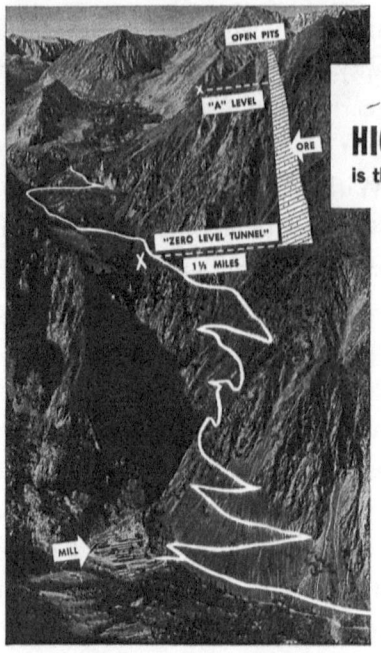

FIGURE 3.8 The Pine Creek mine took form in the 1950s thanks in part to the drilling capacity of its own product, the hard metal tungsten.

Courtesy of County of Inyo, Eastern California Museum.

from its original open pits and shallow "A" tunnel to a new section (the "Zero level") carved out thanks in part to tungsten-carbide drill bits (figure 3.8).[27]

The resulting mine's form directly shapes the film's circuitous structure. *Tungsten* opens high above the Sierra Nevada mountains, home of Pine Creek. Long shots of mountaintops and aerial footage, moving from the mountains down past the mine and into the valley below, set the scene, which the film combines with a similarly high-level description of tungsten's broad industrial and commercial applications. From there, the film zooms in closer, both literally and figuratively, to the mine and its workers, with footage of worker housing close to the mine and in the nearby town of Bishop. Shots of Union Carbide shuttle buses leaving Bishop dissolve back to the mine, "ground zero" of the film's eponymous subject. Having been spiraled down from the mountain peaks, out to the surrounding environs, and back to the mine, the viewer can rightly expect, finally, to proceed into the depths, as any mining film presumably should. At this point, however, we learn that Pine Creek is no ordinary mine but in fact, as the narrator puts it, is "upside down." In this mine, to "go down," you have to "go up."

With this unexpected flip, the logic behind the film's formal movements—down, back up, and back down again—begin to become clearer. We enter the mine, but instead, as in most mining films, of watching miners pile into elevators for the iconic descent, this time the camera tilts into a low angle shot to follow their trip up. The camera goes with them, and once in the mine, the film becomes generically process oriented. Standard shots follow, with drilling, dynamiting, and then the delivery of the raw ore, which, rather than being dredged up, must be dropped back down a shaft to the processing plant below. Once there, it moves through a series of filtering and processing stages that end with pure tungsten powder that is then loaded into barrels and stacked for delivery back to east-coast chemical and alloy plants for the applications described in the opening shots that establish the location of the Sierras.

With the end of the process sequence, the Sierras again become the visual backdrop. We're back at the top, in other words, having descended from the literal and rhetorical heights down to life on the ground, ascended with the miners, followed the raw ore back down, and resurfaced with it in processed form. We exit the mine, like the tungsten itself, having been processed from "raw material"—the uneducated viewer—into something more refined—an industrial observer learned in the art of tungsten and its value. Getting there is both an aesthetic and rhetorical process, the form of which follows a sophisticated flow like the kind depicted in the corporate flowcharts that outlined the production of Union Carbide's tungsten and the Pine Creek mine's other by-products.

Films about commodity production often pursue something like this formal logic, starting with their end products, to which they eventually return after following the step-by-step processes of their creation. *Tungsten* does this work, too, tracing the transformation of raw materials into a useful form. But this work, it must be emphasized, is not merely about illustrating or tracing an industrial process but also involves the broader and more complex process by which something unrefined is instrumentalized. In this case, that instrumentalization applies no less to the film's viewer—the subject of the film's ambition to refine—than to its named subject, the refinement of which is never sufficient on its own for instrumentalization but rather must be accompanied by a broader world-making endeavor that includes the refinement of public interest. That the film attempts to achieve the latter form of refinement in synchronicity with the industrial process it documents makes it a fascinating example of what industrial cinema so often tried to achieve.

Having initiated the viewer into this process, *Tungsten* then takes them through it again, this time to prove the mine's environmental bona fides. Like the "upside down" mine, here the film turns on its head, acknowledging the mine's detrimental ecological effects but only, and just as quickly, to demonstrate that what looks bad can just as easily be made good again. The form repeats: starting in the peaks of the Sierra Nevada, the film returns to a broad establishing rhetoric, now about the importance of preserving this pristine environment and its local communities (the workers and Bishop), before turning back toward the mine. Again it ascends to the source of the water used to process the ore, descends with it through the mine, and proceeds through the stages of an extractive process, this time to remove pollution and render a "pure" product (figure 3.9). The film duly ends back where it began, with a penultimate shot that matches the opening image of the Sierra's peaks, before a final slow zoom out returns viewers to ground level with the Pine Creek mine's pines, subtly implying that what follows can only be another iteration of this unending and environmentally harmonious industrial cycle (figure 3.10).

ENTANGLED CINEMAS OF EXTRACTION

In both its title and subject, *Tungsten: A Treasure of the Sierra Nevada* bares a surely unintentional and otherwise strangely misguided but evocative intertextual reference to a more iconic film, John Huston's Warner Brothers classic, *The Treasure of the Sierra Madre* (1948). I deem it unintentional because surely no publicity officer would have found it wise—beyond the potential utility of invoking a vague form of Hollywood notoriety—to associate their business with Huston's damning critique of prospecting, mineral wealth, and U.S. extraction in Mexico. And perhaps it *was* notoriety they were after, a possibility to which I will return. But intentional or not, the connection creates a beguiling pairing, both because Huston's film is such a compelling example of the cinema of extractions as it emerged out of Hollywood's midcentury industrial cinema and because it functions as a distorted commercial mirror through which to reread the elemental form of *A Treasure of the Sierra Nevada*.

The Treasure of the Sierra Madre tells a story about the corrupting temptations of mineral wealth. Expressed most fully through the narrative arc of Humphrey Bogart's Fred Dobbs, the film's lesson about greed takes the form of a nihilistic death spiral of endless accumulation. Dobbs begins as a beggar on the streets of Tampico, Mexico, having presumably been attracted there to work in the

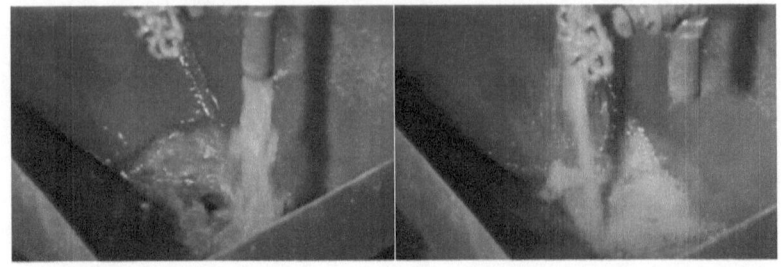

FIGURE 3.9 *Tungsten*'s second extractive process makes dirty water clean again.

FIGURE 3.10 *Tungsten*'s opening and final two shots highlight its repetitive, cyclical form.

region's booming oil fields. Left to rely on handouts from rich U.S. capitalists, his fortunes initially ride on the generosity of strangers. Those fortunes rise when he finds work for the U.S. owner of another nearby oil field. But when the oilman runs off without paying, Dobbs falls back to where he started, exhausted and once again without prospects. A few scenes later, he and friend Bill Curtin track down the oil boss and exact retribution in a barroom brawl. Money in hand and boosted by Dobbs's well-timed luck in the lottery, the two enlist a wizened older prospector, Howard (played by Huston's father, Walter), in a scheme to strike it rich, this time by extracting gold from the desolate hills of Durango. Their plan works, and their fortunes briefly seem sure again, but Dobbs grows increasingly paranoid as the gold accumulates. He eventually tries, unsuccessfully, to kill Curtin and escape with the gold but instead dies at the hands of a group of bandits bent on stealing his burros. In the end, all the gold blows away in a windstorm, leaving Curtin and Howard as poor as they started but with dreams that go beyond gold.

The Treasure of the Sierra Madre's simplistic surface-level moral—that true wealth lies beyond material pursuits—was the kind of public relations message that companies such as Union Carbide used industrial films to associate with their products. *A Treasure of the Sierra Nevada* makes this very argument, both about its community of workers and about the local environment the plant promises to keep clean. *Sierra Nevada*'s story about cleansing the mine's polluted water even loosely echoes fictional Howard's proto-environmentalist insistence that, as a kind of tribute to the mountain, the trio of goldminers must clean up their mine before departing the Sierra Madre. So, too, *Sierra Nevada* reproduces *Sierra Madre*'s emphasis on the value of labor and its embeddedness in the extractive process. For Union Carbide, valorizing labor made for good public relations, and to the degree to which it is a process film, *Sierra Nevada*'s depiction of process begins and ends with laboring bodies.

In contrast, *Sierra Madre*'s account of labor diverges radically from the rhetoric of extractive industries, especially when read through the lens of the film's formation.[28] Huston adapted the screenplay from the Marxist writer B. Traven's novel, a damning account of Spanish colonial and U.S. capitalist exploitation of Mexican mineral wealth. Although some of Traven's strongest criticisms failed to make the final cut, the film still includes numerous stridently anticapitalist messages, often delivered most clearly in Walter Huston's Academy Award–winning performance as Howard. It is Howard who insists that gold's value lies not in its scarcity but rather in the intense labor required to extract it. Howard also comes the closest, in the film's final version, to associating Dobbs's greed with capitalism and appealing for a more socialist approach to the prospectors' work.

Some of Traven's harsher critique made Huston's script but didn't pass muster with studio executives or the Hollywood censors. An opening scene set in a Tampico bank that would have highlighted U.S. corruption and its violent military undertones was cut, as was another speech in which Howard would have denounced America's approach to its Mexican mining operations and drawn an equivalence between U.S. profit seekers and the film's stereotyped bandits. "We're as much thieves as they are," he would have argued. Extracting the treasure of the Sierra Madre, as these scenes might have made clear, relied not on the virtues of U.S. labor and the ingenuity of technical processes but rather on the systematic exploitation of a place, its land, and its people. Wary of what such a message might mean for U.S. cultural diplomacy in the era of the Good Neighbor policy, however, Warner Brothers producers and the Production Code Administration head Joseph Breen expressed reservations about the film, if not an outright ultimatum to change it.[29]

That these debates unfolded while the film was being shot in Mexico (among the first Hollywood location shoots outside the United States) adds another layer to its complex extractive theme.[30] Durango made for an ideal production site, but not so much for its landscape. The latter could easily have been staged closer to Los Angeles and does not even, as James Naremore has emphasized, appear in the kinds of landscape shots standard to the western genre—to the point that it would be hard to classify the film, formally speaking, as a western.[31] Instead, the location mattered more for the unseen thematic and formal richness of a place long mined for its mineral wealth and that had indeed undergone an oil boom like the one depicted in the film.

Here again, in other words, the Hollywood cinema of extractions took form in the balance of brief on-screen depictions of this extractive industry and how that industry imposed itself on the production more so as its material backdrop and structuring logic than as part of its story. The backdrop entangled Hollywood and extractive industries in unseen but important ways, including Huston's extensive use of the Warner Brothers research department to learn about the histories of oil prospecting in Mexico, the "look and feel of the work camps and derricks from the perspective of the average laborer," and the legal status of U.S. land claims to Mexico's mineral-rich soil.[32] Answering these questions—formal questions about industry formations, aesthetic forms, and legal codes—gave Huston the raw material for a film whose structure and themes closely follow those of the industries it depicts.

Dobbs's story, in particular, ends in doom because it pursues extraction's logic of endless accumulation to its inevitable endpoint: resource exhaustion. Howard once again voices this danger, warning that a true prospector never stops no matter how much he gains. He tries to save Dobbs and Curtin from that fate by arguing that they should cut their extraction process short and go home satisfied with a healthy profit rather than digging for every speck of gold. But Dobbs cannot countenance leaving anything in the ground, even if, as the film emphasizes, he has no real goal beyond wealth itself. Having pursued a dream of limitless growth, he ultimately finds only exhaustion— of the mine and his own mind and body—and ends up with more

FIGURE 3.11 To exhaust the extraction site's gold, Dobbs exhausts himself and duly meets his end scrambling for another limited resource, water. *The Treasure of the Sierra Madre* (dir. John Huston, 1948).

gold than he can carry but dying of thirst, face down in a puddle of muddy water (figure 3.11). That the film nearly ends with this grim outcome—to the chagrin of executives and no doubt some audiences accustomed to Hollywood happy endings—underscores how a formal critique of capital becomes both the film's narrative form and, arguably, a formal critique of tidy but profitable Hollywood resolutions.

But the film does not quite end there, still needing to resolve the status of the gold and Dobbs's partners. The bandits who kill Dobbs mistakenly pour out the gold to lighten their load, only to be captured trying to sell the burros, while Howard and Curtin arrive just in time to hear the firing squad and race off in pursuit of the gold as it blows away. The film closes with a shot that starts on Curtin riding off to a presumably less materialistic future but then tilts down to reveal one last bag of gold, possibly still full. Had Huston's intended opening at the Tampico bank been included, this closing image would have put a fine point on the film's political economy: if you trace the sources of wealth back to their origins, you end up with raw extracted stuff and all the corrupt tales that come with it. Instead, it opens with a shot of Dobbs's losing lottery numbers, making for a less obvious but no less powerful pairing with that bag of gold (figure 3.12). Much as

FIGURE 3.12 *The Treasure of the Sierra Madre*'s political economy tracks exploitation from financial figures through oil and mineral extraction back to ground level.

lotteries, with their small but endlessly accumulating entry costs and long odds, prey on the poor, so too extracting wealth from colonial and neocolonial settings depends on cheap labor in sacrificed land. That message can be seen only on the ground, and Huston's film has the virtue of taking and leaving us there.

Tungsten: A Treasure of the Sierra Nevada of course has no interest in anything like that kind of criticism. But its association with *Sierra Madre* invites us to read it accordingly not just as a promotional film about tungsten but rather, and against its form, as an unlikely cautionary tale about extraction's inevitable ends. Although the film's cyclical structure strains to prove the opposite, endless accumulation can move only in a straight line to an inevitable endpoint when the resources have finally been exhausted. Along the way, the consequences pile up, not least of which is the pollution the film reveals only to disavow, and even more so the unseen damage to the area around Pine Creek and the mine's workers, which index both the slow and immediate violence Union Carbide's practices involved there and elsewhere.

Union Carbide clearly saw things differently, and the history of Huston's film offers one last way to understand what Hollywood notoriety and its marketing strategies might have meant to a corporation invested in film promotion. As Naremore explains, one of the challenges Warner Brothers faced when it came time for the release was how to market the film using its biggest star, Bogart, when his character Dobbs was so despicable. The studio opted simply to swap the film's reality for the one it preferred, selling *Sierra Madre* through "slickly lit photos" of Bogart "modeling topcoats, sport shirts, tuxedos, hats, and pipes."[33] In other words, studio publicity transformed what was, at its core, an anticapitalist film with a doomed antihero into an image of performed wealth and endless accumulation, as if Dobbs had, in fact, lived to see his dreams fulfilled. If the producers of *A Treasure of the Sierra Nevada* meant for viewers to think about *The Treasure of the Sierra Madre*, surely this is what they had in mind. Banking on surface-level associations with Hollywood glamour, Union Carbide's film simply chose the reality it preferred, imagining that it, too, was a story not about the risks and consequences of a world with limited resources but rather about the world of limitless growth that it and its producers hoped they might create.

CONCLUSION: ELEMENTAL ENERGY FOR MOTION PICTURES

Although often classified as a western, *The Treasure of the Sierra Madre*, as Naremore has emphasized, mostly looks like something else. With its shadowy visual form, dark underlying theme, nihilistic protagonist, and bleak conclusion, it arguably shares as much, if not more with the era's famous films noir.[34] That category doesn't quite fit either, at least insofar as *Sierra Madre* mostly takes place far removed from noir's typical urban settings.[35] But if we understand noir's environment more capaciously as "unnatural" and "human made," as Jennifer Fay has described, it would be hard to argue against *Sierra Madre*'s inclusion. After all, as Huston knew thanks to his Warner Brothers research team, Durango had been shaped for more than a century by extractive industries that stripped the land, crossed it with railroads, dotted it with settlements, and defined it as a place to be extracted. The resulting "inhospitable" environment, to use Fay's term, defines the film's settings, aesthetics, and the "anti-humanist ecologies" of precisely what Traven and Huston sought to critique: "the ends of a consuming capitalist culture without the promise of renewal, redemption, or hope for regeneration." In contrast to those idealized cyclical forms, Dobbs's exhausted death epitomizes noir's logical linear endpoint and its role as what Fay describes as a genre lesson in "how to die in the Anthropocene."[36]

Fay's gripping ecocritical rereading of film noir, particularly its characters' bleak listlessness, finds a material counterpart in the story of projected light with which this chapter began. Among the questions film industry scientists explored as they attempted to perfect theater illumination was just how much energy was necessary to ensure that sufficient light reached the screen. One 1914 manual estimated, for example, that a projection powered by alternating current would require a constant flow of up to 53 watts per square centimeter of film, about 3.2 watts of which would reach the screen as visible light.[37] The latter amount depended, in part, on the projected film's visual form. Put simply, the darker the film—and thus the opaquer the film strip—the less light would reach the screen, its energy instead captured by the film strip as heat. Such darkness mattered, in part, because the darker the film, the hotter it would get, and the more it risked catching fire. Film noir was, in this respect, among the most dangerous motion picture forms.[38] In a material sense that doubled its narrative and allegorical listlessness, it was also the least energetic. Although it required no less energy to project, noir refused, in its literal darkness, to energize the spectator by withholding its energy qua light.

Industrial films such as *A Treasure of the Sierra Nevada*, in contrast, offered something like the opposite: an energy forged in spectacular images, optimistic narratives, and harmonious cycles of boundless growth and limitless accumulation without consequences. Lighting up the screen with their seemingly transparent paeons to progress, such films taught viewers how to *live* in the Anthropocene—or at least what privileged forms of "good" living were supposed to look like, if you could have them. They illustrate the role media industries have played in defining the natural world as a set of extractible resources as well as the reflexive quality of media texts that represent extractive processes. Moreover, they highlight the dialectical relationship between media and extraction, in which media act as world-defining agents of the extractive industries upon which they depend and the extracted materials become visible and knowable as more-than-material components (i.e., images, symbols, and spectacles) of modern life. The form such narratives and spectacles took, and how their "usefulness" was forged in synchronicity with idealized visions of their extracted subjects' forms, is the subject of the next, final, chapter.

4

INDUSTRIAL FILM'S SPECTACULAR AND PROSAIC POETICS

By the second half of the twentieth century, the cinema of extractions had become a largely industrial affair. Hollywood's "industrial cinema" continued to make extractions a part of popular screen culture that at times, as films such as *The Treasure of the Sierra Madre* (dir. John Huston, 1948) demonstrate, reflexively exposed its material backdrops. For most viewers, however, extraction appeared more often in images curated by extractive industries and their promoters. In the United States, the parallel film business these industries supported picked up steam during the two decades before World War II. By the 1920s, private oil and automobile companies had adopted film; federal government institutions, such as the Bureau of Mines, were producing films about coal, oil, and other resources; and trade organizations, such as the American Petroleum Institute, followed suit.[1] By the end of the 1930s, the field could support its own trade magazine, *Business Screen*, and similar developments were found in western European countries such as France, Germany, and Britain, where state institutions such as the Empire Marketing Board made cinema, as Lee Grieveson argues, "an important element in fostering the wealth of the nation and the elaboration of a capitalist and imperialist governmentality."[2] During the 1950s and 1960s, these industrial and corporate cinemas rode waves of economic recovery and industrial growth, not least thanks to profits from hydrocarbon energy, which often was extracted by colonial and, increasingly, neocolonial industries that continued after decolonization. Their products included not only large catalogs of films but also new production companies, portable projectors, exhibition venues, and even their own film festivals. The midcentury Great Acceleration that spelled potential climate disaster thus included an industrial film acceleration that tracked and helped trigger it.[3]

One of the critical stories the industrial cinema of extractions told in these years had to do with form. Selling material, corporate, and cinematic malleability, films made by extractive industries extended the world-making ambitions found in the early cinema of extractions from the broadest vision of large-scale technologies and infrastructure—roads, bridges, and buildings; trains, tankers, and steamships—to everyday consumer objects and domestic devices. Just as Union Carbide, for example, sold tungsten, in *Tungsten: A Treasure of the Sierra Nevada*, on its wide range of applications, so too did other extractive industries stake their products' utility on their formal malleability. The 1956 American Petroleum Institute–sponsored short *Destination Earth*, for instance, tells this story about oil. Directed by Carl Urbano for the firm founded by Disney-veteran John Sutherland, its animation celebrates oil's presence in seemingly every part of everyday life, which is best exemplified by a scene in which two chemists-cum-magicians conjure a cornucopia of colorful objects out of two oil barrels (figure 4.1). Synching animated and petrochemical plasticity, the film exemplifies oil's material and formal interconnections with cinema.

That extracted materials and movies connected in this way resulted in part from how industries needed to frame their products. Selling not so much tungsten, coal, oil, or gas as those materials' uses in other technologies and industrial and consumer products, this cinema of extractions required narratives and aesthetics of formal transformation. Film offered one important medium for that formal

FIGURE 4.1 Oil's malleability as animated form in *Destination Earth* (dir. Carl Urbano, 1956).

transfer, and film companies, in turn, sold their medium's versatility. Magazines like *Business Screen* and advertisers, such as the Jam Handy company, pitched themselves precisely on film's capacity to conform to whatever industry required. A 1967 advertisement for the industrial film division of the documentary firm Wolper Productions exemplifies this formal dream. Selling "motion pictures for business," the ad envisions film's formal integration with all the major industries and industrial products, from trains, trucks, tankers, and jets to petrochemicals, pipelines, communications, finance, and agriculture (figure 4.2). Film, the ad promises, can adapt itself to any industry, and so too can every industry be formed in the image of film.

For all the idealism such images expressed, however, the important question of just how this malleability took form on screen has largely gone unexplored. This despite the fact that the corporate- and industry-sponsored film sector that produced films such as *Tungsten* and *Destination Earth* has become such an important part of cinema's historical and historiographic narrative. During the past two decades, persuasive arguments have been made that this parallel film industry's products were shown, seen, and, it is at least implied, therefore mattered, at least as much as, if not more than, the commercial features, art cinema, and documentaries shown in film theaters. The numbers alone make a powerful argument. As Haidee Wasson's research shows, by 1969, "portable, self-operated [projection] machines outnumbered

FIGURE 4.2 "Motion Pictures for Business," Wolper Productions, Industrial Film Division, *Business Screen* 28, no. 1 (1967).

theatrical screens by a ratio of more than 875:1" in the United States. That's more than 8.5 million projectors, many used to show the films pioneered by these devices' "early adopters," that is, U.S. industry. Taking advantage of what Wasson describes as their film "apparatus's elasticity," these "authoritative, centralized, and powerful organizations and institutions" sought control of the U.S. visual imaginary.[4]

Part of their films' importance lies in one of the adjectives used to describe them: "useful." Implicitly more so, or at least more explicitly so than those other film categories, these films *do things*, things with value. As Wasson and Charles Acland put it in the introduction to one of this subfield's early defining volumes, as a form of "useful culture" (Tony Bennett's phrase), this cinema "shapes debates, moves populations, directs capital, furthers authority, and ordains the self." In short, it does social, political, and economic work. To understand how it does so has required, Acland and Wasson rightly argue, a "reorientation of the kinds of questions we ask of our film and media history."[5]

Those questions have pushed research in many important new directions, but they have not tended to be about film form.[6] Instead, attention to form has been replaced by devotion to context under the more historicist rubric of the New Film History.[7] To understand industrial and corporate films, we need to understand industrial and corporate contexts that pull us away from the film text. Thomas Elsaesser's contribution to another of the field's defining volumes, *Films That Work*, perhaps most succinctly systematizes this approach, with its three contextualizing categories of analysis: who commissioned the film, for what purpose, and for what use.[8] Answering such questions may lead one back to films and their form, but that return has rarely materialized. In the introduction to *Films That Work*, Vinzenz Hediger and Patrick Vonderau point to one reason for this methodological shift when they describe industrial films as "far from self-sufficient entities for aesthetic analysis."[9] Their point is that we need context to make sense of industrial film aesthetics, but in practice, it has often meant that aesthetic analysis has simply been replaced by context and more context. It may come as no surprise, then, that studies of industrial film more often include rote accounts of content or narrative, sometimes with associated formal *description* but seldom with any sustained formal *analysis*.[10] The upshot of this methodological shift has been an immense gain in historical knowledge, not least including the knowledge that "cinema" need not mean theatrical commercial cinema, that the contemporary practice of carrying screens everywhere has long roots in mobile media technologies, and that screen culture, both inside and beyond the film theater, has long been—and in many ways continues to be—dominated by persuasive cultures of industry and the state.

A perhaps unforeseeable corollary of this shift has been that persuasive film culture's formal aesthetic strategies have become something of a black box. Wasson's important book, for example, has "movies" in its title but includes little analysis of them. We may still assume that the films projected on those eight million projectors do their work and achieve their usefulness, but how they do so goes largely unexplored.[11] What if we closed that circle by returning to the question of form with eyes newly trained by the valuable contextualization created in "useful" cinema studies and the questions required to understand other places and ways films have worked?[12] This chapter does so with a focus on one of useful cinema's significant branches, the cinema of extractions.[13] Taking as its primary example the 1965 Shell-sponsored short, *Shellarama* (dir. Richard Cawston), it asks two broad questions: First, what form does usefulness take in "useful" cinema? And, second, when and with what consequence does that usefulness—and its form—tip over into excess and spectacle, or what we might go so far as to describe as its "uselessness?"

As I have argued so far, the "cinema of extractions" emerged in the nineteenth century as a cinema that did seemingly useful work—promoting industry, selling products, and, more broadly, creating ways of seeing the world in the image of capitalism and industry. With the emergence of Hollywood and other resource-integrated, Hollywood-like film industries, the early cinema of extractions split. Beyond the feature films and documentaries focused on extraction that continued to be produced, this cinema took two general forms: one appearing in the margins and as the reflexive backdrop of the commercial "industrial film" industry named by David James; and the other as what we have now come to know as "industrial film," or useful cinema. When named, as James does, in this way, the commercial industry more clearly did "work" and had the kind of "usefulness" now associated with industrial and corporate film. After all, few would dispute that commercial cinema has played a fundamental role in "shaping debates" and "ordaining the self," to use Acland and Wasson's terms. As Grieveson has demonstrated, moreover, Hollywood had a clear use value for industry as a site for reinvestment (i.e., doing "useful" things, such as directing capital and furthering authority).[14]

It is arguably just as true, and more to the point, that "useful" cinema may not always have been quite as useful as the name implies. Corporations and industry may have commissioned and projected films with use value and utility in mind, but did they always succeed? We know, at least anecdotally, that audiences learned to arrive late to miss the short films before commercial features, and it is not hard to imagine that spectators (in theaters, schools, conference rooms, and elsewhere) ignored or mocked them, nodded off, or in other ways refused to allow "films that work" to do any work.[15] In this respect, we must acknowledge that useful films may have sometimes been something closer to "useless," or, put less provocatively, that they may simply have been ancillary products of corporate spectacle and excess, and not the integral corporate and industrial instruments that descriptors like "useful" and "work" imply.[16] Creating an industrial culture that could produce 8.5 million projectors—and the associated screens and libraries of small-format film prints—was already an arguably excessive pursuit, the material consequences of which paralleled Hollywood's resource integration and contributed even more clearly and materially than Hollywood production to the midcentury Great Acceleration.[17]

As those material consequences suggest, to unravel the difference between utility and excess, we could continue to do what industrial and useful cinema scholars have done so well: read the archive to give context for what corporate public relations people wanted from film, how they attempted to achieve it, and what we can glean about the results from things like projector counts, distribution figures, test screening questionnaires, festival awards, and reviews. But we could also look to form and the interplay between what I describe as industrial film's spectacular and prosaic poetics. Examining these films formally will not tell us if they "worked," but it will tell us something about what "working" was understood to mean. It will also tell us something about how "usefulness" so often attempted to navigate the dueling imperatives to create, on the one hand, arresting (often excessive) spectacle and, on the other hand, prosaic (potentially uninspiring) utility. More important, it once again illustrates the utility of linking form to (the form of its) content and recognizing how extractive industries shaped, in ways that become reflexively legible, the forms of their capture.

THE MORALITY OF THE TRACKING SHOT

My interest in writing this chapter began while watching the spectacular sequence of aerial tracking shots in *Shellarama*, a fifteen-minute short that roughly tracks the life cycle of petroleum from prospecting sites and wells to pipelines and tankers to petrol stations and moving machines. The sequence in question follows a pipeline from deep in a desert oil field, up over a steep mountain pass, and finally down to a waiting tanker at the seashore below. Tracking swiftly forward, then climbing, banking left and right, and swooping down, these shots exude energy and spectacle, both in their exuberant form and in the cost required for extensive aircraft shots and distribution in the seventy-millimeter Super Technirama format. Watching this spectacle and contemplating its excessive form, I was reminded of a comment by Jean-Luc Godard published in the July 1959 *Cahiers du cinéma* roundtable about *Hiroshima mon amour* (dir. Alain Resnais, 1959). The conversation quickly turns to form, including the political stakes of Resnais's remarkable tracking shots. Eric Rohmer proposes that some viewers may find the film "jarring in places," to which Jacques Doniol-Valcroze responds with a question: "Morally or aesthetically?" "It's the same thing," interjects Godard, "tracking shots are a question of morality."[18]

Godard's remark referred to an article by Luc Moullet, published four months earlier in the *Cahiers*, about Samuel Fuller. Hoping to separate the confused, seemingly conservative politics of Fuller's films from their aesthetic achievements, Moullet had argued that "the question of morality" was not only a question of its narrative or thematic politics but also its form. Morality was "a question of tracking shots."[19] Whatever Godard meant to say by flipping Moulet's formula, at stake in this exchange, with its subtle formal reversal, was, as Antoine de Baecque has argued, and James Cahill has described in the context of Jacques Cousteau and Louis Malle's underwater traveling shots in *Le Monde du silence* (1956), nothing less than the changing politics of form in post-1944 French film and its criticism.[20] To highlight these stakes, de Baecque tracks forward to Jacques Rivette's 1961 review of Gillo Pontecorvo's film *Kapo*, the fictionalized story of a concentration camp that Rivette denounces for what he sees as its aestheticization of mass death. Particularly reprehensible, in Rivette's view, was a tracking shot that ends on a close-up of Emannuelle Riva's character dying after throwing herself onto an electric fence. If, for Moullet, it had been possible to dissociate form from politics—so that an ideologically dubious film could nonetheless feature formal achievements independent of politics—for Godard, "all cinematic gestures," in de Baecque's words, involve "the taking of a moral stand."[21] This fact was well illuminated by the apparently immoral cinematic beautification of extermination that made Pontecorvo, in Rivette's famous description, a man "worthy of the most profound contempt."[22]

Pontecorvo's infamous tracking shot reminds us just how much our experience of form changes over time. Moving but a few feet in a matter of a few seconds, the shot looks decidedly restrained from the perspective of what Daniel Morgan has described as our contemporary "age of the moving camera." In *The Lure of the Image*, Morgan returns to this shot and its reception to argue, in part, that what Rivette and especially subsequent critics such as Serge Daney found so inexcusable was not so much the disjuncture between its content and form but rather how it positioned the spectator. "It is this aspect of camera movements," Morgan writes, "their ability to generate epistemological fantasies, that worries Daney when he thinks about the 'tracking shot in Kapo.'" Driving this epistemological fantasy—the idea that cinematic vision creates reliable knowledge—is the camera, the movement of which, Morgan continues, "pulls the viewer along with it, into the world of the film; the viewer is made to inhabit the camera's position . . . to identify with its way of showing the world."[23]

It is this epistemological fantasy, this attempt to make the viewer inhabit the camera's position, to share its literal—and, more broadly, its sponsoring company's figurative—point of view, that corporate oil films like *Shellarama* attempted to make reality. Whether or not it always (or ever) worked is, at best, difficult to confirm, but creating a shared point of view is part of what they sought to achieve. Their goal, in this sense, was not simply to *represent* but also to *create* and to bring mass publics into alignment—or, as I also argue, perceptual resonance—with a new oil-centric point of view.[24] The tracking shot represents one formal mechanism, and one of the most spectacular, for doing so. The remainder of this chapter uses *Shellarama* to consider how this technique, and other, more prosaic formal strategies have defined industrial film's poetics. At stake is not a judgment about tracking (and other) shots' relative morality but rather a greater understanding of how industrial and corporate films achieved their politics not simply through content—understood in context—but also through form.

OIL'S SPECTACULAR AND PROSAIC INDUSTRIAL POETICS

An industrial or corporate film poetics would no doubt share a great deal with poetic approaches traditionally applied to commercial and art cinema. It would similarly involve an interest in historically contextualized production norms and methods to examine the changing importance and meaning of devices and techniques, including tracking, panning, and zooms; cuts, fades, and dissolves; and lighting and mise-en-scène. Often, such devices have comparable aims in industrial and other types of film: to direct vision, to mark the passage of time, to create tension and drama, to generate ways of thinking, or otherwise to move and persuade. Identifying those devices, their relative use in production contexts, and how they are likely to have been understood by film viewers has the upshot of creating what David Bordwell has well summarized as "a conceptual framework within which particular questions about films' composition and effects can be posed" and with the broader ambition of supporting other critical and theoretical projects.[25]

Developing a full poetics of industrial cinema that would attend to the changing production norms found across industrial film's long history and geographic diversity far exceeds this chapter's scope, particularly if done in the expansively comparative "serial" form proposed by Hediger and Vonderau.[26] I seek to demonstrate, instead, the richness of doing historicized formal analysis for a type of cinema that has largely evaded formal concerns. More important, I will use this case to argue that any industrial film poetics must be attuned to the specificity of nonfilm industrial contexts.[27] Put simply, the forms of industry shaped the forms of industry films. We should thus ask, for example, if a dissolve means the same thing in films about nuclear power as it does in films about water treatment? Or do long shots and close-ups, long takes and montage sequences, have the same utility in films about hydroelectric dams as they do in films about coal mines? What may most distinguish an industrial film poetics from the kind of commercial and art cinema poetics found in work by Bordwell and others is how the differing forms and aims of nonfilm industries shaped the practices, forms, and, ultimately, the meanings of their industrial film products. Analyses of industrial film should approach content through form and vice versa.

Any poetics of industrial film must also consider the possibility that the aestheticization of the industrial world may at times have produced not so much a "useful" as a "useless" cinema, a superfluous form of expenditure created out of what Georges Bataille described in 1949 in the first volume of *The Accursed Share* as an "effect of a wild exuberance."[28] This exuberance arose in part from sudden, immense, and arguably excessive oil wealth, wealth that *Shellarama* expresses both materially and formally. Shot in Technicolor and released in widescreen seventy-millimeter Super Technirama, the film, as a material object and an iteration of a large-scale cinematic format, already conveys the kind of excessive expenditure through which oil companies poured money into public relations in the 1960s. Although its creation was no doubt driven in part by useful persuasive ambitions, it was also about the arguably useless creation of cultural products by oil companies and their public relations people, who were selling, as the basis of modern existence, nothing less than, as Bataille put it at the time, a "luxurious squandering of energy in every form."[29]

The conditions that made this squandering possible represent one shaping component of industrial oil cinema's poetics. Because oil companies could often amass more significant financial resources for film production than other kinds of firms, they tended, by the middle part of the twentieth century, to produce what were known in the trade as "prestige films." So named for their esteem-garnering ambitions, such films directed their big budgets to expensive production values, including formal characteristics such as color and widescreen formats, aerial cinematography, and longer running times. On the content side, larger production budgets supported the more geographically ambitious shoots required by an industry shaped by the often-long distances separating extraction sites from refineries and consumer markets. It should thus come as little surprise that industrial oil films were often colonial films that could also involve the further genre mixing of travelogues and shallow ethnographic accounts of exoticized people and places. Their big budgets and corresponding formal flourishes put such films on the spectacular side of industrial poetics, but here, too, we find the more prosaic strategies seen in other industrial films of the time.

Shellarama, as the title's reference to Cinerama already implies, exemplifies the spectacular formal heights achieved in industrial prestige cinema, but it does so slowly and then in combination with otherwise standard formal devices.[30] Together, these devices give the film the general form of a series of vectors that shoot up and out from oil's upstream origins to its downstream destinations. "Upstream" and "downstream" are industry terms that naturalize oil's inevitable flow from source to market, but in this case, they imply the very opposite of the film's directional approach. From start to finish, *Shellarama* places its viewer in an oil-centric perspective that first normalizes and then glamorizes oil through a *rising* narrative shot on an ever-upward moving trajectory.

The film begins by placing the viewer in the position of oil (figure 4.3). Forgoing a traditional establishing shot, it opens down in the muck, where the oil lies. It is a sensible formal approach for a film about stuff: start, as closely as possible, where it comes from. Panning up, the camera finds feet, stretching across and gripping a dark slippery surface. Climbing, like oil, out of the ground, the next shot rises just above the surface, where feet become legs, before cutting

FIGURE 4.3 *Shellarama*'s (1965) opening scene, up and out of the muck.

to a wider shot of ten men—eight Black, two white—waist-deep in murky water. As the two white men plant a tripod-mounted theodolite, a story begins to take form. Led by their Black guides, these men are here to search and survey, a story confirmed in two final opening shots: first, a more traditional establishing shot of the men arriving in a new location by boat, and then a medium shot of one of the surveyors planting a pole in the ground. The preamble duly ends with a drilling site found and marked for extraction.

In these five shots lasting less than sixty seconds, the film establishes, in both content and form, its basic subject and conceit. Its celebration of oil will be formed and guided by oil's movement from its subterranean origins to applications in places farther away, a movement quickly established formally by the sequence's tracked, panned, and montaged shift from its close-up, down in the dark depths, up and out to wider views. The ensuing credit sequence accordingly replays, now more abstractly, the form and rhetoric of rising, with the film's title letters filling with color before the camera again tracks to the surface, this time passing sediment layers as it moves up what appears to be the inside of a well (figure 4.4).

As the titles conclude, the next sequence confirms the pattern by again opening not with a standard establishing shot but from the same oil-centric view. Here we get a prototypical example of one of oil cinema's most iconic views: an extreme low-angle shot, looking up into a derrick and face to face with an oncoming drill. Just as the tricone reaches the camera and wellbore, Cawston cuts to a wide-angle view of the scene. Another, wider shot comes next, followed by a sequence that pauses on the work of drilling, moving between close-ups of the drill, medium shots of workers managing the addition of new sections, and eventually a stream of oil that sprays into the sky. Here again, the camera rises, panning up slowly into a low-angle shot that follows this oil with a formal reverence confirmed in the shot that closes the sequence: another slow pan, this time moving horizontally to capture the proud faces of workers gazing up, like the camera, at the gushing product of their labor.

INDUSTRIAL FILM'S SPECTACULAR AND PROSAIC POETICS • 121

FIGURE 4.4 *Shellarama*'s rising form makes its title.

The ensuing shots span out to similar sites, documenting geographically diverse locations of drilling and pumping, and ending with the rise and fall of pump jacks that animate oil's never-ending rise to the surface. This sequence underscores the formal logic established in the opening. Now operating as a kind of oil travelogue, the film radiates out, like oil and its influence, farther and farther from its origins in the wells. Following the format of its precursor and lodestar, Mike Todd's 1952 film *This Is Cinerama!*, *Shellarama* soon traffics in big images of recognizable places, including Paris's Arc de Triomphe and the Roman Colosseum. But first and foremost, it catalogs a less iconic, largely colonial world of extraction and distribution sites. Like the early film travelogues analyzed by Jennifer Peterson and others, *Shellarama* frames this world as "a series of consumable places" and as "endlessly representable commodities."[31] But whereas, in many of those early films, consumption remains, for the most part, immaterial (their resources are images; their consumption metaphorical) films like *Shellarama* make it literal. The places and natural resources it depicts are meant to be removed and consumed, not just viewed. Giving new meaning to the early film company slogan "the whole world within reach," *Shellarama* teaches viewers a material version of the early film lesson that, as Tom Gunning puts it, "no longer are even the most remote reaches of the planet inaccessible."[32]

Tracing oil's movement from these now-accessible places to energy-hungry Western markets, the film accelerates in the next sequence, the ninety-three-second series of aerial tracking shots that trace the trajectory of a pipeline from desert to coast (figure 4.5). Racing forward and rising, rolling, and eventually falling like the rollercoaster in *This Is Cinerama!*, *Shellarama*'s pipeline sequence creates an especially exuberant vehicle for the experience Anne Friedberg termed the "mobilized virtual gaze."[33] This sequence exemplifies one of the film's key ideological approaches. Put in formal terms, it seeks a kind of alignment among viewer, camera, and corporation. From the French *aligner* (or "into line," *à ligne*), alignment captures both this sequence's linear logic—defined by its oil and gas pipelines, with cinema's form made to match the forms of oil infrastructure—and the film's attempt to bring the viewer's point of view into line with Shell's.

Perhaps even more so, the film capitalizes on what Scott Richmond has described as cinema's "proprioceptive modulation." By this Richmond means that when we watch films featuring these kinds of camera movements, cinema's technical apparatus becomes part of the perceptual and affective system through which "we orient ourselves with the

FIGURE 4.5 *Shellarama*'s tracking shots align infrastructural and film form.

world." Proprioception, as Richmond explains, always involves the mediation of inside and outside through which we attain our sense of self and our position in a world we experience in motion. Cinema's moving camera adds another layer of mediation to this experience and to its subject-forming nature by repositioning us artificially. This process does not, Richmond stresses, involve a one-to-one correspondence between normal perception and cinematic perception. The latter is, of course, an illusion—a technological form of vision that we come to inhabit only momentarily as spectators.[34]

Richmond's account of cinematic proprioception illuminates an important component of the world and subject-forming work deployed in films like *Shellarama*. These films seek two kinds of illusion: first, the perceptual, phenomenological kind described by Richmond—the kind that encourages viewers to give themselves over to the pleasures of the moving-image—and second, an ideological kind of illusion that this perceptual illusion and entertainment supports and engenders. The ideological illusion is the impression such films give that oil power is seamless and immaterial; that its extraction is safe, efficient, and even spectacular; and that cheap modern mobility can be taken for granted. The cinematic illusion through which we experience flying across deserts and mountains and moving seamlessly around the world thus reproduces one of the ideological illusions of oil, which sells just this kind of seamless, immaterial motion.[35] The "cinematic perception" that makes the first kind of illusion work is, Richmond argues, a perception that does not belong to the viewer, nor to cinema, but rather to the experiential relationship created in their ongoing encounter.[36] To engage in this encounter, as Richmond argues through media theorist Mark Hansen, is to open oneself to technics (i.e., the technical modulation that cinema offers). That openness of self-perception, or of individuation, is part of how this film works on its viewer—how, that is, it uses form to persuade the viewer to embrace and to see and understand themselves in the world created by oil's infrastructural system. That the film was shot and screened in Super Technirama with stereophonic sound contributed to this formal strategy. Synching the spectator perceptually and ideologically extended from the film's form to its exhibition format, where the experience of technological immersion enhanced the illusion.

The origin of this perceptual and ideological illusion takes us back to the early cinema of extractions and the coal-powered railroad industry. Coal and rail helped encourage the same kind of cinematic mobility, sponsoring the first corporate films in the 1890s and, over the next two decades, making film a key tool in campaigns promoting colonization, tourism, and industrial development.[37] "Cinema's locomotive, panoramic past," as Annette Michelson put it, has often been described, including by Wolfgang Schivelbusch, Lynn Kirby, and others.[38] The two technologies' fusion in early cinema's so-called phantom rides—that is, films shot from the front of moving trains and sometimes screened in repurposed rail cars, again to create an immersive technological illusion that anticipates widescreen—set the standard for the literal tracking shots reproduced half a century later on *This Is Cinerama*'s roller-coaster tracks, which we see echoed in *Shellarama*'s aerial race to the sea.[39]

In one of the earliest and most enduring accounts of these phantom rides, a reviewer of one titled *The Haverstraw Tunnel* (1897) sources that film's locomotive power in an "unseen energy [that] swallows up space and flings itself into the distances" (figure 4.6). The resulting effect, the reviewer continues, is "as mysterious and impressive as an allegory." Unsurprisingly, given its evocative language, the quote appears frequently in early film scholarship, not least including several essays by Gunning, one of which puts "unseen energy" in its title.[40] But never, to my knowledge, has the source of this "energy" been considered beyond the fact that camera and operator are of course mounted on a train. Perhaps the

FIGURE 4.6 *Haverstraw Tunnel* [American Mutoscope and Biograph, 1897 (©1903)], in which "unseen energy" becomes visible infrastructure, notably including the pylons and wires that run parallel with the tracks.

oversight has to do with the simple fact that we know it is coal, so why bother to mention it? But to take this fact for granted misses an opportunity to consider the triangulation of form, infrastructure, and point of view that these films made both distinctly visible and, as that 1897 reviewer suggests, allegorical.

In *Allegories of Cinema*, David James reminds us that every film allegorizes its own making, in part because "the financial and technological resources employed and the social relations of a film's manufacture and consumption mark the limits of its formal possibilities."[41] In other words, every film tells at least two stories: whatever story it means to tell and a story about the potentials and limits involved in its own creation. The first story lies right on the surface as the film's literal meaning; the latter requires interpretation and the deciphering of clues that become visible in formal choices, for instance, in the color and spectacular aerial tracking shots seen in prestige films like *Shellarama*, or in the black-and-white, often more static long takes found in low-budget films made for other industries.

James's point comes in the context of an argument about the avant-garde and the "industrial cinema" otherwise known as classical Hollywood, but the method readily applies to the industrial cinema seldom studied back then but that has now become prominent in film scholarship. In this context, it encourages us to read the phantom ride, as that 1897 reviewer suggests, allegorically as the reflexive documentation of the unseen and subsequently unremarked-on energetic relation through which coal, rail, and cinema merge to make culture. Their merger most often lies behind and out of view in the operation of infrastructure, but films like *The Haverstraw Tunnel* and *Shellarama* bring it to the surface and the screen. Part of what is distinct about industrial and corporate films is how they make this unseen energy seen, creating a form of what Lisa Parks has termed "infrastructural visibility."[42] The "unseen energy" that swallows space in *Shellarama* is the very stuff the film is about: the oil and the infrastructural and social relations that made its movement possible. Put another way, and more broadly, the phantom of every phantom ride is the fossil fuel power that mobilizes its mobilized virtual gaze.

The tracking shots in these films thus mark the convergence of content and form and the adaptation of cinematic form to industrial and infrastructural content. Here we find cinema being shaped, in formal terms, by that which it seeks to represent. The resulting convergence of visual form and infrastructural context is a defining element of the industrial poetics found in the midcentury industrial cinema of extractions, a cinema that makes visible the correspondence, the interchange, and the feedback between cinematic forms and the forms of their extracted contents. To see that correspondence requires that we take seriously not just how images depict infrastructure but also the role images and aesthetics play in infrastructural development. In her work about the jet age, for example, Vanessa Schwartz examines how infrastructural aesthetics become something more than just the representational or epiphenomenal outgrowth of infrastructure. "Transport and communication media," in particular, "did not just support each other," Schwartz argues, "rather, they served the same end in one network of facilitating circulation."[43] Infrastructures may give rise to images and shape aesthetics, but infrastructure also has been shaped first by aesthetic questions and problems that require and generate both material and visual solutions. The "jet-age aesthetic," as Schwartz calls it, or the aesthetics of an age of oil, as I might also put it, cannot be understood outside this mutually constituting infrastructure-image relationship. At stake, as Brian Larkin has argued, is how infrastructure's "aesthetic address constitutes a form of political action that is linked to, but differs from, [its] material operations." The corporate cinema of extractions emerged as one means to manage infrastructure's "aesthetic address," as part of how, in Larkin's words, infrastructural "visibility or invisibility are made to happen as part of technical, political, and representational processes."[44]

The dynamics of visibility in the infrastructure-aesthetic relationship become uniquely apparent in a world of energy that was driven by a defining material-immaterial connection. Energy was and is a problem of how visual forms actively shape our relationship to material things. By tracing the life cycle of oil, *Shellarama* shows us oil's material and formal transformation from crude to refined stuff and on to its "immaterial" deployment as energy (e.g., gasoline) and culture (e.g., gasoline brands). This representation of energy's material transformation illustrates how oil becomes culture, and in this way, how aesthetics shape oil's material forms (such as gas stations) as well as how those forms then become the raw material for more images in industrial films (see figure 4.7).

This process of material transformation becomes visible in the sequences that follow *Shellarama*'s spectacular aerial tracking shots. After arriving at sea, the film slows down, first in a section that flows along slowly with the waiting *Shell Aramare*, a tanker completed in

FIGURE 4.7 Oil becomes culture becomes image in Shell's spectacular industrial film poetics.

1960 for Shell's Venezuelan subsidiary. After a few moments rising and falling with the waves (the camera and viewer are again synched with oil transport), a slow dissolve carries us from sea back to land and a quiet series of still shots that come next. First, three wide establishing shots introduce a refinery lit up in twilight hours, followed by closer views, all shot, once again, from low angles looking up at rising tanks and towers that will transform upstream crude into useful downstream forms. This quiet interlude continues by intercutting the refinery and storage tanks with shots of calm streets, parking lots, and garages, all full of waiting vehicles. Here again, the film's form—the stillness of the shots, the slow pace of the editing, and the quiet soundtrack—correspond to its story about a world waiting to be put in motion.

This sequence and the one it sets up play on the dynamic created by stillness and a potential to move that for companies like Shell was nothing less than an existential, world-defining problem. In the wake of the rapid aerial tracking shots seen moments earlier, this slow montage creates rising tension by suddenly capturing the world in relative immobility: its streets, squares, and avenues deserted; its parking lots full of motionless cars. The tension builds—and with it, potential energy—until finally a Shell tanker truck appears, followed by another image of rising oil, this time in the form of gasoline filling a waiting tank (figure 4.8). The pace and volume of the soundtrack rises, too, followed by one last moment of calm as the tank finally fills, now ready to repower and reanimate the world and the film with nothing more than the press of a button.

This sequence gave the film an alternate release title, *Push Button Go*, that tidily encapsulates the more instrumentalist argument it also makes, in part through a prosaic poetics of carefully framed shots and deliberately paced cuts.[45] In contrast to the exuberance implied by *Shellarama*, with its roots in the Greek *horama*, for sight or spectacle, and its fast-paced aerial shots and remarkable travelogue views, *Push Button Go* points to the film's parallel argument about oil's utility

INDUSTRIAL FILM'S SPECTACULAR AND PROSAIC POETICS • 131

FIGURE 4.8 Gas fills the tank, and then "push button go."

and usefulness as it arrives downstream and becomes integrated in an automatic consumer process. The difference underscores the underlying dynamic, or tension, in this and so many other "useful" films, between usefulness and the kind of wild exuberance and spectacular squandering of excess energy described by Bataille.

The remainder of the film, up to its final shots, attempts to sell this exuberance not as excess but rather as utility—as the very basis for modern life and happiness. This rhetorical shift coincides with a shift from "midstream" oil infrastructure to oil's deployment as an unseen source of power and pleasure. In this sequence, derricks, pipelines, and tankers make way for cars, trucks, and scooters, and the image of gushing crude gives way to oil as it takes cultural and social form as the petrol station, the automobile, and the experience of driving. Formally speaking, the shift involves three primary techniques. First, in its narrative structure, the film uses a pattern of repetition with difference, circling back, first to repeat the calm streets and parking lots seen earlier but now reanimated by moving vehicles (figure 4.9). A few minutes later, it doubles down on this technique, similarly repeating the shift from exuberant movement to calm and quiet, and

FIGURE 4.9 Potential energy becomes oil culture formally through repetition with difference.

then back to automobile energy, triggered yet again by the sound of an engine starting—push button, go.

Second, the tracking shots return, now filmed from car-mounted cameras that sync cinematic power and pleasure with the joy of gas-fueled automobility. Hopping between vehicles and locations, these shots again define the film as a travelogue while also typifying the tracking shot's power to move us, as underscored by the device's description in French as *le travelling*. To be modern, the film implies, is to travel, whether by way of its immersive form of moving-image media or the fossil-fueled moving machines in which it immerses its viewer—and upon which it relied to be produced at all. Placing its viewers in the virtual position of moving machines, the film seeks to move them into literal seats as drivers.

Finally, to move from vehicle to vehicle and place to place, the film adopts a more rapid montage format that includes a series of match cuts designed to deliver the key, if only implicit, argument that modern oil-powered life is shared equally by everyone, everywhere. Early in the sequence, for instance, match cuts create the formal equivalence of three people—a white woman, a white man, and a Black man—all driving cars (figure 4.10). The pattern then repeats to create a similar match-cut association between white, bikini-clad women, Londoners in suits, and Black Africans in flowing robes, all seen from behind riding scooters (figure 4.11). Conjuring a utopian

FIGURE 4.10 *Shellarama*'s match-cut universalism, side view.

vision of gas-powered equality, the shots recall "The Family of Man," the 1955 photo exhibition curated by Edward Steichen, one of the goals of which was to offer, as Fred Turner describes it, "a view of humanity in which all people, including former and contemporary enemies, could be seen as equal."[46] For companies such as Shell that relied on access to former colonial sites like those seen in the film's opening, a similar universalist ideal needed to be sold, and film's formal capacity for moving-image photomontage was no less up to the task than photobooks or exhibition layouts.[47]

FIGURE 4.11 *Shellarama*'s match-cut universalism, phantom ride view.

One is nonetheless left to wonder what viewers might have made of the ensuing juxtaposition of this universalist whitewashing of colonial and neocolonial relations with the version of American Manifest Destiny that followed for those who saw the film when it was released theatrically as the preamble to John Sturges's 1965 Super Cinerama spectacle, *The Hallelujah Trail*. Often described as a spoof of the western framed within a mockumentary, Sturges's film takes parodic aim, in part, at the problem of resource scarcity. The material in question, however, is not water, or oil and gas, or even that more favored western subject, gold, but instead whiskey, the resource no western town can do without. The film flopped at the box office despite its arguably brilliant conceit, whiskey being one of the western genre's unremarked-on but ever-present necessities. More to the point, it fittingly ends with a joke that might have resonated with anyone whose memory and attention could sustain nearly three hours of bad jokes, misogyny, and a depiction of Native Americans—as violent, liquor-thirsty kidnappers—that is staggeringly racist even by midcentury Hollywood standards. The joke is that the ill-fated whiskey, which everyone fears has been lost in a bed of quicksand, just will not stay down. Like Shell's rising oil, it must resurface, a predestined return that generates a healthy profit for one alcoholic weather prophet and a soldier with a homestead claim.

CONCLUSION: PHASE CHANGES AND FORMAL TRACES

Films such as *Shellarama* demonstrate how easily extracted materials like oil could be transformed, in the span of a short film reel, from crude materials to cultural objects and idealized social experiences. When treated as texts worthy of close interpretation, they allow us to see this reformation as it takes form—and as it is sold—through devices such as montage, match cuts, and exuberant tracking shots. Consider two final examples of the spectacular and prosaic poetics with which Shell closed its film. *Shellarama* ends by decisively ceding itself, in two striking ways, to the most spectacular form of industrial poetics. The most obvious way comes in the final shot, which begins as seemingly just another phantom ride filmed from the front of a moving car but then suddenly veers off the road and takes flight, soaring into an aerial tracking shot, out over a river, under a bridge, and steadily into a drawn-out closing dissolve that blends road and sky (figure 4.12). Driving is flying, the shot implies, and with boundless horizons tailor-made for cinema's biggest screens.

136 • INDUSTRIAL FILM'S SPECTACULAR AND PROSAIC POETICS

Preceding this gravity-defying shot, the film diverges in a second, quieter way, from prosaic norms to industrial spectacle. One of the well-known rules guiding Shell's industrial film poetics was that the Shell brand should never appear in its films except in the opening and closing title cards. As Rudmer Canjels puts it, "with a few

FIGURE 4.12 In *Shellarama*'s closing spectacle, driving becomes flying with boundless horizons.

exceptions, prestige was to be obtained through association instead of by clear propaganda," a rule that set Shell apart from many of its oil competitors, who also sought prestige in this subtle way but were often much less reticent about showing and selling their brand, too.[48] *Shellarama* breaks this rule twice, first, and most innocuously, when the name of the *Shell Aramare* tanker fills the screen about halfway through, and then in one of its final shots, which races past a roadside Shell service station (see figure 4.7). In both cases, the film seemingly cannot help but put its sponsor on screen, as if the spectacular event of Super Technirama demands it. But both are also reflexive moments that underscore the feedback loop between infrastructure and culture. The *Shell Aramare* tanker holds, in its name, the film's title, and there it becomes a mise-en-abyme—a literal vehicle for oil that mirrors the film's figurative one from within. This simple moment becomes more significant when understood in the logic of the cinema of extractions, a cinema, as I have been arguing, that always involved an inherent degree of reflexivity about the material requirements of its creation. The Shell gas station serves this same purpose, while also, in a more straightforward way, illustrating oil's transformation into material culture and that culture's utility as immaterial signifier and (filmed) image.

* * *

Seeing oil and its infrastructure as material and cultural form, as I have modeled in this chapter, is just part of what we gain if we take seriously Godard's insistence that tracking (and other) shots are a question or matter of morality. We know by now that global warming driven by fossil fuel consumption has spawned a climate crisis, with already devastating consequences, particularly for the most vulnerable populations and those marked by histories of colonization and resource extraction celebrated in the opening of *Shellarama* and films like it. But we need not take the simple kind of moralistic stand that sometimes drives work in the environmental humanities, where restating the causes and consequences of climate change often passes for final arguments or self-evident stakes. Judging the "morality" of tracking shots and other film forms may be one useful way to analyze the kind of public relations work through which companies like Shell knowingly misled the world about the world-altering consequences of their work. But treating it only as ideological deception misses a crucial opportunity to recognize the genuine outburst of enthusiasm that oil and gas and their mobility created, including the many forms of modern pleasure that made up that "wild exuberance" described by Bataille. One moral of this story, then, is that films like *Shellarama* are not only documents of an immoral process's history or even cultural markers, as I have described previously, of a new geological epoch's emergence.[49] They are not, in other words, simply epiphenomenal products of the fossil fuel age. Such films also helped drive that age and both to create and to express part of its real pleasure by propagating its ideas and worldviews and giving them persuasive and moving visual form.

The student and scholar of images knows no simple one-to-one correspondence exists between ideas and their images—or between infrastructure and images of it—but rather that the movement of idea or design to visual form or object and back again requires formal translations, or phase changes, that leave traces for analysis and interpretation. As David James again puts it so well, "a given stylistic vocabulary is never merely itself; rather it is the trace of the social processes that constitute a practice."[50] To this we should add that social processes and their practices take form through aesthetic and formal logics. Style, or form, in other words, operates in a relational circuit, not just as the outcome of social practice but also as part of what constitutes that practice in the first place. A cinema and media studies up to the task of analyzing infrastructure, energy, and environment should be invested in analyzing—in both the images and the materials and practices that create them, and that they in turn create—that trace we call form.

CONCLUSION

Counter-Cinemas of Extraction

The history of the industrial cinema of extractions, even in its most enticingly spectacular mode, can make for rather dispiriting reading, much less close analysis. I have seen even the most engaged classes worn down by weeks of watching such films and reading their histories, and I have experienced what I imagine to be a similar feeling after hours of archival viewing and combing through the documents that give context to these films' celebratory scenes of terrestrial and human domination. Corporate films such as Shell's *Shellarama*, Union Carbide's *Tungsten: A Treasure of the Sierra Nevada*, and thousands of others like them demonstrate how effectively extractive industries marshalled film culture to create and narrate the worlds they desired. These films taught viewers that the land was there to be used, that its resources were inexhaustible, and that their applications lay elsewhere, far from the places, societies, and cultures their extraction required but all too often disavowed and destroyed. Even films that slyly criticized the industries they were commissioned to celebrate were the exceptions that proved the more disheartening rule that by the middle of the twentieth century, if not years earlier, image power had become corporate power.[1] Thus, even if their films were sometimes "useless," corporations had so powerfully made film aesthetics conform to their industrial politics that they could afford some exuberant excess.

Acknowledging the image power extractive industries had acquired need not, of course, lead one to assume that resistance was nonexistent or futile. Exceptions exist, and counter-cinemas have emerged. We may take heart in the fact that extractive films and the strategies and ideologies they make visible place us firmly in the realm of corporate realities typically kept hidden from public scrutiny or more carefully mediated to manage it. If we want to understand extractive systems and the ideologies behind them, the cinema of extractions puts it right on the surface, or at least within reach of contextualized interpretation and analysis. Seen in retrospect, these films are often surprisingly frank about the dangerous working conditions extraction required, the damage they did to workers and the environment, and the beliefs and corporate visions underlying it all. In this respect, surface-level reading already captures important scenes and stories that many extractive industries would rather see forgotten. What we see in these films is also more than simply the epiphenomenal reflection of what their sponsors did; they are also both mediated interpretations of industrial work and one of the world-making tools that attempted to make that work possible. To understand this world-making requires more than just "surface reading."[2] Instead, as I have proposed, it works best when done using contextual knowledge to inform formal readings of two kinds of context—the film's subject and its production history—and then turning those readings back to the text.

The same method applies to the cinema of extractions found in the commercial feature film industry. Understanding that cinema as a form of "industrial cinema," as David James named it, has the virtue of pushing us to read for the material backdrops that Hollywood and other illusionary cinemas were similarly designed to make us forget.[3] Although materialist history has revealed a great deal—and can still be used to teach us more—about the realities mostly concealed behind the scenes, materialism need not be an end in itself. Enormous value remains in interpretation, "symptomatic" readings, and what material knowledge can bring back to texts that emerge in dialogue with (and not just as the product of) the conditions of their making.

When read together, these two cinemas—two sides of the same extractive coin developed in the 1890s and split in the 1910s—narrate a worldview founded long before cinema but consolidated in the twentieth century. Charlie Chaplin summed it up well as the age of oil, film, and aeronautics. That age's media of transport made Western experience ever more mobile and ever more virtual, leading, as Vanessa Schwartz has argued, straight into a new age in which many of us accept, and even expect or demand, life lived at a mediated distance. The jet age and its aesthetics prepared people "who could," Schwartz argues, "better mediate between the material and image worlds, saw less antagonism between the human and the technological spheres, and were comfortable rather than distressed at seeing themselves as spectators of their changing world."[4] The result has been a great deal of pleasure and possibility for those who can afford it and a higher standard of living for many others but still driven by ever-growing degrees of inequality and built on disavowed histories of colonial domination and violent subjugation. Corporate cinemas of extraction and Hollywood's glamorous stories of extracted wealth taught people how to enjoy the upside while ignoring or explaining away the downside—how, that is, to live in an Anthropocene coded *not* as an age of climate change catastrophe and colonial suppression but rather of the kind of human domination that makes a "good life" possible.

READING FOR EXTRACTIONS

Part of what may seem remarkable about the cinema of extractions is that it puts so much of the dangerous, damaging, and devastating stuff required to create this good life right in front of us. Extractive industries saw these "negative externalities" as little more than the cost of doing business, but eventually they had to be concealed when their visibility threatened to taint the corporate or industrial image. One of my goals in this book is to encourage forms of analysis that look at this cinema more closely and consider more carefully what it reveals whether in the form of celebratory corporate vehicles or reflexive Hollywood diversions. I have proposed that doing so involves three general steps that I outline, one final time, as a call to methodological action, especially for the student interested in developing a more expansive and intricate formal practice.

Step One: Read for the Forms of the Contents

Neoformalist literary analysis points the way to a more engaged manner of approaching a film's subject as a series of forms. We already know this, in part, from anthropologists and social historians, who have long been invested in developing systematic knowledge of social structures and studying the intricacies of cultural formations. The film analyst, too, can enrich their analysis of any film by learning more about its depicted subject, be it oil prospecting, coal mining, factory labor, office work, apartment living, architecture, or the film business.[5] The task, however, is not only to learn the history and practices of whatever subject but also to consider that subject's *forms*. What form does factory or mining or office work involve? How would one characterize the form of auto racing or espionage, marriage or mourning, electioneering or cooking and cleaning? Every subject may be defined by a set of forms that can usefully draw out abstract principles and logics that underpin practices.

These abstract forms need not—indeed, they *must* not—become universalizing dogma or determinist ahistorical shackles that limit analysis. Forms are contingent, malleable, and shaped by social experience and difference. In the preceding chapters, I have, for example, argued that the oil industry may be defined by various forms, including the rise and fall of boom and bust, the vector form of lines connecting nodes, the industry language of "upstream" and "downstream" movement, and the formal logic of concentric circles that radiate out from extraction and distribution sites. I have similarly schematized mining as a line and node system with a temporal logic of extraction and delivery times, as a linear processual system leading from the crudest raw materials to refined products, and as an idealized looping system of endless accumulation. In the broadest strokes, such forms may define most petroleum or mining industries and infrastructures, but they also vary according to historical and geographic contexts and need to be assessed accordingly. Industrial, political, and social systems take on varying forms shaped by the times and places of their creation. This is why film and media scholars need to write and read deeply researched histories of media materials and their connected extractive industries. The work of analysis requires attention to the resulting formal possibilities and sufficient rigor not to assume that just any formal reading will do.

Step Two: Read for the Forms of Production

I have often returned to David James's *Allegories of Cinema* in this book because James so clearly articulates the analytic stakes of connecting the modes of film production to their textual products. James's historical materialist method has renewed value today, I believe, as one means to marshal the new materialist knowledge generated by studies of media and extraction. Using what we might call raw materialist history, we may reconnect new materialist knowledge to textual interpretation. In the past two decades, scholars working in production studies and media industry studies have also considerably expanded how we understand the modes of production. This work will continue to bear fruit as their analyses of contemporary practices steadily become historical data about media industries past. Just as we may read the forms of the contents, we should also read these accounts for the forms of the production contexts, which again may at times follow standardized logics but also vary widely across time, place, genre, and medium. In this book, I have emphasized how production forms so often must be molded to follow the forms of their films' subjects. But the shaping influence may also go the other way, which would explain why, for example, mining films shot on studio sets may look nothing like mining films shot in mines.

Step Three: Read Textual Forms with and Against the Forms of Their Contents and the Forms of Their Production

Mastering film's formal language remains one of the primary prerogatives of many film and media undergraduate programs, and I assume any student will read this book having learned to identify and interpret cuts, fades, and dissolves, long shots and long takes, zooms and pans, and the most spectacular and prosaic of tracking shots. As Lee Grieveson has demonstrated, this approach has roots, at least in the United States, in Hollywood-supported efforts to define film analysis as a *belle-lettrist* practice of "film appreciation" that foreclosed more critical methods—historical, political economic, and reception-oriented—that might have cast the industry in a very different light.[6] By pushing for a mode of analysis that takes seriously modes of production and contextualized subject histories, one of my aims is to redirect formal knowledge to those more critical paths.[7]

The student engaged in this practice will ask how and why tracking shots are deployed to mobilize the linear formal logics of oil distribution or how high- and low-angle shots give form to ways not just of seeing but also of thinking about and valuing drilling and mining. At stake is a way of understanding film not simply as the epiphenomenal depiction, documentation, or reflection of extractive (and other) practices, but also as a world-making force whose forms work in concert with the forms, practices, and ideologies of their subjects. A film does not become "useful" or do its "work" merely by existing in a corporate film catalog or being shown in a boardroom, in a classroom, or at an industrial film festival but rather through specific formal strategies that merit close attention. Devoting that attention, especially with the contextual knowledge "useful" cinema studies has been so good at developing, can take us far from film appreciation and into the work of criticism and political analysis.

COUNTER-CINEMAS OF EXTRACTION

With this approach in mind, I want to end with a different kind of cinema of extractions, a counter-cinema that at times upsets or disrupts the extractive forms seen elsewhere in this book and at other times performs something akin to a cinematic version of the kinds of analyses this book seeks. I take inspiration, in part, from a question received after presenting an early version of this book's opening chapter about how I might define, in concert with the cinema of extractions, a "cinema of reparations."[8] I do not have a complete answer to this question, but one component would surely involve cinemas that have either resisted and refused the kinds of extractive world-making practices seen and deployed in films such as *Shellarama* or developed counter-narratives about extractive industries that create opportunities to recover alternative histories of places and peoples whose stories have, for too long, been shaped and defined by those industries, their films, and their archives. Generations of feminist film historians have demonstrated the historical, conceptual, and political necessity of refusing to accept the historical narratives we have been given.[9] So, too, have historians of colonial cinema and scholars more attentive to race within national frameworks shown us how to adjust our historical geographies and reading practices to account for histories occluded by dominant narratives and archival absences.[10]

While writing this conclusion, I have been thinking, in particular, about Jennifer DeClue's analysis of Black feminist avant-garde films and her argument "that liberation can be attained by searching the past for evasions and distortions as a means to see anew," in part by reading films "that work and rework visual terrain and in so doing expose perversions that are embedded in archival material."[11]

Here I offer two examples that demonstrate some of the potential films have shown to perform this visual working and reworking of extractive industries and their histories through form. I am not necessarily arguing that these films are representative of broader cinematic trends or movements—that would require a more detailed history. Rather, I see them as useful texts through which to consider alternative formal engagements with, respectively, extractive industry and its history. The first example, Margot Benacerraf's documentary about salt extraction in Venezuela, *Araya* (1959), models a film treatment of resource extraction that challenges corporate and industrial ways of seeing—and does so especially through its formal engagement with industrial form. The second, Sanaz Sohrabi's recent short feature, *Scenes of Extraction* (2023), enacts, in its formal strategies, an approach to history and industrial form very much like the one I have attempted to define and encourage.

Written with Pierre Seghers and shot by Benacerraf and Giuseppe Nisoli, *Araya* documents salt production and other elements of daily life and labor among the salt-mining and fishing families of the Araya Peninsula on Venezuela's northern Caribbean coast. It details a laborious extractive process that begins with day and night shifts digging salt out of the coastal marsh, then proceeds to shore, where the salt is dried and stacked in neat rows of pyramids, pulled back down into carefully weighed bags, lifted again onto trucks, and finally put back out to sea on boats destined for markets and on to unseen houses and tables elsewhere. Benacerraf encourages us to see this process formally, whether through the sheets of raw salt pulled from the marsh, or the piles of salt pushed by the cutters in their shallow boats, or the scaled-up salt pyramids formed on shore and the orderly lines of men who mount and descend them.

First and foremost, however, the film pursues salt production's forms across the repetitive series of what the narration voiced by Jose Ignacio Cabrujas describes as the "same ancient gestures" that have defined "the daily ritual of the salt" for centuries. These ancient gestures tie together the workers who perform their connected ritualistic forms. The men who lift baskets of salt and dump them into piles, for example, share a gestural form with the men who raise sacks of salt to be tossed onto boats, and similar gestures connect these actions to the women who carry buckets and pails to retrieve fresh water; the men who carry baskets of fish to be cleaned, cut, and salted; and the women who carry the fish to be sold (figure c.1). Everyone in Araya has their gesture, whether it is sewing and tying salt sacks or sewing and tying fish nets; cutting salt or cutting fish; passing tokens or pushing wheelbarrows.

Benacerraf and Nisoli immerse us in these forms and their steady rhythms and tie us into the connected systems of resources and labor that form what the film describes as Araya's "closed economy." About halfway through, for example, a remarkable sequence shows how four young men break down sacks of salt into the finer grains used for preserving fish. We hear them, first, pounding in unison, and we just begin to see their shadows in the left foreground of a shot initially focused on two boys carrying heavy baskets of fish we have just seen rinsed in the previous shot (figure c.1). Just as one of the boys dumps his basket, the camera pans down to the pile of salt and another sack being dumped—that ancient gesture twice repeated—pulling us from one step in a connected process to the next (figure c.2). These fish, the sea's "sustenance," the narrator explains as part of this transition, "must be salted, and fast." The camera slowly pans back up to four large clubs and the shadows cast across the salt by the men pounding them. A new shot then reverses field, still trained on salt and ground, before we shift again, this time putting the men between us and the

148 • CONCLUSION

FIGURE C.1 *Araya*'s (dir. Margot Benacerraf, 1959) connected gestural forms.

salt so we can see their feet rise and fall and rise and fall, alternating with each strike. The next shot reveals this gesture's corresponding upper form from a low angle that looks up at a blank sky rhythmically interrupted by the men raising their clubs, arms, and torsos, alternating, like their feet, with each new strike. The sequence ends

FIGURE C.2 Immersed in *Araya*'s "closed economy" of gestural forms.

by cutting back out to a medium shot of the four men and then to a wider view that shows them continuing their work in the background while another man carries a box of the crushed salt into the foreground to begin the next section of the film and the next phase of work: preparing the waiting fish.

This connecting formal logic shows us how the people of Araya, through the forms they perform, become individuals and families and a community. As the salting process begins, the narrator explains that "the salt of Dámaso and Nemesio, of Beltrán and Fortunato, thus complements Adolfo's fishing." By this point, we know these men by name and how their work and lives are woven together through their labor. We know whose son is cutting salt and whose is carrying it; whose daughter is fetching water and whose is sewing nets; and whose wife is weighing salt sacks, whose is directing water distribution, and whose is selling fish. Put simply, *Araya* insists that extractive stories can be individual stories, family stories, and community stories. They can be human narratives, not resource narratives; they can be human images, not resource images. And all this in ways that contrast starkly with the kind of "human" stories told even in industrial films, such as *Tungsten*, that make a point of highlighting the unnamed workers who make extraction possible, or, even more so, those like *Shellarama* that make workers little more than on-screen guides for how to admire the stuff they extract.

Araya knows the difference and makes it part of its story and its form. Having opened with a short history of the region's colonization by the Spanish and the violent origins of a system of salt extraction still overseen by a fortress that towers over the salt pyramids, the film concludes with the violent arrival of industry. Introduced by blasts of dynamite, the sequence takes on the style of a short industrial film, moving quickly through a series of shots showing how modern machines turn giant boulders into tiny rocks and the land into the beginnings of productive industrial infrastructure. The formal contrast, in both image and sound, could not be clearer. Benacerraf puts a fine point on it formally by cutting from a low-angle shot of a bulldozer pushing dirt to a high-angle shot of a waiting basket of salt, the false continuity of which underscores the difference between manual and machine labor and the two systems' incompatibility.

The subsequent scene cuts together shots that contrast the forms we now know so well—the lines of salt carriers and their pyramids and the gestures of Araya's men and women—with new lines made by diggers and dump trucks and the forms of earth-processing machines. "Will the hardships of men disappear," Benacerraf asks, and "will machines finally replace the arms of Benito, of Beltrán and Fortunato? . . . Is this the end of the turning wheel of salt?" The film offers no definitive answer. Having spent the previous hour documenting the toil and torments that make this wheel turn, but also the individuals and the community around it, *Araya* questions, perhaps earnestly, whether industrialization could bring a better way of life, all the while still betraying, through its form, a sense of doubt. Generational change, the film implies, happens in deep dialogue with the lived past and those who turned the wheel and performed the ancient gestures before. We see this especially through the story of young Carmen, who collects shells and flowers to decorate gravestones with her grandmother. Who will plant the real and metaphorical seeds that may, as the final lines hopefully imagine, one day bloom for Araya's long departed? *Araya* leaves little doubt that its faith lies with the Carmens of the world, and not with the faceless machines that blow the land asunder.

SCENES OF EXTRACTION

The question of people and how they move into and out of extractive histories drives a second example of a counter-cinema. *Scenes of Extraction* reached me late in writing this book but quickly captured my interest as a particularly engaging example of the new work being produced by artists and scholars invested in telling stories about the worlds extractive industries have made and how those industries have attempted, so often through images, to control how we know their worlds and remember—or strategically forget—the work of their creation. Based on Sohrabi's extensive research in the archives of British Petroleum, the film focuses on the development of oil and transportation infrastructure in Iran and their roots in geological surveying. The film's primary and powerful argument is that this surveying and other oil work relied on indigenous knowledge and labor while simultaneously working, through photography and film, to define indigenous subjects as little more than accessories to extraction or its primitive analogs and forever to fix that idea in the corporate visual record that forms the film's primary source. Its implicit question is what role film might play in revealing that work and in unfixing its ideological legacies.

Scenes of Extraction takes BP's visual archive of extractions as its raw material and subjects it to forms of critical and close visual analysis much like the reading methods I pursue and advocate in this book. The method begins to come into focus in the film's five-minute opening, which introduces the construction of the Trans-Iranian Railway (1927–1938), a major infrastructural project partly funded with revenues from the Anglo-Persian, then Anglo-Iranian Oil Company (AIOC), an antecedent of BP. The Trans-Iranian Railway, the film argues, was more than just a new railroad. By linking modernization and nation building with foreign-controlled oil extraction, the Railway became the material expression of a political relationship. Only by ceding control of its extractable resources to the British, this politics implied, could Iran become "modern." The film goes on to show how the Railway and the political argument it embodied became the raw material for images carefully curated by AIOC publicity officers in photographs and industrial films documenting the construction. Much like the Shell-branded service stations and tankers seen in films such as *Shellarama*, here the Railway becomes an element of culture that normalizes its structuring political relationships and their "promise."[12]

Scenes of Extraction uses a 1930 AIOC film, *The Trans-Persian Railway*, to show this transformative process in action and to introduce the stakes of looking closely not just at what such films reveal but also what they exclude. Describing one of the AIOC film's phantom-ride sequences, Sohrabi's voiceover highlights its strategic synching of film and industrial infrastructure. "Here the camera not only moves in parallel to the infrastructure," she explains, "it also becomes one with it." As other examples in this book have similarly shown, here we find cinema conforming itself to the Railway's form (figure c.3). Both are driven by an unseen energy that structures not just the infrastructure but also, as *Scenes of Extraction* highlights by historicizing the Railway's origins, a broader political configuration that this infrastructure represents. In the margins, meanwhile, we see another form of energy, the railroad's construction workers, who are also in the process of becoming unseen, reduced, in Sohrabi's words, to "specters" whose "disembodied social experiences," strategically lost or buried in the AIOC/BP archives and in the "shadow of infrastructure," become one of the film's driving concerns.

FIGURE C.3 Inset films display industrial and colonial logics of infrastructural synchronicity and geological world mastery that the film reproduces to overturn.

Film stills from *Scenes of Extraction* (2023), 44 minutes, Canada/Iran. Copyright: Sanaz Sohrabi/VOX, Center for Contemporary Images, Montréal. Images reproduced with the permission of BP p.l.c.

What makes *Scenes of Extraction* such a compelling work—and an example of a counter-cinema of extractions—is how it uses the industrial film and photographic archive, exposing and dismantling its strategies and forms to turn it into a cinema that reveals some of what has been concealed. The extractive archive becomes the guide for this process. BP's films and photo albums provide a route through what becomes legible, in Sohrabi's words, as a "colonial network and [the] accumulation of imperial capital." Tracing that network through the "parallel pathways between the infrastructures of oil and the infrastructures of image," *Scenes of Extraction* makes visible the system of colonial power and knowledge that linked British oil extraction in places like colonized Burma (Myanmar) and geologists operating across the British Empire, especially the geological survey teams based in India. The corporate photo albums whose images fill Sohrabi's film documented these networks and the racial hierarchies reproduced at each node, eventually including Iran, where the search for oil reserves generated a corresponding image reserve.

Industrial films captured and spread this work in yet more images. Sohrabi includes an extended excerpt from *Survey of Anglo-Iranian Oil Company Operations in Iran* (1938), which includes a revealing lesson in corporate image production that becomes a cipher for *Scenes of Extraction*'s countervailing form. British survey work, we learn from the inset film, begins with extensive aerial photography. Back on the ground, the developed and printed photographs, the narrator explains, "are laid on a table in the mosaic room, the prints overlapping so that common details coincide," and eventually "a complete photograph map is built up" (figure c.3). Meanwhile, other prints are used to create stereoscopic images, "showing everything in relief." For the prospector or colonizer, such images promised visual mastery and totalizing knowledge that, when shown more widely, became an important component of what Priya Jaikumar has analyzed as colonial cinema's multifaceted effect of "visual objectivity." For the geological surveyors Sohrabi follows in *Scenes of Extraction* no less than the colonial geographers analyzed by Jaikumar, colonial space was not merely something to be studied but also a "product" to be generated through maps, photographs, mosaic rooms, and stereoscopes. These space-making images abstracted real places, turning them, Jaikumar argues, into artefacts.[13]

Scenes of Extraction exposes and dismantles this instrumental process by turning itself into an alternative mosaic room filled with artifacts culled from the image archive. The resulting form, with its reassembled and layered fragments of images, challenges the formal logics behind the AIOC's approach to things like foreground and background, center and margin, presence and absence, and whole and fragment. "Common details," to use the AIOC narrator's terms, "coincide" here, but instead of forging extractive geological knowledge, their commonality connects the historical processes and human relations normally effaced or obscured by industrial public relations. We see, for example, layered onto photographs of Iranian geological surveyors, the Burmese workers whose colonial labor became a model for the AIOC's work in Iran (figure c.4). We later see similar

FIGURE C.4 Cutting, layering, and recontextualization as depth-making forms.

Film stills from *Scenes of Extraction* (2023), 44 minutes, Canada/Iran. Copyright: Sanaz Sohrabi/VOX, Center for Contemporary Images, Montréal. Images reproduced with the permission of BP p.l.c.

connections between Iranian work and subsequent prospecting operations in other parts of the British Empire. Putting such connections at the center of the story is both a rhetorical and a formal strategy enacted by repurposing and reworking techniques like those used by the AIOC and the visual material it left behind.

In other parts of the film, Sohrabi challenges the rhetorical and visual marginalizing work found in the AIOC's treatment of indigenous labor. Jaikumar again offers one way to understand this work, arguing that even colonial films designed to turn their subjects into mere artifacts nonetheless retain traces of the lives and liveliness of the workers they depict. *Scenes of Extraction* activates this enduring liveness by focusing on the people documented in the AIOC image archive. But more so, Sohrabi pushes us to contemplate what it meant for these workers to be framed and captured in this way. This extractive "image regime," she argues, was not merely a corollary to the surveying and prospecting it documented, but in fact represented critical "corroborating" work that supported colonial labor by establishing racial hierarchies and ideas about supposed primitiveness. "What we are left with," as she puts it most powerfully, "is the horror of inhabiting the images of extraction." Even if every image of colonial labor and indigenous subjects may have its enduring liveness and presence, those subjects nonetheless risk remaining mere artifacts, stripped of history and thereby entombed in colonial forms and logics. Sohrabi's film works to counter that process by slicing these people from the extractive image and archive and reinserting them into a history in which they were more than just marginal.[14]

One way we may read this reprocessing of the colonial archive is as a form of refinement designed to counter the "refining" work performed by extractive industries and their publicity regimes. The industrial cinema of extractions always modifies its industries' visual content by stripping away crude realities to leave behind only the cleanest one, the reality most "refined" (from the verb "fine," to clarify a liquid by removing its sediment, or to make thinner, both from the

Latin *finire*, to finish). A counter-cinema of extractions like the one I see at work in *Scenes of Extraction* tracks that refining process and seeks its enduring sediment, whether in historical contexts or where it remains in the image, waiting to be reread and thereby reprocessed—re*formed*—in the work of interpretation. Sohrabi's film, with its cut, fragmented, collaged, and layered form, shows some of the directions this work may follow.

UNSETTLED WAYS OF SEEING

At stake in any counter-cinema of extractions and in any critical method of extractive reading is both how we see the world and who conditions that seeing. "Seeing," as John Berger put it most simply long ago, "establishes our place in the surrounding world." But so too does that world, in turn, condition how we see it. "The relation between what we see and what we know," Berger continues, "is never settled.... The way we see things is affected by what we know or what we believe." Influenced by Walter Benjamin, Berger recognized the critical role modern media had come to play in shaping that knowing, and, in a reflexive mode of critical world-making, he developed "Ways of Seeing" first as a television show to explore visual media's power. Berger's approach to world-making acknowledged the many factors that determined what we know and thus what we see, not least including gender and class, which "Ways of Seeing" emphasized. We would now add to this additional ways of thinking about the complex intersecting roles of race, ethnicity, and sexual orientation, among other factors that condition how we see and know the world around us. Berger also recognized the power corporations had come to play in influencing this knowing, in part as they attempted to control not just what we see but also how we know ourselves in the first place (e.g., as gendered, as classed). In an intensely image-dense culture, the publicity image had become,

Berger observed, a nagging impetus to transform oneself, one's world, and, in so doing, one's ways of seeing.[15]

Reading for extractions means, in part, seeking the material realities underpinning that unsettled dynamic between what we see and what we know. Doing so must include attending to the important role played by extractive industries for whom the stakes could not be higher. Corporations and industries must create worlds, and they do so both literally and in the way Berger and others recognized: by shaping how we see and thus know. Through their own films as well as their influence on extraction-dependent commercial film industries, it would be difficult to overestimate the role of extractive industries' structuring importance in how we see the world. Understanding that role materially has immense value and has brought a great deal to film and media (and art and literary) scholarship by offering another way of understanding how art and media change with, respond to, and even sometimes help remake the broader material world. Those insights can go still further when reconnected to analyses of texts and the forms through which material realities come to be influential textual ones. Texts alternately stabilize and unsettle our understanding of the material world, but they only do so within the shifting limits of material constraints that put pressure on, without necessarily determining, what texts can be and do. Tremendous interpretative insight lies in this unsteady balance.

Material and textual analysis may thus work best, as I have tried to show in this book, in tandem, united by a way of thinking about form that connects text and context. Leaping between the two, the formalist approach modeled here seeks new and unexpected readings of both texts—one of our most important ways of seeing the world—and the material worlds that create those texts and that those texts, in turn, help create again. In that feedback loop, no text, context, or reading of them can ever be final or sure. And as it should be. Let us take some small comfort in the fact that while criticism will never, on its own, change the world, the world can still be changed.

CONCLUSION • 159

This is just one reason the goal of the work proposed in this book cannot, as Jaikumar and Grieveson noted about the study of media and extraction more broadly, simply be a way "to castigate media as an extension of technological and social modernity, nor bemoan the ills of industrialization and decry economic development as an unmitigated evil" but must instead contribute to "educating us on the extractive pasts of media and modernity." Whether or not doing so can, as Jaikumar and Grieveson propose, "enable different futures" feels highly uncertain to me as I finalize these pages in early 2024.[16] I nonetheless find value in what generating this knowledge can do to help us understand how our world looks and how its ways of looking, shaped by their material histories, influence our ways of seeing, however unsettled this knowledge may leave us. Let us read through that unsettled position, from the forms of the text to the forms of the context, and back and forth again.

NOTES

INTRODUCTION: EXTRACTIVE AND EXTRACTED MEDIA

1. Charlie Chaplin added the narration to footage from an unreleased 1918 film project, *How to Make Movies*.
2. Vanessa R. Schwartz, *Jet Age Aesthetic: The Glamour of Media in Motion* (New Haven, CT: Yale University Press, 2020).
3. See, for example, Estelle Caron, "Images de la mine et des mineurs," *Les cahiers de la cinémathèque*, no. 71 (December 2000): 47–52; Stephanie LeMenager, *Living Oil: Petroleum Culture in the American Century* (New York: Oxford University Press, 2014); Sheena Wilson, Adam Carlson, and Imre Szeman, eds., *Petrocultures: Oil, Politics, Culture* (Montreal-Kingston: McGill-Queen's University Press, 2016); Macarena Gómez-Barris, *The Extractive Zone: Social Ecologies and Decolonial Perspectives* (Durham, NC: Duke University Press, 2017); Siobhan Angus, "Mining the History of Photography," in *Capitalism and the Camera: Essays on Photography and Extraction*, ed. Kevin Coleman and Daniel James (London: Verso, 2021), 55–73; Karen Redrobe and Jeff Scheible, eds., *Deep Mediations: Thinking Space in Cinema and Digital Cultures* (Minneapolis: University of Minnesota Press, 2020); and Marina Dahlquist and Patrick Vonderau, eds., *Petrocinema: Sponsored Film and the Oil Industry* (London: Bloomsbury Academic, 2021).
4. For a summary of this field and its stakes, see Priya Jaikumar and Lee Grieveson, "Media and Extraction: A Brief Research Manifesto," *Journal of Environmental Media* 3, no. 2 (2022): 197–206. See also Imre Szeman and

Jennifer Wenzel, "What Do We Talk About When We Talk About Extractivism?," *Textual Practice* 35, no. 3 (2021): 505–23.

5. The best description of modernity and its application to cinema is still Leo Charney and Vanessa R. Schwartz, introduction to *Cinema and the Invention of Modern Life*, ed. Leo Charney and Vanessa R. Schwartz (Berkeley: University of California Press, 1995), 3. Key texts in this now vast literature also include Miriam Hansen, "Benjamin, Cinema and Experience: 'The Blue Flower in the Land of Technology,'" special issue on Weimar film theory, *New German Critique* 40 (Winter 1987): 179–224; Anne Friedberg, *Window Shopping: Cinema and the Postmodern* (Berkeley: University of California Press, 1993); Giuliana Bruno, *Streetwalking on a Ruined Map: Cultural Theory and the Films of Elvira Notari* (Princeton, NJ: Princeton University Press, 1993); Tom Gunning, "The Whole Town Is Gawking: Early Cinema and the Visual Experience of Modernity," *Yale Journal of Criticism* 7, no. 2 (1994): 189–201; Lynne Kirby, *Parallel Tracks: The Railroad and Silent Cinema* (Durham, NC: Duke University Press, 1997); Vanessa R. Schwartz, *Spectacular Realities: Early Mass Culture in* Fin-de-Siècle *Paris* (Berkeley: University of California Press, 1998); Miriam Hansen, "The Mass Production of the Senses: Classical Cinema as Vernacular Modernism," *Modernism/Modernity* 6, no. 2 (April 1999): 59–77; Ben Singer, *Melodrama and Modernity: Early Sensational Cinema and Its Contexts* (New York: Columbia University Press, 2001); Tom Gunning, "Systematizing the Electric Message: Narrative Form, Gender, and Modernity in *The Lonedale Operator*," in *American Cinema's Transitional Era: Audiences, Institutions, Practices*, ed. Charles Keil and Shelley Stamp (Berkeley: University of California Press, 2004), 15–50; Tom Gunning, "Modernity and Cinema: A Culture of Shocks and Flows," in *Cinema and Modernity*, ed. Murray Pomerance (New Brunswick, NJ: Rutgers University Press, 2006), 297–315; and Kristen Whissel, *Picturing American Modernity: Traffic, Technology, and the Silent Cinema* (Durham, NC: Duke University Press, 2008).

6. Lewis Mumford, *Technics and Civilization* (New York: Harcourt, Brace, 1934), 337.

7. See, for example, Lee Grieveson, *Cinema and the Wealth of Nations: Media, Capital, and the Liberal World System* (Berkeley: University of California Press, 2018); Alice Lovejoy, "Celluloid Geopolitics: Film Stock and the War Economy, 1939–47," *Screen* 60, no. 2 (2019): 224–41; and Kirsty Sinclair Dootson, *The Rainbow's Gravity: Colour, Materiality, and British Modernity* (New Haven, CT: Yale University Press, 2023).

8. A rough lineage of this historiography would include (among others) books such as Barry Salt, *Film Style and Technology: History and Analysis* (London: Starword, 1983); Steve Neale, *Cinema and Technology: Image, Sound, Colour* (London: BFI, 1985); Kirby, *Parallel Tracks*; Frances Guerin, *A Culture of Light: Cinema and Technology in 1920s Germany* (Minneapolis: University of Minnesota Press, 2005); Brian Larkin, *Signal and Noise: Media, Infrastructure, and Urban Culture in Nigeria* (Durham, NC: Duke University Press, 2008); Whissel, *Picturing American Modernity*; Brian R. Jacobson, *Studios Before the System: Architecture, Technology, and the Emergence of Cinematic Space* (New York: Columbia University Press, 2015); Lisa Parks and Nicole Starosielski, eds., *Signal Traffic: Critical Studies of Media Infrastructures* (Urbana-Champaign: University of Illinois Press, 2015); Doron Galili, *Seeing by Electricity: The Emergence of Television, 1878–1939* (Durham, NC: Duke University Press, 2020); Rahul Mukherjee, *Radiant Infrastructures: Media, Environment, and Cultures of Uncertainty* (Durham, NC: Duke University Press, 2020); and Luci Marzola, *Engineering Hollywood: Technology, Technicians, and the Science of Building the Studio System* (New York: Oxford University Press, 2021).

9. In this respect, work on extractions also hearkens back to Jean-Louis Comolli's attempt to articulate a "materialist theory of the cinema" that required, Comolli insisted, a more capacious view of the "apparatus" not reduced to the camera alone. Noting the lack of writing about "film stock (and the devices feeding it through the camera), emulsion, and the black space between the frames" as well as "laboratory processes" and "color grading and sound mixing," Comolli emphasized that such absences risked, among other things, "the masking and effacement of labor." For Comolli, a "materialist theory" built on this more-refined definition of cinema's technological underpinnings needed to account both for cinema's "scientific heritage" (the historical and technical details of its devices and techniques) and its "ideological heritage" (e.g., the profit motive that drove, in Comolli's account, cinema's ultimate appearance as a commodity form in the late nineteenth century). Recovering this scientific and ideological heritage was not, however, sufficient on its own. The medium's scientific and ideological formation and the aesthetic styles they made possible (things "*of* the camera") next needed to be put in dialogue with the "ideological investments which have been made *in* the camera"— that is, in the content of film texts. Here we have, in other words, one attempt to reconcile text and material context, one to which scholars of extraction may fruitfully return with more detailed knowledge of cinema's scientific and

ideological "heritage" in raw materials. See Jean-Louis Comolli, "Technique and Ideology: Camera, Perspective, Depth of Field," in *Cinema Against Spectacle*, ed. Jean-Louis Comolli and trans. Daniel Fairfax (Amsterdam: Amsterdam University Press, 2015), 152–53, emphasis added. Originally published in six parts, beginning with Jean-Louis Comolli, "Technique et idéologie: Caméra, perspective, profondeur du champ," *Cahiers du cinéma*, no. 229 (May 1971): 4–21. See also Daniel Fairfax's overview and lucid historicization of Comolli's essay in his introduction to *Cinema Against Spectacle* and in Daniel Fairfax, *The Red Years of* Cahiers du cinéma *(1968–1973)*, vol. 1, *Ideology and Politics* (Amsterdam: Amsterdam University Press, 2021), 149–72.

Bordwell, Staiger, and Thompson's monumental study of classical Hollywood in many ways met the call for this more detailed technical history. Bordwell tidily dismissed Comolli's attempt to read ideology through material and style, but Comolli's methodological imperative to read between historically situated materialist, technical, and stylistic forms of analysis remains important, even if his execution of it, as Bordwell did not fail to point out, was wrong on the technical details. See David Bordwell, Janet Staiger, and Kristin Thompson, *The Classical Hollywood Cinema: Film Style and Mode of Production to 1960* (New York: Columbia University Press, 1985); and David Bordwell, *On the History of Film Style* (Cambridge, MA: Harvard University Press, 1997), 159–63. Recent scholarship has further extended our knowledge of the "black space between the frames." See, for example, Lovejoy, "Celluloid Geopolitics"; Marzola, *Engineering Hollywood*; Mal Ahern, "Climate Control, Modernism, and Mass Production," *Discourse* 45, no. 1–2 (2023): 3–32; and Dootson, *Rainbow's Gravity*.

10. See Thomas Elsaesser, "The New Film History," *Sight and Sound* 55, no. 4 (Autumn 1986): 246–51. See also the books reviewed in Elsaesser's essay: Robert C. Allen and Douglas Gomery, eds., *Film History Theory and Practice* (New York: Knopf, 1985); Salt, *Film Style and Technology*; Neale, *Cinema and Technology*; and Elisabeth Weis and John Belton, eds., *Film Sound: Theory and Practice* (New York: Columbia University Press, 1985).

11. See Friedrich A. Kittler, *Discourse Networks, 1800/1900*, trans. Michael Metteer (Stanford, CA: Stanford University Press, 1990); and Friedrich A. Kittler, *Gramophone, Film, Typewriter*, trans. Geoffrey Winthrop-Young and Michael Wutz (Stanford, CA: Stanford University Press, 1999).

12. Geoffrey Winthrop-Young and Michael Wutz, "Translators' Introduction: Friedrich Kittler and Media Discourse Analysis," in *Gramophone, Film, Typewriter*, xxix. Materiality, for Kittler, may be understood as "that which has

no meaning," as Bernhard Siegert has summarized it. "These sense-making machines, these sense-making dispositifs or apparatuses," Siegert explains, "are based on materialities that themselves do not make sense, are blind, dumb—but are all the more powerful for it." Geoffrey Winthrop-Young, "Material World: Geoffrey-Winthrop Young Talks with Bernhard Siegert," *Artforum International* 53, no. 10 (Summer 2015): 324.

13. Jon Lewis and Eric Smoodin, eds., *Looking Past the Screen: Case Studies in American Film History and Method* (Durham, NC: Duke University Press, 2007); and Karen Beckman, *Crash: Cinema and the Politics of Speed and Stasis* (Durham, NC: Duke University Press, 2010), 1.

14. Michael Baxandall, *Painting and Experience in Fifteenth Century Italy: A Primer in the Social History of Pictorial Style* (Oxford: Oxford University Press, 1972), 1; and Svetlana Alpers, *The Art of Describing: Dutch Art in the Seventeenth Century* (Chicago: University of Chicago Press, 1983), xxiv.

15. "A pictorial style," Baxandall argues, "gives access to the visual skills and habits and, through these, to the distinctive social experience." Baxandall, *Painting and Experience in Fifteenth Century Italy*, 151–52.

16. Indeed, they helped shape film scholarship in an earlier moment when art history provided important methodological models. Bordwell, for example, consistently turned to Baxandall and Alpers, although with less focus on their materialist accounts of art than on their attention to historical practices of reading and their detailed treatment of style. See, for example, his appeal to Baxandall's application of eye-movement analysis and account of viewing practices in Bordwell, *On the History of Film Style*, 317n93, 321n15. In *Figures Traced in Light*, Bordwell also returns to Alpers and Baxandall's detailed approach to form in their study of Tiepollo. See David Bordwell, *Figures Traced in Light: On Cinematic Staging* (Berkeley: University of California Press, 2005), 10; and Svetlana Alpers and Michael Baxandall, *Tiepolo and the Pictorial Intelligence* (New Haven, CT: Yale University Press, 1994).

17. Jaikumar and Grieveson, "Media and Extraction," 199.

18. Vanessa R. Schwartz and Jeannene M. Przyblyski, "Visual Culture's History: Twenty-First Century Interdisciplinarity and Its Nineteenth-Century Objects," in *The Nineteenth-Century Visual Culture Reader*, ed. Vanessa R. Schwartz and Jeannene M. Przyblyski (New York: Routledge, 2004), 8.

19. Eugenie Brinkema, *Life-Destroying Diagrams* (Durham, NC: Duke University Press, 2022), 259–60.

20. Roland Barthes, "Myth Today," in *Mythologies*, trans. Annette Lavers (New York: Hill and Wang, 1972), 112.

21. Key exceptions, as outlined further in chapter 4, include Edward Dimendberg's masterful reading of *Le chant du styrène* (dir. Alain Resnais, Pechiney, 1958) and Salomé Skvirsky's analysis of industrial films included in what she terms the "process genre." See Edward Dimendberg, "'These Are Not Exercises in Style': *Le Chant du styrène*," *October*, no. 112 (Spring 2005): 63–88; and Salomé Aguilera Skvirsky, *The Process Genre: Cinema and the Aesthetic of Labor* (Durham, NC: Duke University Press, 2020). On "industrial and corporate film" and "useful cinema," see Vinzenz Hediger and Patrick Vonderau, eds., *Films That Work: Industrial Film and the Productivity of Media* (Amsterdam: Amsterdam University Press, 2009); Charles R. Acland and Haidee Wasson, eds., *Useful Cinema* (Durham, NC: Duke University Press, 2011); and Devin Orgeron, Marsha Orgeron, and Dan Streible, eds., *Learning with the Lights Off: Educational Film in the United States* (Oxford: Oxford University Press, 2012). These often-cited volumes notably appeared alongside work on colonial cinema that shared many methodological investments but have not tended to be included in the "industrial," "useful," or "nontheatrical" literature. See, for example, Lee Grieveson and Colin MacCabe, eds., *Empire and Film*, Cultural Histories of Cinema (London: BFI, 2011); and Lee Grieveson and Colin MacCabe, eds., *Film and the End of Empire* (Houndmills, UK: Palgrave Macmillan, 2011).

22. See Anna Kornbluh, *Realizing Capital: Financial and Psychic Economies in Victorian Form* (New York: Fordham University Press, 2014); Caroline Levine, *Forms: Whole, Rhythm, Hierarchy, Network* (Princeton, NJ: Princeton University Press, 2015); and Timothy Aubry and Florence Dore, "Introduction: Formalism Unbound," *Post45*, no. 5 (December 2020), https://post45.org/2020/12/aubry-dore-introduction/. See also the earlier returns to formalism in the special issues: Susan J. Wolfson and Marshall Brown, eds., "Reading for Form," *Modern Language Quarterly* 61, no. 1 (2000); and Stephen Best and Sharon Marcus, eds., "Surface Reading: An Introduction," *Representations* 108, no. 1 (Fall 2009): 1–21. Historians have long been interested in the analytical relationship between content and form, for instance, as examined closely by Hayden White, whose analysis of the "content of the form" underscored the role that narrative and other forms of relating history play in the creation of historical meaning. Without dismissing White's important intervention in the study of historical *writing*, Levine positions her mode of literary *reading* as its inverse: "Rather than hunting for the buried *content of the form*, I propose here to read *the forms of the content*, the many organizing principles that encounter one another inside as well as outside of the literary text." Hayden

White, *The Content of the Form: Narrative Discourse and Historical Representation* (Baltimore, MD: Johns Hopkins University Press, 1987); and Levine, *Forms*, 16.

23. Because I approach cinema as a world-making system, I also share with Anna Kornbluh a strong investment in form as a building mechanism and in how forms "structure new possibles." But I also explore this building in cinemas of industrial and corporate extraction and world domination in which case such "possibles" offer perhaps less "inspiration for new figuring, projecting, [and] building" than they allow us to see how similar inspiration has been marshaled for often divergent or directly opposed political aims. Identifying how these corporate and industrial building projects have been achieved formally—and not just denouncing their ideologies—has tremendous value, even if it also makes the part of Levine's method that emphasizes "unsettling and unmaking" equally appealing. Put somewhat banally, we need both approaches—formalisms that make and unmake, assemble and disassemble, settle and unsettle. See Anna Kornbluh, *The Order of Forms: Realism, Formalism, and Social Space* (Chicago: University of Chicago Press, 2019), 7, 4. See also the "twofold, reflexive approach to reading and imagination" that Jennifer Wenzel uses to get at that which "remains 'external' to representation, just outside the frame, or difficult to recognize within it." Jennifer Wenzel, *The Disposition of Nature: Environmental Crisis and World Literature* (New York: Fordham University Press, 2020), 6.

24. Hans Ulrich Gumbrecht and K. Ludwig Pfeiffer, eds., *Materialität der kommunikation* (Frankfurt: Suhrkamp, 1988); and Hans Ulrich Gumbrecht and K. Ludwig Pfeiffer, eds., *Materialities of Communication*, trans. William Whobrey (Stanford, CA: Stanford University Press, 1994).

25. K. Ludwig Pfeiffer, "The Materiality of Communication," in *Materialities of Communication*, 6.

26. Friedrich A. Kittler, "Afterword to the Second Printing," in *Discourse Networks, 1800/1900*, trans. Michael Metteer (Stanford, CA: Stanford University Press, 1990), 371.

27. Friedrich Kittler, *Optical Media: Berlin Lectures 1999*, trans. Anthony Enns (Cambridge: Polity, 2010), 34, 38.

28. Kittler, *Gramophone, Film, Typewriter*, xxxix.

29. If, as Geoffrey Winthrop-Young and Michael Wutz have argued, part of Kittler's goal, following in Nietzsche's footsteps, was to bracket off and ultimately squeeze out the "noise" of things such as media content that "cover[ed] up" the underlying work done by media technologies, I attempt to pull those

brackets back open. Winthrop-Young and Wutz, "Translators' Introduction," xxix–xxx.
30. John Durham Peters, "Introduction: Friedrich Kittler's Light Shows," in *Optical Media: Berlin Lectures 1999*, by Friedrich Kittler, trans. Anthony Enns (Cambridge: Polity, 2010), 2.
31. David. E. Wellbery, foreword to *Discourse Networks, 1800/1900*, by Friedrich A. Kittler, trans. Michael Metteer (Stanford, CA: Stanford University Press, 1990), xvii, xiv.
32. Wellbery, foreword, xiii.
33. Kittler, *Optical Media*, 145, 144.
34. Winthrop-Young and Wutz, "Translators' Introduction," xxxv.
35. Peters, "Introduction," 6–7.
36. Kittler's "favorite interpretation," for example, departed from, if not completely undermined, traditional literary readings of Friedrich Schiller's *Don Carlos* by treating the play as a "mirror" for the discourse network that produced it. Geoffrey Winthrop-Young, "Implosion and Intoxication: Kittler, a German Classic, and Pink Floyd," *Theory, Culture, and Society* 23, nos. 7–8 (2006): 77–78.
37. Winthrop-Young, "Implosion and Intoxication," 78.
38. In Winthrop-Young's words, Kittler read the poem as a "linguistic event that gestures toward certain rules and conditions that gave rise to it as well as the ways in which it is interpreted." Winthrop-Young, "Implosion and Intoxication," 80.
39. Or again as Winthrop-Young describes it, Kittler reads the song as a "technoacoustic event . . . whose seductive qualities are due to a sophisticated performance of the technological progression that enabled these qualities." Winthrop-Young, "Implosion and Intoxication," 83.
40. Winthrop-Young, "Implosion and Intoxication," 86.
41. White, *The Content of the Form*, 45.
42. David E. James, *Allegories of Cinema: American Film in the Sixties* (Princeton, NJ: Princeton University Press, 1989), 12.
43. Some standard volumes include Richard Maxwell and Toby Miller, *Greening the Media* (New York: Oxford University Press, 2012); Nadia Bozak, *The Cinematic Footprint: Lights, Camera, Natural Resources* (New Brunswick, NJ: Rutgers University Press, 2012); Parks and Starosielski, *Signal Traffic*; Nicole Starosielski and Janet Walker, eds., *Sustainable Media: Critical Approaches to Media and Environment* (London: Routledge, 2016); Sean Cubitt, *Finite Media: Environmental Implications of Digital Technologies* (Durham, NC: Duke

University Press, 2017); and Hunter Vaughan, *Hollywood's Dirtiest Secret: The Hidden Environmental Costs of the Movies* (New York: Columbia University Press, 2019).

44. For cinema studies, a field that has, in many of its subfields, moved further away from interpretation than literary studies, this return to allegory may have correspondingly greater value. Reading films as allegories of their means of production means something different for a medium with a different material form. Attending to extracted materials also draws the interpretative method partly away from James's Marxist-rooted historical materialism. Fredric Jameson makes the difference explicit in *The Political Unconscious*, in which he emphasizes that Marxist historical materialism "does not assert the primacy of matter so much as it insists on an ultimate determination by the mode of production." At stake is how we understand the role of matter in interpretation. "The grounding of materialism in one or another conception of matter," Jameson cautions, "is rather the hallmark of bourgeois ideology from the eighteenth-century materialisms all the way to nineteenth-century positivism and determinism." This too-easy approach, he argues, is rooted in "intellectually [dishonest]" and even "fatuous" attempts to draw "a tacit homology between the 'production' of language in writing and speech, and economic production" that ignore the difference between writing and "real work on the assembly line and . . . the experience of the resistance of matter in genuine manual labor." The approach to matter pursued here is duly wary—and indeed critical—of the kind of positivism found in many recent materialist analyses of art and media. It nonetheless finds value in stressing the materials of historical materialist analysis, in part by highlighting the raw materials and "resistance of matter" always involved in cinema and media's modes of production (e.g., Redrobe's point about cinema's "high and hybrid technology" and Comolli's insistence on the importance of not effacing labor). See Fredric Jameson, *The Political Unconscious: Narrative as a Socially Symbolic Act* (Ithaca, NY: Cornell University Press, 1981), 45–46.

45. Schwartz and Przyblyski, "Visual Culture's History," 3.

46. For more about cinema's role in "engineering consent," see Lee Grieveson, "Introduction: Film and the End of Empire," in *Film and the End of Empire*, ed. Lee Grieveson and Colin MacCabe (Houndmills, UK: Palgrave Macmillan, 2011), 4. David Nye makes a similar argument about industry's need to create worlds through images in David E. Nye, *Image Worlds: Corporate Identities at General Electric, 1890–1930* (Cambridge, MA: MIT Press, 1985).

47. Where the "cinema of attractions" names the "relation to the spectator" established by films before 1906, the "cinema of extractions" names the relation to the means of production. Each of these relations takes form in the moment of production with feedback from, on the attractions side, past and anticipated reception, and, on the extractions side, the available materials, infrastructure, and labor. Neither need perforce supersede the other, they simply explain different aspects of the film text's formation. See Tom Gunning, "The Cinema of Attractions: Early Film, Its Spectator and the Avant-Garde," *Wide Angle* 8, nos. 3–4 (1986): 63–70. Early cinema work more focused on production includes, for example, Charles Musser, *Before the Nickelodeon: Edwin S. Porter and the Edison Manufacturing Company* (Los Angeles: University of California Press, 1991); William Uricchio and Roberta Pearson, *Reframing Culture* (Princeton, NJ: Princeton University Press, 1993); and Schwartz, *Spectacular Realities*.

48. André Gaudreault, "Narration and Monstration in the Cinema," *Journal of Film and Video* 39, no. 2 (Spring 1987): 29–36.

49. A preliminary list of such films might include, for instance: *Behemoth* (dir. Zhao Liang, 2015), *Manufactured Landscapes* (dir. Jennifer Baichwal, 2006), *Lessons of Darkness* (dir. Werner Herzog, 1992), *The Wages of Fear* (dir. Henri-Georges Clouzot, 1953), *Blind Shaft* (dir. Li Yang, 2003), and *There Will Be Blood* (dir. Paul Thomas Anderson, 2007).

50. Daryl Meador, "The Cinema of Extractions in Dallas, Texas," *Social Text Online*, June 7, 2018, https://socialtextjournal.org/periscope_article/the-cinema-of-extractions-in-dallas-texas/.

51. Rosalind Galt, *Pretty: Film and the Decorative Image* (New York: Columbia University Press, 2011), 6, 230. "If the pretty offers an optic for analyzing film form," she writes in the postscript, "it refuses the shibboleths of 'formalism,' insisting that the decorative is historically and geographically embedded" (300).

52. Karl Schoonover and Rosalind Galt, *Queer Cinema in the World* (Durham, NC: Duke University Press, 2016), 29. See also chapter 4, "Who Owns the Kampung? Heritage, History, and Postcolonial Space," in Rosalind Galt, *Alluring Monsters: The Pontianak and Cinemas of Decolonization* (New York: Columbia University Press, 2021), 159–96.

53. John David Rhodes, *Spectacle of Property: The House in American Film* (Minneapolis: University of Minnesota Press, 2017), 7.

54. In a similar vein, Kartik Nair perfectly summarizes the reading steps required to analyze the relationship between the materiality of production

design and its appearance on screen: "It is . . . only by feeling and looking, reading and researching that the *mise en scene* can come into view as a site of presence, first, concealment next and revelation last." Kartik Nair, "Striking Out: Visual Space, Production Design, and Labor History in *Joker*," *Quarterly Review of Film and Video* 39, no. 8 (2022): 1909.

55. Priya Jaikumar, *Where Histories Reside: India as Filmed Space* (Durham, NC: Duke University Press, 2019), 4, 7.

56. Rochona Majumdar, *Art Cinema and India's Forgotten Futures: Film and History in the Postcolony* (New York: Columbia University Press, 2021), 21, 13–14.

57. See also the approach to cinema as a site of political thinking in Mauro Resmini, *Italian Political Cinema: Figures of the Long '68* (Minneapolis: University of Minnesota Press, 2022).

58. Jerome Christensen, *America's Corporate Art: The Studio Authorship of Hollywood Motion Pictures* (Stanford, CA: Stanford University Press, 2012), 3.

59. John T. Caldwell, "Televisuality as a Semiotic Machine: Emerging Paradigms in Low Theory," *Cinema Journal* 32, no. 4 (Summer 1993): 28, 25; and Jeff Menne, *Post-Fordist Cinema: Hollywood Auteurs and the Corporate Counterculture* (New York: Columbia University Press, 2019), 29.

60. See John T. Caldwell, "Industrial Geography Lessons: Socio-Professional Rituals and the Borderlands of Production Culture," in *MediaSpace: Place, Scale and Culture in a Media Age*, ed. Nick Couldry and Anna McCarthy (London and New York: Routledge, 2004), 164; and John T. Caldwell, *Production Culture: Industrial Reflexivity and Critical Practice in Film and Television* (Durham, NC: Duke University Press, 2008).

61. J. D. Connor, *The Studios After the Studios: Neoclassical Hollywood (1970–2010)*, POST•45 (Stanford, CA: Stanford University Press, 2015), 1–2; and J. D. Connor, *Hollywood Math and Aftermath: The Economic Image and the Digital Recession* (London: Bloomsbury, 2018), 8. In the latter book, Connor makes the provocative argument that "to justify the continuing importance of close reading to the study of media industries one would need to demonstrate that the reading of those movies is important to the industry itself, to demonstrate that such texts play an essential role within the equation of pictures." (31) I am not sure the burden of proof need always extend so far (because our understanding of media industries may be enhanced by reading its practices and forms in dialogue with its films even if the industry itself does not do so), but Connor persuasively shows just how evocative such readings can be, for instance in the case of a film such as *Moneyball* (dir. Bennett Miller, 2011), the content of which *was* a corporate media strategy.

62. Some important work in the vast and growing field of scholarship focused on how films engage with and mediate our knowledge about nature and the nonhuman world includes Gregg Mitman, *Reel Nature: America's Romance with Wildlife on Film* (Cambridge, MA: Harvard University Press, 1999); David Ingram, *Green Screen: Environmentalism and Hollywood Cinema* (Exeter: University of Exeter Press, 2000); Patrick Brereton, *Hollywood Utopia: Ecology in Contemporary American Cinema* (Bristol: Intellect Books, 2005); Robin L. Murray and Joseph K. Heumann, eds., *Ecology and Popular Film: Cinema on the Edge* (Albany: State University of New York Press, 2009); Adrian J. Ivakhiv, *Ecologies of the Moving Image: Cinema, Affect, Nature* (Waterloo, Canada: Wilfred Laurier University Press, 2013); James Leo Cahill, "Animal Photogénie: The Wild Side of French Film Theory's First Wave," in *Animal Life and the Moving Image*, ed. Michael Lawrence and Laura McMahon (London: BFI, 2015), 23–41; Selmin Kara, "Anthropocenema: Cinema in the Age of Mass Extinctions," in *Post-Cinema: Theorizing 21st-Century Film*, ed. Shane Denson and Julia Leyda (Falmer, UK: REFRAME Books, 2016), 750–84; and Graig Uhlin, "The Anthropocene's Nonindifferent Nature," *Journal of Cinema and Media Studies* 58, no. 2 (Winter 2019): 157–62.
63. Jennifer Fay, *Inhospitable World: Cinema in the Time of the Anthropocene* (New York: Oxford University Press, 2018), 5, 99.
64. As James Cahill argues in his important study of Jean Painlevé, any account of cinema's world-making power should also attend to its "Copernican vocation," the anti-Anthropocentric shift in perspective through which cinema makes possible new ways of seeing the nonhuman world by decentering human vision. That "vocation," as Cahill shows, was partly inhered in the "indifferent gaze" filmmakers and theorists attributed to the cinematic apparatus but was also achieved through form. See James Leo Cahill, *Zoological Surrealism: The Nonhuman Cinema of Jean Painlevé* (Minneapolis: University of Minnesota Press, 2019), 16–25.
65. Debashree Mukherjee, *Bombay Hustle: Making Movies in a Colonial City* (New York: Columbia University Press, 2020), 189, 196. See also Debashree Mukherjee, "The Aesthetic and Material Force of Landscape in Cinema: Mediating Meaning from the Scene of Production," *Representations* 157, no. 1 (Winter 2022): 115–41.
66. This field is succinctly summarized in Adam Wickberg and Johan Gärdebo, "Editors' Introduction: What Are Environing Media?," in *Environing Media* (London: Routledge, 2023), 1–12.

67. See also Eva Horn's earlier capacious account of media studies: "Doors and mirrors, computers and gramophones, electricity and newspapers, television and telescopes, archives and automobiles, water and air, information and noise, numbers and calendars, images, writing, and voice—all these highly disparate objects and phenomena fall into media studies' purview." Eva Horn, "Editor's Introduction: 'There Are No Media,'" *Grey Room* 29 (2007): 7–8; and John Durham Peters, *The Marvelous Clouds: Toward a Philosophy of Elemental Media* (Chicago: University of Chicago Press, 2015).
68. Some important works include: Inga Pollmann, "Invisible Worlds, Visible: Uexküll's Umwelt, Film, and Film Theory," *Critical Inquiry* 39, no. 4 (Summer 2013): 777–816; Jussi Parikka, *A Geology of Media* (Minneapolis: University of Minnesota Press, 2015); Weihong Bao, *Fiery Cinema: The Emergence of an Affective Medium in China, 1915–1945* (Minneapolis: University of Minnesota Press, 2015); Antonio Somaini, "Walter Benjamin's Media Theory: The Medium and the Apparat," *Grey Room* 62 (Winter 2016): 6–41; and Yuriko Furuhata, *Climatic Media: Transpacific Experiments in Atmospheric Control* (Durham, NC: Duke University Press, 2022).
69. See, for example, Wickberg and Gärdebo, "Editors' Introduction," 4–5.
70. James Leo Cahill, Brian R. Jacobson, and Weihong Bao, "Media Climates: An Introduction," *Representations* 157, no. 1 (Winter 2022): 12–13.
71. For Metz, Hjelmslev's model allowed him to escape the traditional "form/content" pair ("one of the most frequently relied on in debates about the cinema"), which failed to allow sufficient distinction between different categories of "signified" and "signifier." See, for example, Christian Metz, "Methodological Propositions for the Analysis of Film," trans. Diana Matias, *Screen* 14, nos. 1–2 (1973): 89–101; and Christian Metz, *Film Language: A Semiotics of Cinema*, trans. Michael Taylor (Chicago: University of Chicago Press, 1991).
72. For Gumbrecht, Hjelmslev offered a way of mapping a "nonhermeneutic field" of inquiry. See Hans Ulrich Gumbrecht, *Production of Presence: What Meaning Cannot Convey* (Stanford, CA: Stanford University Press, 2004), 14. First developed in Hans Ulrich Gumbrecht, "A Farewell to Interpretation," in *Materialities of Communication*, 389–404.
73. Metz anticipated something like this move. See, for example, the page-spanning footnote in *Film Language* in which he comes closest to opening film analysis to the formalist approach to "content" I develop here. Metz puts it like this: "I want to insist on the presence of a specific level of 'figures' that by definition, relate to the filmic vehicle itself—and these are the figures

that actually define 'cinematographic language'—and to distinguish it from another semiological level, which is, incidentally, doubly contrasted to the first in that it is both less general (since it concerns particular films) and more general (*since it incorporates systems that are very broadly cultural and that extend beyond the cinema itself*)." Metz, *Film Language*, 223–24, emphasis added. Jameson, too, uses Hjelmslev's model, which he adapts, for example, to genre theory. See Jameson, *Political Unconscious*, 147.

74. Bordwell, Staiger, and Thompson, *Classical Hollywood Cinema*.
75. Charles Musser, *The Emergence of Cinema: The American Screen to 1907*, vol. 1, *History of the American Cinema* (New York: Scribner, 1990), 17.

1. EARLY CINEMAS OF EXTRACTION

1. Tom Gunning, "The Cinema of Attractions: Early Film, Its Spectator and the Avant-Garde," *Wide Angle* 8, nos. 3/4 (1986): 63–64.
2. Fernand Léger, "A Critical Essay on the Plastic Quality of Abel Gance's Film *The Wheel* [*Comoedia*, 1922]," in *Functions of Painting*, ed. Edward Fry, trans. Alexandra Anderson (New York: Viking, 1973), 20.
3. Among the many possible works one might cite, see Bill Brown, *A Sense of Things: The Object Matter of American Literature* (Chicago: University of Chicago Press, 2003); Jane Bennett, *Vibrant Matter* (Durham, NC: Duke University Press, 2010); and Timothy Morton, *Hyperobjects: Philosophy and Ecology After the End of the World* (Minneapolis: University of Minnesota Press, 2013).
4. Important work about early film's relationship to rail includes Annette Michelson, "Track Records, Trains of Events: The Limits of Cinematic Representation," in *Junction and Journey: Trains and Film*, ed. Alexandra Bonfante-Warren (New York: Museum of Modern Art, 1991), 24–31; and Lynne Kirby, *Parallel Tracks: The Railroad and Silent Cinema* (Durham, NC: Duke University Press, 1997).
5. André Gaudreault, "Narration and Monstration in the Cinema," *Journal of Film and Video* 39, no. 2 (Spring 1987): 29–36.
6. Note how some early observers already rejected the notion that cinema had reproduced fairground or circus attractions. As Luka Arsenjuk notes, for example, Vsevolod Meyerhold saw cinema not so much as a new kind of attraction but as a form of "electrified naturalism." Although Meyerhold, with his emphasis on figural movement, rejected the naturalist part, the fact that early cinema and media scholarship was less invested in the attractions model

tells us a great deal about the implications of cinema's electrification. See Luka Arsenjuk, *Movement, Action, Image, Montage: Sergei Eisenstein and the Cinema in Crisis* (Minneapolis: University of Minnesota Press, 2018), 70. On connections to electricity, see Doron Galili, *Seeing by Electricity: The Emergence of Television, 1878–1939* (Durham, NC: Duke University Press, 2020); and Brian R. Jacobson, *Studios Before the System: Architecture, Technology, and the Emergence of Cinematic Space* (New York: Columbia University Press, 2015), 148–52. On a slightly later period, see Frances Guerin, *A Culture of Light: Cinema and Technology in 1920s Germany* (Minneapolis: University of Minnesota Press, 2005). On Hollywood's debt to electricians and electrical engineering, see Luci Marzola, *Engineering Hollywood: Technology, Technicians, and the Science of Building the Studio System* (New York: Oxford University Press, 2021).

7. I use the term *Anthropocene* advisedly, not as a straightforward way of describing an epoch of universal human control but rather to invoke all the criticism of the term, including the alternative names (e.g., capitalocene, plantationocene), that highlight not only the social inequities of global warming and climate change but also how scholars have sometimes failed but at other times powerfully managed to turn the term's limits into conceptual gains. To cite only a few better-known examples of the latter, see Donna J. Haraway, "Tentacular Thinking: Anthropocene, Capitalocene, Chthulucene," *E-Flux* 75 (September 2016), http://www.e-flux.com/journal/tentacular-thinking-anthropocene-capitalocene-chthulucene/; T. J. Demos, *Against the Anthropocene: Visual Culture and Environment Today* (Berlin: Sternberg, 2017); and Kathryn Yusoff, *A Billion Black Anthropocenes or None* (Minneapolis: University of Minnesota Press, 2018).

8. Early film historians helped pioneer this nontextual method and what became known as the New Film History by emphasizing the importance of context. As I discuss in chapter 4, the method's relative disinterest in film texts, which made some early film history closer to social and cultural history with only glancing attention to film aesthetics, was immediately recognized and questioned. To cite one example, scholars such as Charles Musser, whose 1991 study of Edwin S. Porter was also a corporate/industrial history of the Edison Company, could go so far as to ask if it was even *film* history anymore. Building on that important work, with its investment in materialist history, I stress the role played by the literal materials that had to be mined and made into film's machines and working practices. See, for example, the many non-film-focused chapters and the general emphasis on contextual

factors—importantly including urbanization and technological change—in the key volume Leo Charney and Vanessa R. Schwartz, eds., *Cinema and the Invention of Modern Life* (Berkeley: University of California Press, 1995). Other representative books include Giuliana Bruno, *Streetwalking on a Ruined Map: Cultural Theory and the Films of Elvira Notari* (Princeton, NJ: Princeton University Press, 1993); Anne Friedberg, *Window Shopping: Cinema and the Postmodern* (Berkeley: University of California Press, 1993); Laurent Mannoni, *Le grand art de la lumière et de l'ombre: Archéologie du cinéma* (Paris: Nathan Université, 1994); and Vanessa R. Schwartz, *Spectacular Realities: Early Mass Culture in* Fin-de-Siècle *Paris* (Berkeley: University of California Press, 1998). Musser's question about film's place in broader cultural histories of early cinema appears in Charles Musser, *The Emergence of Cinema: The American Screen to 1907*, vol. 1, *History of the American Cinema* (New York: Scribner, 1990), 17.

9. See Jon Crylen, "Living in a World Without Sun: Jacques Cousteau, Homo Aquaticus, and the Dream of Dwelling Undersea," *Journal of Cinema and Media Studies* 58, no. 1 (Fall 2018): 1–23; and Brian R. Jacobson, "Prospecting: Cinema and the Exploration of Extraction," in *Cinema of Exploration: Essays on an Adventurous Film Practice*, ed. James Leo Cahill and Luca Caminati (New York: AFI, 2021), 280–94.

10. This form of worlding took form in a context, as James Leo Cahill argues, of a broader "reconceptualization and re-exploration of the world, of what the world or a world is, of what or who constitutes and counts as part of the world, and more broadly of what sort of world was worth (or being) reconstructed." I thank Cahill for sharing this unpublished manuscript, "On the Plurality of Worlds: Jacques Yves Cousteau and Louis Malle's *Silent World*."

11. For more about these material requirements, see especially Hunter Vaughan, *Hollywood's Dirtiest Secret: The Hidden Environmental Costs of the Movies* (New York: Columbia University Press, 2019). Paramount's forest is described in "From Forest to Film," *Photoplay*, April 1918.

12. For more about the "human-built world" and its applications to early cinema, see Jacobson, *Studios Before the System*. As Jennifer Fay has put it more recently, "film enjoys a rather unique relationship to the material, elemental world through which we may appreciate both the artificiality of human world-making and the ambitions to design an artificial, unhomely planet." Jennifer Fay, *Inhospitable World: Cinema in the Time of the Anthropocene* (New York: Oxford University Press, 2018), 5.

13. For more about the limits of that control, see, for example, H. Mark Gosser, "The Bazar de la charité Fire: The Reality, the Aftermath, the Telling," *Film History* 10, no. 1 (1998): 70–89; and Brian R. Jacobson, "Fire and Failure: Studio Technology, Environmental Control, and the Politics of Progress," *Cinema Journal* 57, no. 2 (Winter 2018): 22–43. See also Nadine Chan's forthcoming work about the failure and breakdown of film technologies in tropical climates.

14. That hidden resource and environmental work has become a key area of film studies inquiry, including important work dating to the early 2010s by Nadia Bozak, whose book *The Cinematic Footprint* challenged the discursive "immateriality" of digital media, and Toby Miller and Richard Maxwell, whose *Greening the Media* similarly emphasized the resource costs of an industry whose image products could easily be untethered, at least in the popular imaginary, from their material origins. More recently, Hunter Vaughan has traced such costs to classical Hollywood's resource-hungry backlots, from the fire-scorched remains of Atlanta in *Gone with the Wind* (1939) to the soaked sets of Hollywood itself in *Singin' in the Rain* (1952). Recent and forthcoming studies of film stock by Alice Lovejoy and Elena Past promise to considerably enhance our knowledge of cinema's resource requirements. See Nadia Bozak, *The Cinematic Footprint: Lights, Camera, Natural Resources* (New Brunswick, NJ: Rutgers University Press, 2012); Richard Maxwell and Toby Miller, *Greening the Media* (New York, NY: Oxford University Press, 2012); Nicole Starosielski and Janet Walker, eds., *Sustainable Media: Critical Approaches to Media and Environment* (London: Routledge, 2016); Vaughan, *Hollywood's Dirtiest Secret*; and Alice Lovejoy, "Celluloid Geopolitics: Film Stock and the War Economy, 1939–47," *Screen* 60, no. 2 (2019): 224–41.

15. Lee Grieveson, *Cinema and the Wealth of Nations: Media, Capital, and the Liberal World System* (Berkeley: University of California Press, 2018), 2, 34.

16. See also, for example, my account of Gaumont's and Pathé's early financial entanglements with electricity companies in Jacobson, *Studios Before the System*, chap. 4.

17. Or, as Martin Johnson puts it, "in the beginning, all moving images were local." Martin L. Johnson, *Main Street Movies: The History of Local Film in the United States*, Cinema and the American Experience (Bloomington: Indiana University Press, 2018), 1.

18. As Charles Musser has noted, "The assertion that the predominant function of motion pictures in the kinetoscope era and beyond was to advertise and promote might be debated, but it is not obviously wrong." Charles Musser,

"Early Advertising and Promotional Films, 1893–1900: Edison Motion Pictures as a Case Study," in *Films That Sell: Moving Pictures and Advertising*, ed. Bo Florin, Nico de Klerk, and Patrick Vonderau (London: BFI, 2016), 83.

19. See, for example, Jennifer Peterson, "Workers Leaving the Factory: Witnessing Industry in the Digital Age," in *The Oxford Handbook of Sound and Image in Digital Media*, ed. Carol Vernallis, Amy Herzog, and John Richardson (New York: Oxford University Press, 2013), 598–619; and Brian R. Jacobson, "Found Memories of Film History: Industry in a Post-Industrial World; Cinema in a Post-Filmic Age," in *New Silent Cinema*, ed. Paul Flaig and Katherine Groo (New York: AFI, 2015), 243–62.

20. Siegfried Kracauer, *Theory of Film: The Redemption of Physical Reality*, pbk. ed. (Princeton, NJ: Princeton University Press, 1997).

21. Leo Charney and Vanessa R. Schwartz, introduction to *Cinema and the Invention of Modern Life*, 1–12.

22. Lewis Mumford, *Technics and Civilization* (New York: Harcourt, Brace, 1934), 337.

23. David E. Nye, *Image Worlds: Corporate Identities at General Electric, 1890–1930* (Cambridge: MIT Press, 1985), 148.

24. Ian Christie, "'The Captains and the Kings Depart': Imperial Departure and Arrival in Early Cinema," in *Empire and Film*, ed. Lee Grieveson and Colin MacCabe (London: BFI, 2011), 21–34.

25. The cinema of extractions helped drive racial capitalism even if, as Vanessa Schwartz has proposed, its films may *also* have "contributed to the slow but steady process of decolonization" by presenting to Western viewers the returned gaze of imperial subjects. See Vanessa R. Schwartz, "On the Move: Seeing the World in Early Transport Films," in *City of Cinema: Paris 1850–1907*, ed. Leah Lehmbeck, Britt Salvesen, and Vanessa R. Schwartz (Los Angeles: Los Angeles County Museum of Art, 2022), 132. On early ethnographic films, see Fatimah Tobing Rony, *The Third Eye: Race, Cinema, and Ethnographic Spectacle* (Durham, NC: Duke University Press, 1996); and Alison Griffiths, *Wondrous Difference: Cinema, Anthropology, and Turn-of-the-Century Visual Culture* (New York: Columbia University Press, 2002).

26. Applied to New York, the phrase comes from Max Page, *The Creative Destruction of Manhattan, 1900–1940*, Historical Studies of Urban America (Chicago: University of Chicago Press, 1999).

27. For more about these films, see Brian R. Jacobson, "Infrastructural Affinity: Film Technology and the Built Environment in New York circa 1900," *Framework* 57, no. 1 (Spring 2016): 7–31.

28. See, for example, the first chapter of Robin L. Murray and Joseph K. Heumann, eds., *Ecology and Popular Film: Cinema on the Edge* (Albany: State of New York Press, 2009). On Michon, see Aydin Kazimzade, "Cinema in Azerbaijan: The Pre-Soviet Era," *Azerbaijan International* 5, no. 3 (Autumn 1997): 30–35; and Rahman Badalov, "Cinema: Oil and Revolution," *Azerbaijan International* 5, no. 3 (Autumn 1997): 57–64.
29. "Rivalry in the Oil Fields," *Moving Picture World* 6, no. 16 (April 23, 1910): 642.
30. Later that year, Griffith again made California oil country the setting for drama in *The Message of the Violin* (1910).
31. Schwartz, "On the Move," 123.
32. Grieveson, *Cinema and the Wealth of Nations*, 51. For more about the Edison war films, see Kristen Whissel, *Picturing American Modernity: Traffic, Technology, and the Silent Cinema* (Durham, NC: Duke University Press, 2008), 21–61.
33. On railroad sponsorship, see Musser, *The Emergence of Cinema*, 1:164.
34. I seek, in other words, to move beyond what Siobhan Angus rightly describes as "the obvious yet underexplored thesis that resource extraction is one condition of possibility for photography and visual culture." See Siobhan Angus, "Mining the History of Photography," in *Capitalism and the Camera: Essays on Photography and Extraction*, ed. Kevin Coleman and Daniel James (London: Verso, 2021), 57.
35. On Ford, see Lee Grieveson, "The Work of Film in the Age of Fordist Mechanization," *Cinema Journal* 51, no. 3 (Spring 2012): 25–51. On municipal booster films, see Johnson, *Main Street Movies*, 16–55. For more about the extensive work on industrial and sponsored film, see chapter 4.

2. FROM EXTRACTIONS TO RESOURCE INTEGRATION

1. Caroline Levine, *Forms: Whole, Rhythm, Hierarchy, Network* (Princeton, NJ: Princeton University Press, 2015). Levine's reading of *The Wire* appears in chapter 6.
2. Key texts include John T. Caldwell, *Production Culture: Industrial Reflexivity and Critical Practice in Film and Television* (Durham, NC: Duke University Press, 2008); Jennifer Holt and Alisa Perren, eds., *Media Industries: History, Theory, and Method* (Malden, MA: Wiley-Blackwell, 2009); Vicki Mayer, Miranda J. Banks, and John T. Caldwell, eds., *Production Studies: Cultural Studies of Media Industries* (New York: Routledge, 2009); Miranda Banks, Bridget Conor, and Vicki Mayer, eds., *Production Studies, The Sequel! Cultural*

Studies of Global Media Industries (London: Routledge, 2015); and Lisa Parks and Nicole Starosielski, eds., *Signal Traffic: Critical Studies of Media Infrastructures* (Urbana-Champaign: University of Illinois Press, 2015).

3. Kristin Thompson, "The Lonedale Operator," in *The Griffith Project*, ed. Paolo Cherchi Usai, vol. 5, *Films Produced in 1911* (London: British Film Institute, 2002), 18.

4. Tom Gunning, "Systematizing the Electric Message: Narrative Form, Gender, and Modernity in *The Lonedale Operator*," in *American Cinema's Transitional Era: Audiences, Institutions, Practices*, ed. Charles Keil and Shelley Stamp (Berkeley: University of California Press, 2004), 15; and Raymond Bellour, "To Alternate/To Narrate (on *The Lonedale Operator*)," in *The Analysis of Film*, by Raymond Bellour, ed. Constance Penley, trans. Inge Pruks and Roxanne Lapidus (Bloomington: Indiana University Press, 2000), 262.

5. *Biograph Bulletin*, March 23, 1911, cited in Thompson, "The Lonedale Operator," 19.

6. Gunning, "Systematizing the Electric Message," 26, 26–27, 27, 45, 27.

7. Levine, *Forms*, 12.

8. One limitation of Gunning's analysis may be that he roots Griffith's "systematic order" only in the film's diegesis, not in what I would describe, following Levine and Hjelmslev, as the form of the film's pro-filmic content. Christian Metz, in his turn to Hjelmslev's more complex model of signification, recognized the limit of the standard form and content division and went to Hjelmslev, as I'm doing here, in search of a more nuanced field of relations. See Christian Metz, "Methodological Propositions for the Analysis of Film," trans. Diana Matias, *Screen* 14, nos. 1–2 (1973): 89–101.

9. See Paul Young's terrific analysis of early depictions of the telegraph, in which he also develops "a counter-history of the emergence of classical cinema" founded on "the pleasures of watching the cinema *work*" taught in part by images of telegraphic exchange. Paul Young, "Media on Display: A Telegraphic History of Early American Cinema," in *New Media 1740–1915*, ed. Lisa Gitelman and Geoffrey B. Pingree (Cambridge, MA: MIT Press, 2003), 232.

10. John David Rhodes makes a similar argument about the Fort Lee, New Jersey, shooting location of *The Lonely Villa* (dir. D. W. Griffith, 1909), emphasizing how "the pressure of this place and its geography" becomes legible in the film. See John David Rhodes, *Spectacle of Property: The House in American Film* (Minneapolis: University of Minnesota Press, 2017), 47. Rhodes brilliantly

reads the film as a "fable of property" that indexes both broader anxieties about modernity's "newly intensified unequal distribution of wealth" (45) and the specific property relations that made Fort Lee, with its comparatively cheap real estate, a good place for New York film companies to shoot on location and to establish new studios. The standard history of Fort Lee's film industry is found in Richard Koszarski, *Fort Lee: The Film Town* (Rome: John Libbey, 2004).

11. As Steve Ross puts it, beyond his "brilliant but racist *The Birth of a Nation* . . . Griffith was, during his Biograph years, one of the most powerful critics of class injustice that the movie industry ever produced," achieved in part thanks to his use of a parallel editing finely tuned to contrasting class difference. Steven J. Ross, *Working-Class Hollywood: Silent Film and the Shaping of Class in America* (Princeton, NJ: Princeton University Press, 1998), 36–37; 49–50. See also Tom Gunning, *D. W. Griffith and the Origins of American Narrative Film* (Urbana: University of Illinois Press, 1991), 241; and Constance Balides, "Cinema Under the Sign of Money: Commercialized Leisure, Economies of Abundance, and Pecuniary Madness, 1905–1915," in *American Cinema's Transitional Era: Audiences, Institutions, Practices*, ed. Charles Keil and Shelley Stamp (Berkeley: University of California Press, 2004), 299.

12. Charlie Keil, "Transition Through Tension: Stylistic Diversity in the Late Griffith Biographs," *Cinema Journal* 28, no. 3 (Spring 1989): 25.

13. Lee Grieveson, *Cinema and the Wealth of Nations: Media, Capital, and the Liberal World System* (Berkeley: University of California Press, 2018), 36.

14. One of the founding documents of industry-oriented film ecocriticism focuses on Hollywood. See Charles J. Corbett and Richard P. Turco, "Sustainability in the Motion Picture Industry" (Los Angeles: UCLA Institute of the Environment and Sustainability, November 2006), https://www.ioes.ucla.edu/wp-content/uploads/mpisreport.pdf. See, especially, Hunter Vaughan, *Hollywood's Dirtiest Secret: The Hidden Environmental Costs of the Movies* (New York: Columbia University Press, 2019).

15. The arrival by the early 1920s of the technology firms needed to service production studios with cameras, lights, labs, and other materials further consolidated the resource integration that made Hollywood an "industrial cluster." See Luci Marzola, *Engineering Hollywood: Technology, Technicians, and the Science of Building the Studio System* (New York: Oxford University Press, 2021), 4; 43–44.

16. Tom Gunning, "The Cinema of Attractions: Early Film, Its Spectator and the Avant-Garde," *Wide Angle*, no. 8.3/4 (1986): 70.

17. "Seeing Los Angeles Film Studios Through the Megaphone; A 'Travel and Scenic,'" *Motion Picture News*, July 17, 1915, 62; and "Morosco-Bosworth Brings Out Features of Distinctive Quality," *Motion Picture News*, July 17, 1915, 68. An earlier article published that April described the studio as "modern in every respect, being built of reinforced concrete with the main stage, 90 by 150 feet, covered with a glass roof." "Progress of Bosworth–Morosco," *Moving Picture World*, April 10, 1915, 217.
18. Note that *Sunshine Molly* was not unique for using California's oil fields as a setting for film action. As discussed briefly in chapter 1, Los Angeles's first film companies shot films in California's oil fields immediately on their arrival in 1910. Other mid-1910s films set and shot in the oil industry included a Lasky production shot in the same fields as *Sunshine Molly* titled *Where the Trail Divides* (dir. Oscar Apfel and James Neil, 1914), *Mrs. Plum's Pudding* (dir. Al E. Christie, 1915), *What Love Can Do* (dir. Jay Hunt, 1916), *Sunny Jane* (dir. Sherwood MacDonald, 1917), *The Jaguar's Claws* (dir. Marshall Neilan, 1917) starring Sessue Hayakawa, *A Branded Soul* (dir. Bertram Bracken, 1917), which features an oil well fire, and *Real Folks* (dir. Walter Edwards, 1918), which features footage shot south of Los Angeles of an oil well coming in. See "Oil Gusher Caught in 'Real Folks,'" *Motography* 19, no. 7 (February 16, 1918): 313.
19. Shelley Stamp, *Lois Weber in Early Hollywood* (Oakland: University of California Press, 2015), 57.
20. See, for example, Dheeshana S. Jayasundara et al., "Exploratory Research on the Impact of the Growing Oil Industry in North Dakota and Montana on Domestic Violence, Dating Violence, Sexual Assault, and Stalking: A Final Summary Overview" (U.S. Department of Justice, 2016); and Lily Grisafi, "Living in the Blast Zone: Sexual Violence Piped onto Native Land by Extractive Industries," *Columbia Journal of Law and Social Problems* 53, no. 4 (Summer 2020): 509–39.
21. Stamp, *Lois Weber in Early Hollywood*, 40.
22. "From Forest to Film," *Photoplay*, April 1918.
23. "Doings at Los Angeles," *Moving Picture World*, February 20, 1915, 1124.
24. The southern edge is home to the famous La Brea tar pits, the Los Angeles County Museum of Art, and the new Academy Museum of Motion Pictures. Many historians of U.S. cinema will have visited the Margaret Herrick Library, located just to the southwest.
25. Paul W. Prutzman, *Petroleum in Southern California, 1913* (Sacramento: California State Mining Bureau, 1913), 216; 227–28; and R. P. McLaughlin,

"First Annual Report of the State Oil and Gas Supervisor of California for the Fiscal Year 1915–16" (Sacramento, CA: Department of Petroleum and Gas of the State Mining Bureau, 1917), 177.

26. For a succinct account of the development see Mary Mallory, *Hollywoodland*, Images of America (Charleston, SC: Arcadia, 2011), 9–23.
27. "Oil Well Craze Is Fad Among Film Stars," *Variety*, May 10, 1923. Thanks to Polly Rose for bringing this and the following articles about oil, early Hollywood, and Keaton to my attention.
28. "Untitled," *Photoplay*, July 1923.
29. Buster Keaton, *My Wonderful World of Slapstick* (Garden City, NY: Doubleday, 1960), 278–80; and "Keaton Well Sold—Paid 100 percent," *Variety*, March 11, 1925.
30. Hilary Hallett, *Go West, Young Women! The Rise of Early Hollywood* (Oakland: University of California Press, 2013), 16.
31. On the importance that cars played, for example, in early slapstick comedies shot in Los Angeles, see Mark Shiel, *Hollywood Cinema and the Real Los Angeles* (London: Reaktion, 2012), 69–127. On cars in early studio publicity photos, see Brian R. Jacobson, "Fantastic Functionality: Studio Architecture and the Visual Rhetoric of Early Hollywood," *Film History* 26, no. 2, "Early Hollywood and the Archive" (2014): 62.
32. In addition to those mentioned earlier, a partial list of films featuring burning oil wells would include the following: MGM's star-studded 1940 western *Boomtown* (dir. Jack Conway), the same year's Warner Brothers oilfield drama, *Flowing Gold* (dir. Alfred E. Green), *Tulsa* (dir. Stuart Heisler, 1949), Ebrahim Golestan's *Yek atash (A Fire)* (1961), the John Wayne biopic *Hellfighters* (dir. Andrew V. McLagen, 1968) about oil-well firefighter Paul "Red" Adair, and Sam Mendes's Gulf War film, *Jarhead* (2005), not to mention short documentaries and industrial films sponsored by oil firms and associated companies like Adair's or the offshoot Boots & Coots International Well Control Inc.
33. See "Canine Kings Have Competitor," *Camera!* 6, no. 35 (December 15, 1923): 10; and "Tully Gives Filmdom Real Chill," *Camera!* 6, no. 38 (January 5, 1924): 5.
34. As one article put it, "The chief worry now is to find some philanthropic soul who is willing to donate a few producing wells to art, or at least who is willing to permit the cremation of several gushers for an important sequence in the story.'" "'Flowing Gold' the Cause of Great Oil Boom," *Exhibitors Trade Review*, December 1, 1923, sec. Round About the Studios. The shoot is described in "Elements Rage at United Studios," *Camera!* 6, no. 38 (January 5, 1924): 13; and

"Tully Oil Well Fire Gives Hollywood Thrill," *Motion Picture News* 29, no. 6 (February 9, 1924): 627.

35. John Bengtson, "Buster Keaton—More Backlot Scenes from Our Hospitality," *Chaplin-Keaton-Lloyd Film Locations (and More)* (blog), April 26, 2020, https://silentlocations.com/2020/04/26/buster-keaton-more-backlot-scenes-from-our-hospitality/. The history of United Studios and its acquisition by Paramount is documented in "Paramount Pictures Master Plan Project: Final Environmental Impact Report, Appendix F" (Los Angeles: Department of City Planning, Major Projects Section, April 2016), 141.

36. See, for example, "Rex Beach Oil Tale Is Well Acted," *Exhibitors Herald* 18, no. 10 (March 1, 1924): 49.

37. See Stephanie LeMenager on Doheny's critical role in "creat[ing] a genre of pro-oil propaganda in the 1920s that has a recognizable legacy in U.S. popular culture through oil epics such as the film *Giant* (1956) and even the television series *Dallas* (1978–1991)." Stephanie LeMenager, *Living Oil: Petroleum Culture in the American Century* (New York: Oxford University Press, 2014), 94–96.

38. George T. Pardy, "Hectic, Lurid Melodrama," *Exhibitors Trade Review*, March 8, 1924, sec. Box Office Reviews.

39. "Teapot Dome Scandal Is Busting Washington Wide Open," *Film Daily* 27, no. 40 (February 18, 1924): 4.

40. See "When Oil Cans Went Big," *Film Daily* 29, no. 45 (August 22, 1924): 6; and "Stunts That Are Building Patronage," *Exhibitors Trade Review*, November 22, 1924.

41. "A Shower of 'Flowing Gold,'" *First National Franchise* 4, no. 1 (May 1924): 19.

42. "Oil 'Came In' for Flowing Gold Run," *Moving Picture World* 72, no. 3 (January 17, 1925): 230.

43. "Mechanical Pump for Flowing Gold," *Moving Picture World* 68, no. 7 (June 14, 1924): 659; and "[Flowing Gold Window Display in Eugene, Or.]," *Exhibitors Herald* 18, no. 24 (June 7, 1924): 48. Some evidence suggests that the display's owner, the "Guaranty Oil Company of Oregon" was either a scam business or just never discovered any oil, contributing to the financial ruin of the local Eugene Bible University. See Harry R. Baird, "E. C. Sanderson" (master's thesis, Butler University, 1957), 62–63.

44. During the 1920s, films set in cold atmospheres of snow and ice similarly prompted exhibitors to dress their movie houses in the image of cold, even before, and then again after, the introduction of theater air conditioning. See "Coldsploitation" in Nicole Starosielski, *Media Hot and Cold*, Elements (Durham, NC: Duke University Press, 2021), 72–108.

45. "In this *industrial cinema*, film came into being as a commodity, as *industrial film*." David E. James, *Allegories of Cinema: American Film in the Sixties* (Princeton, NJ: Princeton University Press, 1989), 7.

3. MINING MEDIA, OR, ELEMENTAL ENERGY FOR MOTION PICTURES

1. Simon Henry Gage, *Optic Projection: Principles, Installation and Use of the Magic Lantern, Projection Microscope, Reflecting Lantern, Moving Picture Machine* (Ithaca, NY: Comstock, 1914), 570.
2. The material costs and consequences of distribution and exhibition in the digital age have received greater scholarly attention than their precursors. See, for example, important work including Mel Hogan, "Data Flows and Water Woes: The Utah Data Center," *Big Data and Society* 2, no. 2 (2015), https://doi.org/10.1177/2053951715592429; Sean Cubitt, *Finite Media: Environmental Implications of Digital Technologies* (Durham, NC: Duke University Press, 2017), 16–22; Mel Hogan, "The Data Center Industrial Complex," in *Saturation: An Elemental Politics* (Durham, NC: Duke University Press, 2021), 283–305; and Nicole Starosielski, *Media Hot and Cold*, Elements (Durham, NC: Duke University Press, 2021), 191–218.
3. For more about Hollywood lighting, see David Bordwell, Janet Staiger, and Kristin Thompson, *The Classical Hollywood Cinema: Film Style and Mode of Production to 1960* (New York: Columbia University Press, 1985), 273.
4. John Durham Peters, *The Marvelous Clouds: Toward a Philosophy of Elemental Media* (Chicago: University of Chicago Press, 2015), 2; see also Jussi Parikka, *A Geology of Media* (Minneapolis: University of Minnesota Press, 2015).
5. My approach to "image worlds" derives from the historian of technology David Nye's pioneering analysis of G.E.'s use of photographs. See David E. Nye, *Image Worlds: Corporate Identities at General Electric, 1890–1930* (Cambridge, MA: MIT Press, 1985).
6. For more about wartime shortages, see Luci Marzola, *Engineering Hollywood: Technology, Technicians, and the Science of Building the Studio System* (New York: Oxford University Press, 2021), 19–20.
7. M. H. Schoenbaum, "The European War and American Films," *Motion Picture News* 10, no. 7 (August 22, 1915): 24; and M. H. Schoenbaum, "The Corner in Film Chemicals and the Way Out for the Manufacturers," *Motion Picture News* 10, no. 8 (August 29, 1915): 17–18.

8. J. W. Martin, "Says War Will Not Affect Price of Carbons," *Motion Picture News* 10, no. 7 (August 22, 1915): 18.
9. "The Making of an American Projection Carbon," *Motion Picture News* 14, no. 13 (September 30, 1916): 2080–82.
10. *Black Magic: The Story of Manufactured Carbon, 1899–1949* (St. Mary's, PA: Speer Carbon Company, 1949).
11. Although critics of digital media's material costs often (and rightly) cite the "rare earths" found in cameras and other devices such as iPhones, more remains to be written about how these materials were sourced and circulated from (and before) cinema's origins. See, for example, the important, field-defining work in Nadia Bozak, *The Cinematic Footprint: Lights, Camera, Natural Resources* (New Brunswick, NJ: Rutgers University Press, 2012). An important exception to the tendency to focus on the recent past can be found in another important forerunner of today's environmental media and art criticism that already, more than a decade ago, highlighted the material basis of modern forms of media, including now-familiar objects of criticism, such as silver mines and undersea cables. See Richard Maxwell and Toby Miller, *Greening the Media* (New York: Oxford University Press, 2012), 46–59; 71–80.
12. F. H. Richardson, *F. H. Richardson's Bluebook of Projection*, ed. Aaron Nadell, 7th ed. (New York: Quigley, 1942), 363. See also F. H. Richardson, *Motion Picture Handbook: A Guide for Managers and Operators of Motion Picture Theatres*, 3rd ed. (New York: Moving Picture World, 1916), 284; and W. C. Kunzmann, "The Carbon and Projection Light," *Motion Picture News* 10, no. 7 (August 22, 1915): 39–40.
13. Starosielski, *Media Hot and Cold*, 18.
14. Brian R. Jacobson, "Fire and Failure: Studio Technology, Environmental Control, and the Politics of Progress," *Cinema Journal* 57, no. 2 (Winter 2018): 32.
15. See the ad for National Carbon Company "Silvertip" carbons in *Moving Picture World* (April 6, 1918): 147. Another National Carbon Company ad for studio lamp carbons rhetorically asked: "One sun—or one thousand?" See *American Cinematographer* 10, no. 8 (November 1929): 17.
16. "Trouble Department: Questions and Answers Conducted by F. H. Richardson," *Moving Picture World*, January 7, 1911, 192.
17. Richardson, *F. H. Richardson's Bluebook of Projection*, 384.
18. Kunzmann, "Carbon and Projection Light," 52.

19. Among other notable examples, the "Hawks Nest Tunnel Disaster" involved the deaths of miners from silica exposure in West Virginia in the early 1930s, and a YouTube search for "Union Carbide" turns up page after page of videos about Bhopal and various asbestos-related lawsuits. On "slow violence," see Rob Nixon, *Slow Violence and the Environmentalism of the Poor* (Cambridge, MA: Harvard University Press, 2011).
20. Union Carbide 1 file from ECMC, 4.
21. William D. Coolidge, Tungsten and method of making the same for use as filaments of incandescent electric lamps and for other purposes, US Patent 1,082,933, filed June 19, 1912, and issued December 30, 1913.
22. *General Electric Co. v. De Forest Radio Co.*, No. 28 F.2d 641 (U.S. Court of Appeals for the Third Circuit November 23, 1928).
23. The film is available online through the Internet Archive along with other materials preserved by the Eastern California Museum; see https://archive.org/details/cainecm_000029.
24. As Salomé Skvirsky emphasizes, not all industrial films are process films, and not all process films are sponsored by industry, to which we might add that even industry-sponsored films that *do* include process sequences often embed them in nonprocessual narratives, without which the process would not achieve its ideological aim (underscoring Skvirsky's important point that depicting industrial labor does not, in itself, involve "a reactionary politics of labor"). See Salomé Aguilera Skvirsky, *The Process Genre: Cinema and the Aesthetic of Labor* (Durham, NC: Duke University Press, 2020), 54; 120.
25. See, for example, Brian R. Jacobson, "*The Shadow of Progress* and the Cultural Markers of the Anthropocene," *Environmental History* 24, no. 1 (2019): 158–72.
26. See Richard Abel, *The Ciné Goes to Town: French Cinema 1896–1914* (Berkeley: University of California Press, 1994), 125.
27. See H. L. McKinley, T. W. Holmes, and L. E. Sausa, "How U.S.V.'s Pine Creek Mine Will Increase Tungsten Output," *Engineering and Mining Journal* 152, no. 5 (May 1951): 76–83.
28. My discussion of the film's production history is based on the terrific accounts in James Naremore, "The Treasure of the Sierra Madre," in *An Invention Without a Future: Essays on Cinema* (Oakland: University of California Press, 2014), 215–30; and Megan Black, "Scene/Unseen: Mining for *The Treasure of the Sierra Madre*'s Critique of American Capitalist Exploitation," *Modern American History* 2 (2019): 23–47.
29. Black, "Scene/Unseen," 29, 40, 43.

30. *Sierra Madre* was one of seventeen Hollywood productions shot abroad (five in Mexico) in 1948. See Daniel Steinhardt, *Runaway Hollywood: Internationalizing Postwar Production and Location Shooting* (Oakland: University of California Press, 2019), 202–3.
31. Naremore, "The Treasure of the Sierra Madre," 224.
32. Black, "Scene/Unseen," 27.
33. Naremore, "The Treasure of the Sierra Madre," 225.
34. Especially including Raoul Walsh's 1941, Huston-scripted, *High Sierra*, which again stars Bogart, this time alongside the noir icon and director Ida Lupino. *High Sierra*'s California mountain setting makes it another, perhaps even richer, counterpoint to *A Treasure of the Sierra Nevada*, although it will have to be left to some other adventurous reader to explore that connection.
35. On noir's urban settings, see Edward Dimendberg, *Film Noir and the Spaces of Modernity* (Cambridge, MA: Harvard University Press, 2004).
36. Jennifer Fay, *Inhospitable World: Cinema in the Time of the Anthropocene* (New York: Oxford University Press, 2018), 99, 100.
37. Simon Henry Gage, *Optic Projection: Principles, Installation and Use of the Magic Lantern, Projection Microscope, Reflecting Lantern, Moving Picture Machine* (Ithaca, NY: Comstock, 1914), 570–71.
38. Although it was dangerous, for the most part, only in theory. In practice, nonflammable film stock, among other technical innovations, reduced the fire risk when they were available.

4. INDUSTRIAL FILM'S SPECTACULAR AND PROSAIC POETICS

1. On the Ford Motor Company's early film and photography work, see, respectively, Lee Grieveson, "The Work of Film in the Age of Fordist Mechanization," *Cinema Journal* 51, no. 3 (Spring 2012): 25–51; and Terry Smith, *Making the Modern: Industry, Art, and Design in America* (Chicago: University of Chicago Press, 1993), chap. 3. See also Joni K. Hayward Marcum, "Infrastructural Cinema: Seeing Energy on Film in the Long 1930s" (PhD diss., University of Wisconsin-Milwaukee, 2023).
2. Lee Grieveson, "Cinema and the (Common) Wealth of Nations," in *Empire and Film*, ed. Lee Grieveson and Colin MacCabe (London: BFI, 2011), 73.
3. See Will Steffen et al., "The Trajectory of the Anthropocene: The Great Acceleration," *Anthropocene Review* 2, no. 1 (2015): 81–98; and J. R. McNeill

and Peter Engelke, *The Great Acceleration: An Environmental History of the Anthropocene since 1945* (Cambridge, MA: Harvard University Press, 2016).

4. Haidee Wasson, *Everyday Movies: Portable Film Projectors and the Transformation of American Culture* (Oakland: University of California Press, 2020), 4, 3, 28; for more detail, see 153–56.

5. Haidee Wasson and Charles R. Acland, "Introduction: Utility and Cinema," in *Useful Cinema*, ed. Acland and Wasson (Durham, NC: Duke University Press, 2011), 3, 13; and Tony Bennett, "Useful Culture," *Cultural Studies* 6, no. 3 (1992): 395–408.

6. In the introduction to a volume with some important exceptions to this turn away from form, Patrick Vonderau well summarizes this "general observation that industrial, sponsored, or educational films are better explained in terms of use and functionality, rather than meaning or style." Patrick Vonderau, "Introduction: On Advertising's Relation to Moving Pictures," in *Films That Sell: Moving Pictures and Advertising*, ed. Bo Florin, Nico de Klerk, and Vonderau (London: BFI, 2016), 4. Among the chapters that attend to formal strategies used in advertising, see Michael Cowan, "Advertising and Animation: From the Invisible Hand to Attention Management," in *Films That Sell*, 91–113; and Cynthia B. Meyers, "The Best Thing on TV: 1960s U.S. Television Commercials," in *Films That Sell*, 173–93.

7. In the review essay that named this approach, Thomas Elsaesser repeatedly comes back to the fact that "the films themselves are not the object of study," a tendency that he goes on to describe as "the New Film History's apparent indifference to 'actual films.'" Thomas Elsaesser, "The New Film History," *Sight and Sound* 55, no. 4 (Autumn 1986): 29–30.

8. Thomas Elsaesser, "Archives and Archaeologies: The Place of Non-Fiction Film in Contemporary Media," in *Films That Work: Industrial Film and the Productivity of Media*, ed. Vinzenz Hediger and Patrick Vonderau (Amsterdam: Amsterdam University Press, 2009), 19–34. The murky question of authorship in these films also requires attention to context and form. See Brian R. Jacobson, "Corporate Authorship: French Industrial Culture and the Culture of French Industry," in *A Companion to Documentary Film History*, ed. Joshua Malitsky (Hoboken, NJ: Wiley-Blackwell, 2021), 147–64.

9. Vinzenz Hediger and Patrick Vonderau, introduction to *Films That Work: Industrial Film and the Productivity of Media*, ed. Vinzenz Hediger and Patrick Vonderau (Amsterdam: Amsterdam University Press, 2009), 10.

10. Several essays in the standard industrial and educational cinema volumes devote greater attention to formal analysis. See, for example, Vinzenz Hediger,

"Thermodynamic Kitsch: Computing in German Industrial Films, 1928/1963," in *Films That Work*, 127–49; Frank Kessler and Eef Masson, "Layers of Cheese: Generic Overlap in Early Non-Fiction Films on Production Processes," in *Films That Work*, 75–84; Gérard Leblanc, "*Poussières*: Writing the Real vs. the Documentary Real," in *Films That Work*, 119–26; Miriam Posner, "Communicating Disease: Tuberculosis, Narrative, and Social Order in Thomas Edison's Red Cross Seal Films," in *Learning with the Lights Off: Educational Film in the United States*, ed. Devin Orgeron, Marsha Orgeron, and Dan Streible (Oxford: Oxford University Press, 2012), 90–106; and Gregory A. Waller, "Cornering *The Wheat Farmer* (1938)," in *Learning with the Lights Off*, 249–70.

11. Persuasive techniques described by Wasson include, for example, "narrative, movement, sounds, rhythm, visual effects, and projected light," or, even more generally, "the formal properties of cinema." Wasson, *Everyday Movies*, 79.

12. This includes ways we can learn even without the films, as Allyson Field has most cogently argued and modeled. As Field insists, even "nonextant films can be studied, to varying degrees, for their formal aspects." Allyson Nadia Field, *Uplift Cinema: The Emergence of African American Film and the Possibility of Black Modernity* (Durham, NC: Duke University Press, 2015), 26.

13. In the United Kingdom, for example, "No sector of society made more enthusiastic use of the sponsored film than the oil companies," while in France the oil industry was recognized for its leading role in the development of public relations techniques, including film. See Patrick Russell and James Piers Taylor, "Sponsorship," in *Shadows of Progress: Documentary Film in Post-War Britain*, ed. Patrick Russell and James Piers Taylor (London: BFI, 2010), 88; and Franck Bauer, "Pétrole, dirigisme et relations publiques," *La maison de verre* 4 (April 1960): 36–38.

14. Lee Grieveson, *Cinema and the Wealth of Nations: Media, Capital, and the Liberal World System* (Berkeley: University of California Press, 2018), 247–86.

15. Think also of the many feminist and other criticisms of apparatus theory's universalizing assumptions about how commercial cinema works on its abstract spectator.

16. Unlike the experimental films that, as Mike Zryd has argued, "become useful by being anti-useful, by opposing utilitarian, instrumental pedagogy," the "useless" films that interest me *do* intend—we are to assume, because of what we know about their production and exhibition contexts—to achieve that instrumental mode. See Michael Zryd, "Experimental Film as Useless Cinema," in *Useful Cinema*, 317.

17. The same might be said about the U.S. military's adoption of film, which by 1954 had already generated "over one thousand film libraries housing tens of thousands of film prints." There and in other military contexts, film helped facilitate and sustain, as Grieveson and Wasson put it, "the asymmetries of power, resources, and interests that structure the modern world." Film's military work may thus have been "useful" to military powerbrokers, but it may be better understood as a form of excess that was decidedly useless when weighed against other urgent needs such as education, housing, health care, and so on. See Lee Grieveson and Haidee Wasson, "The Military's Cinema Complex," in *Cinema's Military Industrial Complex*, ed. Haidee Wasson and Lee Grieveson (Oakland: University of California Press, 2018), 2–3.
18. Jean Domarchi et al., "Hiroshima, notre amour," in *Cahiers du cinéma, The 1950s: Neo-Realism, Hollywood, New Wave*, ed. Jim Hillier (Cambridge, MA: Harvard University Press, 1985), 62. Originally published as Jean Domarchi et al., "Hiroshima, notre amour," *Cahiers du cinéma* 16, no. 97 (July 1959): 1–18.
19. Luc Moullet, "Sam Fuller: In Marlowe's Footsteps," in *Cahiers du cinéma*, 148. Originally published as Luc Moullet, "Sam Fuller—sur les brisées de Marlowe," *Cahiers du cinéma*, March 1959.
20. Antoine de Baecque, *Camera Historica: The Century in Cinema*, trans. Ninon Vinsonneau and Jonathan Magidoff (New York: Columbia University Press, 2012), 70–73; and James Leo Cahill, "On the Plurality of Worlds: Jacques Yves Cousteau and Louis Malle's Silent World," draft manuscript, 2022. With thanks to Cahill for kindly sharing this work in progress. De Baecque's book was originally published as *L'histoire caméra* (Paris: Gallimard, 2008)
21. de Baecque, *Camera Historica*, 72.
22. See Jacques Rivette, "De l'abjection," *Cahiers du cinéma*, June 1961, 54–55.
23. Daniel Morgan, *The Lure of the Image: Epistemic Fantasies of the Moving Camera* (Oakland: University of California Press, 2021), 2, 46.
24. For an earlier iteration of this argument focused on BP-sponsored films, see Brian R. Jacobson, "Prospecting: Cinema and the Exploration of Extraction," in *Cinema of Exploration: Essays on an Adventurous Film Practice*, ed. James Leo Cahill and Luca Caminati (New York: AFI, 2021), 280–94.
25. David Bordwell, *Making Meaning: Inference and Rhetoric in the Interpretation of Cinema* (Cambridge, MA: Harvard University Press, 1989), 273.
26. Hediger and Vonderau, introduction, 36–37. See also Yvonne Zimmermann, "'What Hollywood Is to America, the Corporate Film Is to Switzerland': Remarks on Industrial Film as Utility Film," in *Films That Work*, 101–17.

27. I take this to be part of Patrick Vonderau's argument that "industrial film as representational technique" must be understood in light of "a general economic phenomenon" and associated conventions that come from elsewhere. See Patrick Vonderau, "Touring as a Cultural Technique: Visitor Films and Autostadt Wolfsburg," in *Films That Work*, 163.
28. Georges Bataille, *The Accursed Share: An Essay on General Economy*, trans. Robert Hurley, vol. 1 (New York: Zone, 1991), 33. Originally published as Georges Bataille, *La part maudite: Essai d'économie générale: La consumation* (Paris: Editions de Minuit, 1949).
29. Bataille, *Accursed Share*, 1:33.
30. Other industrial films of the time that used similar forms shot and presented in Cinerama include *Renault Dauphine* (Renault, 1959), *Journey to the Stars* (Boeing, 1962), *To the Moon and Beyond* (Graphic Films, KLM-Royal Dutch Airlines, 1964), *Wehrhafte Schweiz/Nous pouvons nous defender* [*Fortress of Peace*] (dir. John Fernhout, Swiss Armed Forces, 1964), *Concorde* (1966), and *Bridge to Space* (dir. Robert Gaffney, NASA, 1968). With thanks to John Belton for bringing these films to my attention.
31. Jennifer Lynn Peterson, *Education in the School of Dreams: Travelogues and Early Nonfiction Film* (Durham, NC: Duke University Press, 2013), 8.
32. Tom Gunning, "'The Whole World Within Reach': Travel Images Without Borders," in *Cinéma sans frontières, 1896–1918*, ed. Roland Cosandey, François Albera, and Richard Abel, Sciences Humaines (Québec: Nuit blanche, 1995), 28.
33. Anne Friedberg, *Window Shopping: Cinema and the Postmodern* (Berkeley: University of California Press, 1993).
34. Scott C. Richmond, *Cinema's Bodily Illusions: Flying, Floating, Hallucinating* (Minneapolis: University of Minnesota Press, 2016), 6, 16.
35. Here we find what Karen Redrobe has described as the "binding" together of cinematic technology and one of "capitalism's industrial systems," in this case for the purpose of a "cinematic quest" of speed that negates the associated risks found in "crash films." See Karen Beckman, *Crash: Cinema and the Politics of Speed and Stasis* (Durham, NC: Duke University Press, 2010), 1, 7.
36. Richmond, *Cinema's Bodily Illusions*, 169.
37. Peterson, *Education in the School of Dreams*, 236, 242.
38. Annette Michelson, "Track Records, Trains of Events: The Limits of Cinematic Representation," in *Junction and Journey: Trains and Film*, ed. Alexandra Bonfante-Warren (New York: Museum of Modern Art, 1991), 26. See also Wolfgang Schivelbusch, *The Railway Journey: The Industrialization of Time and Space in the 19th Century* (Berkeley: University of California Press, 1986);

Lynne Kirby, *Parallel Tracks: The Railroad and Silent Cinema* (Durham, NC: Duke University Press, 1997); and Rebecca Harrison, *From Steam to Screen: Cinema, the Railways and Modernity* (London: I.B. Tauris, 2018).

39. A great deal has been written about "Hale's Tours and Scenes of the World." See, for example, Raymond Fielding, "Hale's Tours: Ultrarealism in the Pre-1910 Motion Picture," *Cinema Journal* 10, no. 1 (Autumn 1970): 34–47; Lauren Rabinowitz, "From Hale's Tours to Star Tours: Virtual Voyages and the Delirium of the Hyper-Real," *Iris* 25 (1998): 133–52; and Christian Hayes, "Phantom Carriages: Reconstructing Hale's Tours and the Virtual Travel Experience," *Early Popular Visual Culture* 7, no. 2 (July 2009): 185–98.

40. See Tom Gunning, "An Unseen Energy Swallows Space: The Space in Early Film and Its Relation to American Avant-Garde Film," in *Film Before Griffith*, ed. John L. Fell (Berkeley: University of California Press, 1983), 363. For more details about the film and the associated quote's origins, see Dan Streible, "66mm 8k Phantoms," *Orphan Film Symposium* (blog), February 29, 2020, https://wp.nyu.edu/orphanfilm/2020/02/29/haverstrawtunnel/.

41. David E. James, *Allegories of Cinema: American Film in the Sixties* (Princeton, NJ: Princeton University Press, 1989), 12.

42. See Lisa Parks, "Around the Antenna Tree: The Politics of Infrastructural Visibility," *Flow*, March 6, 2009, http://www.flowjournal.org/2009/03/around-the-antenna-tree-the-politics-of-infrastructural-visibilitylisa-parks-uc-santa-barbara/.

43. Vanessa R. Schwartz, *Jet Age Aesthetic: The Glamour of Media in Motion* (New Haven, CT: Yale University Press, 2020), 11.

44. Brian Larkin, "Promising Forms: The Political Aesthetics of Infrastructure," in *The Promise of Infrastructure*, ed. Nikhil Anand, Akhil Gupta, and Hannah Appel (Durham, NC: Duke University Press, 2018), 175, 186.

45. Dylan Cave, "*Shellarama* (1965)," BFI Screenonline, accessed March 15, 2023, http://www.screenonline.org.uk/film/id/1056068/index.html.

46. Fred Turner, "The Family of Man and the Politics of Attention in Cold War America," *Public Culture* 24, no. 1 (2012): 75.

47. Its efforts to sell this universalist ideal put *Shellarama* in a long lineage of colonial film work, particularly World War II films, with their "rhetoric of unity," as Grieveson puts it, and late-colonial films, the goals of which included what Tom Rice describes as the transformation of "formally controlled colonies into intra-imperial trade blocks." Lee Grieveson, "Introduction: Film and the End of Empire," in *Film and the End of Empire*, ed. Grieveson and Colin MacCabe (Houndmills, UK: Palgrave Macmillan, 2011), 1;

and Tom Rice, *Films for the Colonies: Cinema and the Preservation of the British Empire* (Oakland: University of California Press, 2019), 4.

48. Rudmer Canjels, "Films from Beyond the Well: A Historical Overview of Shell Films," in *Films That Work*, 246. See also Canjels, *The Dynamics of Celluloid on the Road to Independence: Unliver and Shell in Nigeria* (Hilversum: Nederlands Instituut voor Beeld en Gelu, 2017), 59.

49. See Brian R. Jacobson, "*The Shadow of Progress* and the Cultural Markers of the Anthropocene," *Environmental History*, no. 24 (2019): 158–72. Similarly, we may read these films retrospectively for their variation on what James Cahill describes as old nature films' "disquieting address to a present marked by ecological precarity" and thus as perverse elements of a "natural history of cinema" or from the perspective of what Jennifer Peterson has named "an Anthropocene viewing condition." See James Leo Cahill, "Cinema's Natural History," *Journal of Cinema and Media Studies* 58, no. 2 (Winter 2019): 156; and Jennifer Lynn Peterson, "An Anthropocene Viewing Condition," *Representations* 157, no. 1 (Winter 2022): 17–40.

50. James, *Allegories of Cinema*, 23.

CONCLUSION: COUNTER-CINEMAS OF EXTRACTION

1. One such exception, as Edward Dimendberg has shown through close analysis, is Alain Resnais's *Le chant du styrène* [*The Song of Styrene*] (Pechiney, 1958). Edward Dimendberg, "'These Are Not Exercises in Style': *Le chant du styrène*," *October* 112 (Spring 2005): 63–88.

2. Stephen Best and Sharon Marcus, eds., "Surface Reading: An Introduction," *Representations* 108, no. 1 (Fall 2009): 1–21.

3. David E. James, *Allegories of Cinema: American Film in the Sixties* (Princeton, NJ: Princeton University Press, 1989), 12.

4. Vanessa R. Schwartz, *Jet Age Aesthetic: The Glamour of Media in Motion* (New Haven, CT: Yale University Press, 2020), 185–86.

5. As done, for example, in books such as Pamela Robertson Wojcik, *The Apartment Plot: Urban Living in American Culture and Popular Culture, 1945 to 1975* (Durham, NC: Duke University Press, 2010); and Merrill Schleier, *Skyscraper Cinema: Architecture and Gender in American Film* (Minneapolis: University of Minnesota Press, 2008).

6. Lee Grieveson, *Cinema and the Wealth of Nations: Media, Capital, and the Liberal World System* (Berkeley: University of California Press, 2018), 240–46.

7. Learning contextualized subject histories is one way to escape the closed worlds created by the "traditional disciplinary configurations separating the humanities from the natural or social sciences," as emphasized in Priya Jaikumar and Lee Grieveson, "Media and Extraction: A Brief Research Manifesto," *Journal of Environmental Media* 3, no. 2 (2022): 198.
8. With thanks to Debashree Mukherjee for asking the question.
9. My thinking has been shaped by feminist histories of early cinema, including the ongoing Women Film Pioneers Project (Jane Gaines, Radha Vatsal, and Monica Dall'Asta, eds.). See, in particular, Giuliana Bruno, *Streetwalking on a Ruined Map: Cultural Theory and the Films of Elvira Notari* (Princeton, NJ: Princeton University Press, 1993); Anne Friedberg, *Window Shopping: Cinema and the Postmodern* (Berkeley: University of California Press, 1993); Shelley Stamp, *Movie-Struck Girls: Women and Motion Picture Culture After the Nickelodeon* (Princeton, NJ: Princeton University Press, 2000); Amelie Hastie, *Cupboards of Curiosity: Women, Recollection, and Film History* (Durham, NC: Duke University Press, 2007); Mark Garrett Cooper, *Universal Women: Filmmaking and Institutional Change in Early Hollywood* (Urbana: University of Illinois Press, 2010); and Jane Gaines, *Pink-Slipped: What Happened to the Women in the Silent Film Industries?* (Urbana: University of Illinois Press, 2018).
10. In addition to work cited elsewhere in this book, some of the scholarship that has influenced me includes: Jane Gaines, *Fire and Desire: Mixed-Race Movies in the Silent Era* (Chicago: University of Chicago Press, 2001); Jacqueline Najuma Stewart, *Migrating to the Movies: Cinema and Black Urban Modernity* (Berkeley: University of California Press, 2005); Laura Isabel Serna, *Making Cinelandia: Americans Films and Mexican Film Culture Before the Golden Age* (Durham, NC: Duke University Press, 2014); Allyson Nadia Field, Jan-Christopher Horak, and Jacqueline Najuma Stewart, eds., *L.A. Rebellion: Creating a New Black Cinema* (Oakland: University of California Press, 2015); Nicholas Sammond, *Birth of an Industry: Blackface Minstrelsy and the Rise of American Animation* (Durham, NC: Duke University Press, 2015); and Rielle Navitski, *Public Spectacles of Violence: Sensational Cinema and Journalism in Early Twentieth-Century Mexico and Brazil* (Durham, NC: Duke University Press, 2017).
11. Jennifer DeClue, *Visitation: The Conjure Work of Black Feminist Avant-Garde Cinema* (Durham, NC: Duke University Press, 2022), 6.
12. See chapter 4 and Brian Larkin, "Promising Forms: The Political Aesthetics of Infrastructure," in *The Promise of Infrastructure*, ed. Nikhil Anand, Akhil

Gupta, and Hannah Appel (Durham, NC: Duke University Press, 2018), 175–202.

13. Priya Jaikumar, "An 'Accurate Imagination': Place, Map and Archive as Spatial Objects of Film History," in *Empire and Film*, ed. Lee Grieveson and Colin MacCabe, Cultural Histories of Cinema (London: BFI, 2011), 169, 180.

14. Drawing on Saidiya Hartman's work, DeClue evokes the similar "archival reality for Black women—the archive may be a death sentence or it may be a torture chamber." I see resonance between Sohrabi's work and the Black feminist avant-garde filmmakers whose films engage with the archive not, as DeClue writes, for "recovery and recuperation," but rather to create opportunities for "reckoning and witnessing." DeClue, *Visitation*, 17.

15. John Berger, *Ways of Seeing* (London: BBC, 1972), 7, 8, 131.

16. Jaikumar and Grieveson, "Media and Extraction," 201.

BIBLIOGRAPHY

PRIMARY SOURCES

Bauer, Franck. "Pétrole, dirigisme et relations publiques." *La maison de verre* 4 (April 1960): 36–38.

Black Magic: The Story of Manufactured Carbon, 1899–1949. St. Mary's, PA: Speer Carbon, 1949.

Corbett, Charles J., and Richard P. Turco. "Sustainability in the Motion Picture Industry." Los Angeles: UCLA Institute of the Environment and Sustainability, November 2006. https://www.ioes.ucla.edu/wp-content/uploads/mpisreport.pdf.

Domarchi, Jean, Jacques Doniol-Valcroze, Jean-Luc Godard, Pierre Kast, Jacques Rivette, and Eric Rohmer. "Hiroshima, notre amour." *Cahiers du cinéma* 16, no. 97 (July 1959): 1–18.

———. "Hiroshima, notre amour." In *Cahiers du cinéma, The 1950s: Neo-Realism, Hollywood, New Wave*, ed. Jim Hillier, 59–70. Cambridge, MA: Harvard University Press, 1985.

Gage, Simon Henry. *Optic Projection: Principles, Installation and Use of the Magic Lantern, Projection Microscope, Reflecting Lantern, Moving Picture Machine.* Ithaca, NY: Comstock, 1914.

Grisafi, Lily. "Living in the Blast Zone: Sexual Violence Piped Onto Native Land by Extractive Industries." *Columbia Journal of Law and Social Problems* 53, no. 4 (Summer 2020): 509–39.

Jayasundara, Dheeshana S., Thomasine Heitkamp, Roni Mayzer, Elizabeth Legerski, and Tracy A. Evanson. "Exploratory Research on the Impact of the Growing Oil Industry in North Dakota and Montana on Domestic Violence, Dating Violence, Sexual Assault, and Stalking: A Final Summary Overview." Washington, DC: U.S. Department of Justice, 2016.

Keaton, Buster. *My Wonderful World of Slapstick*. Garden City, NY: Doubleday, 1960.

Kunzmann, W. C. "The Carbon and Projection Light." *Motion Picture News* 10, no. 7 (August 22, 1915): 39–40, 52.

Léger, Fernand. "A Critical Essay on the Plastic Quality of Abel Gance's Film *The Wheel* [*Comoedia*, 1922]." In *Functions of Painting*, ed. Edward Fry, trans. Alexandra Anderson, 20–23. New York: Viking, 1973.

Martin, J. W. "Says War Will Not Affect Price of Carbons." *Motion Picture News* 10, no. 7 (August 22, 1915): 18.

McKinley, H. L., T. W. Holmes, and L. E. Sausa. "How U.S.V.'s Pine Creek Mine Will Increase Tungsten Output." *Engineering and Mining Journal* 152, no. 5 (May 1951): 76–83.

McLaughlin, R. P. "First Annual Report of the State Oil and Gas Supervisor of California for the Fiscal Year 1915–16." Sacramento, CA: Department of Petroleum and Gas of the State Mining Bureau, 1917.

Moullet, Luc. "Sam Fuller—sur les brisées de Marlowe." *Cahiers du cinéma*, March 1959.

———. "Sam Fuller: In Marlowe's Footsteps." In *Cahiers du cinéma, The 1950s: Neo-Realism, Hollywood, New Wave*, ed. Jim Hillier, 145–55. Cambridge, MA: Harvard University Press, 1985.

Pardy, George T. "Hectic, Lurid Melodrama." *Exhibitors Trade Review*, March 8, 1924, sec. Box Office Reviews.

Prutzman, Paul W. *Petroleum in Southern California, 1913*. Sacramento: California State Mining Bureau, 1913.

Richardson, F. H. *F. H. Richardson's Bluebook of Projection*. Ed. Aaron Nadell. 7th ed. New York: Quigley, 1942.

———. *Motion Picture Handbook: A Guide for Managers and Operators of Motion Picture Theatres*. 3rd ed. New York: Moving Picture World, 1916.

Rivette, Jacques. "De l'abjection." *Cahiers du cinéma*, June 1961.

Schoenbaum, M. H. "The Corner in Film Chemicals and the Way Out for the Manufacturers." *Motion Picture News* 10, no. 8 (August 29, 1915): 17–18.

———. "The European War and American Films." *Motion Picture News* 10, no. 7 (August 22, 1915): 24.

SECONDARY SOURCES

Abel, Richard. *The Ciné Goes to Town: French Cinema 1896–1914*. Berkeley: University of California Press, 1994.

Acland, Charles R., and Haidee Wasson, eds. *Useful Cinema.* Durham, NC: Duke University Press, 2011.

Ahern, Mal. "Climate Control, Modernism, and Mass Production." *Discourse* 45, no. 1–2 (2023): 3–32.

Allen, Robert C., and Douglas Gomery, eds. *Film History Theory and Practice.* New York: Knopf, 1985.

Alpers, Svetlana. *The Art of Describing: Dutch Art in the Seventeenth Century.* Chicago: University of Chicago Press, 1983.

Alpers, Svetlana, and Michael Baxandall. *Tiepolo and the Pictorial Intelligence.* New Haven, CT: Yale University Press, 1994.

Angus, Siobhan. "Mining the History of Photography." In *Capitalism and the Camera: Essays on Photography and Extraction,* ed. Kevin Coleman and Daniel James, 55–73. London: Verso, 2021.

Arsenjuk, Luka. *Movement, Action, Image, Montage: Sergei Eisenstein and the Cinema in Crisis.* Minneapolis: University of Minnesota Press, 2018.

Aubry, Timothy, and Florence Dore. "Introduction: Formalism Unbound." *Post45,* no. 5 (December 14, 2020). https://post45.org/2020/12/aubry-dore-introduction/.

Badalov, Rahman. "Cinema: Oil and Revolution." *Azerbaijan International* 5, no. 3 (Autumn 1997): 57–64.

Baecque, Antoine de. *Camera Historica: The Century in Cinema.* Trans. Ninon Vinsonneau and Jonathan Magidoff. New York: Columbia University Press, 2012.

Baird, Harry R. "E. C. Sanderson." Master's thesis, Butler University, 1957.

Balides, Constance. "Cinema Under the Sign of Money: Commercialized Leisure, Economies of Abundance, and Pecuniary Madness, 1905–1915." In *American Cinema's Transitional Era: Audiences, Institutions, Practices,* ed. Charles Keil and Shelley Stamp, 285–314. Berkeley: University of California Press, 2004.

Banks, Miranda, Bridget Conor, and Vicki Mayer, eds. *Production Studies, The Sequel! Cultural Studies of Global Media Industries.* London: Routledge, 2015.

Bao, Weihong. *Fiery Cinema: The Emergence of an Affective Medium in China, 1915–1945.* Minneapolis: University of Minnesota Press, 2015.

Barthes, Roland. "Myth Today." In *Mythologies,* trans. Annette Lavers, 109–59. New York: Hill and Wang, 1972.

Bataille, Georges. *The Accursed Share: An Essay on General Economy.* Vol. 1. Trans. Robert Hurley. New York: Zone, 1991.

——. *La part maudite: Essai d'économie générale: La consumation.* Paris: Editions de Minuit, 1949.

Baxandall, Michael. *Painting and Experience in Fifteenth Century Italy: A Primer in the Social History of Pictorial Style.* Oxford: Oxford University Press, 1972.

Beckman, Karen. *Crash: Cinema and the Politics of Speed and Stasis.* Durham, NC: Duke University Press, 2010.

Bellour, Raymond. "To Alternate/To Narrate (on *The Lonedale Operator*)." In *The Analysis of Film*, ed. Constance Penley, trans. Inge Pruks and Roxanne Lapidus, 262–77. Bloomington: Indiana University Press, 2000.

Bengtson, John. "Buster Keaton—More Backlot Scenes from Our Hospitality." *Chaplin-Keaton-Lloyd Film Locations (and More)* (blog), April 26, 2020. https://silentlocations.com/2020/04/26/buster-keaton-more-backlot-scenes-from-our-hospitality/.

Bennett, Jane. *Vibrant Matter.* Durham, NC: Duke University Press, 2010.

Bennett, Tony. "Useful Culture." *Cultural Studies* 6, no. 3 (1992): 395–408.

Berger, John. *Ways of Seeing.* London: BBC, 1972.

Best, Stephen, and Sharon Marcus, eds. "Surface Reading: An Introduction." *Representations* 108, no. 1 (Fall 2009): 1–21.

Black, Megan. "Scene/Unseen: Mining for *The Treasure of the Sierra Madre*'s Critique of American Capitalist Exploitation." *Modern American History* 2 (2019): 23–47.

Bordwell, David. *Figures Traced in Light: On Cinematic Staging.* Berkeley: University of California Press, 2005.

———. *On the History of Film Style.* Cambridge, MA: Harvard University Press, 1997.

———. *Making Meaning: Inference and Rhetoric in the Interpretation of Cinema.* Cambridge, MA: Harvard University Press, 1989.

Bordwell, David, Janet Staiger, and Kristin Thompson. *The Classical Hollywood Cinema: Film Style and Mode of Production to 1960.* New York: Columbia University Press, 1985.

Bozak, Nadia. *The Cinematic Footprint: Lights, Camera, Natural Resources.* New Brunswick, NJ: Rutgers University Press, 2012.

Brereton, Patrick. *Hollywood Utopia: Ecology in Contemporary American Cinema.* Bristol: Intellect Books, 2005.

Brinkema, Eugenie. *Life-Destroying Diagrams.* Durham, NC: Duke University Press, 2022.

Brown, Bill. *A Sense of Things: The Object Matter of American Literature.* Chicago: University of Chicago Press, 2003.

Bruno, Giuliana. *Streetwalking on a Ruined Map: Cultural Theory and the Films of Elvira Notari.* Princeton, NJ: Princeton University Press, 1993.

Cahill, James Leo. "Animal Photogénie: The Wild Side of French Film Theory's First Wave." In *Animal Life and the Moving Image*, ed. Michael Lawrence and Laura McMahon, 23–41. London: BFI, 2015.

———. "Cinema's Natural History." *Journal of Cinema and Media Studies* 58, no. 2 (Winter 2019): 152–57.

———. "On the Plurality of Worlds: Jacques Yves Cousteau and Louis Malle's Silent World." Draft manuscript, 2022.

———. *Zoological Surrealism: The Nonhuman Cinema of Jean Painlevé*. Minneapolis: University of Minnesota Press, 2019.

Cahill, James Leo, Brian R. Jacobson, and Weihong Bao. "Media Climates: An Introduction." *Representations* 157, no. 1 (Winter 2022): 1–16.

Caldwell, John T. "Industrial Geography Lessons: Socio-Professional Rituals and the Borderlands of Production Culture." In *MediaSpace: Place, Scale and Culture in a Media Age*, ed. Nick Couldry and Anna McCarthy, 163–90. London: Routledge, 2004.

———. *Production Culture: Industrial Reflexivity and Critical Practice in Film and Television*. Durham, NC: Duke University Press, 2008.

———. "Televisuality as a Semiotic Machine: Emerging Paradigms in Low Theory." *Cinema Journal* 32, no. 4 (Summer 1993): 24–48.

Canjels, Rudmer. *The Dynamics of Celluloid on the Road to Independence: Unliver and Shell in Nigeria*. Hilversum: Nederlands Instituut voor Beeld en Gelu, 2017.

———. "Films from Beyond the Well: A Historical Overview of Shell Films." In *Films That Work: Industrial Film and the Productivity of Media*, ed. Vinzenz Hediger and Patrick Vonderau, 243–55. Amsterdam: Amsterdam University Press, 2009.

Caron, Estelle. "Images de la mine et des mineurs." *Les cahiers de la cinémathèque* Cinéma Ouvrier en France, no. 71 (December 2000): 47–52.

Cave, Dylan. "*Shellarama* (1965)." BFI Screenonline. Accessed March 15, 2023. http://www.screenonline.org.uk/film/id/1056068/index.html.

Charney, Leo, and Vanessa R. Schwartz, eds. *Cinema and the Invention of Modern Life*. Berkeley: University of California Press, 1995.

———. Introduction to *Cinema and the Invention of Modern Life*, ed. Leo Charney and Vanessa R. Schwartz, 1–12. Berkeley: University of California Press, 1995.

Christensen, Jerome. *America's Corporate Art: The Studio Authorship of Hollywood Motion Pictures*. Stanford, CA: Stanford University Press, 2012.

Christie, Ian. "'The Captains and the Kings Depart': Imperial Departure and Arrival in Early Cinema." In *Empire and Film*, ed. Lee Grieveson and Colin MacCabe, 21–34. London: BFI, 2011.

Comolli, Jean-Louis. "Technique and Ideology: Camera, Perspective, Depth of Field." In *Cinema Against Spectacle*, trans. Daniel Fairfax, 143–244. Amsterdam: Amsterdam University Press, 2015.

———. "Technique et idéologie: Caméra, perspective, profondeur du champ." *Cahiers du cinéma*, no. 229 (May 1971): 4–21.

Connor, J. D. *Hollywood Math and Aftermath: The Economic Image and the Digital Recession*. London: Bloomsbury, 2018.

———. *The Studios After the Studios: Neoclassical Hollywood (1970–2010)*. POST•45. Stanford, CA: Stanford University Press, 2015.

Cooper, Mark Garrett. *Universal Women: Filmmaking and Institutional Change in Early Hollywood*. Urbana: University of Illinois Press, 2010.

Cowan, Michael. "Advertising and Animation: From the Invisible Hand to Attention Management." In *Films That Sell: Moving Pictures and Advertising*, ed. Bo Florin, Nico de Klerk, and Patrick Vonderau, 91–113. Cultural Histories of Cinema. London: BFI, 2016.

Crylen, Jon. "Living in a World Without Sun: Jacques Cousteau, Homo Aquaticus, and the Dream of Dwelling Undersea." *Journal of Cinema and Media Studies* 58, no. 1 (Fall 2018): 1–23.

Cubitt, Sean. *Finite Media: Environmental Implications of Digital Technologies*. Durham, NC: Duke University Press, 2017.

Dahlquist, Marina, and Patrick Vonderau, eds. *Petrocinema: Sponsored Film and the Oil Industry*. London: Bloomsbury Academic, 2021.

DeClue, Jennifer. *Visitation: The Conjure Work of Black Feminist Avant-Garde Cinema*. Durham, NC: Duke University Press, 2022.

Demos, T. J. *Against the Anthropocene: Visual Culture and Environment Today*. Berlin: Sternberg, 2017.

Dimendberg, Edward. *Film Noir and the Spaces of Modernity*. Cambridge, MA: Harvard University Press, 2004.

———. "'These Are Not Exercises in Style': *Le chant du styrène*." *October* 112 (Spring 2005): 63–88.

Dootson, Kirsty Sinclair. *The Rainbow's Gravity: Colour, Materiality, and British Modernity*. New Haven, CT: Yale University Press, 2023.

Elsaesser, Thomas. "Archives and Archaeologies: The Place of Non-Fiction Film in Contemporary Media." In *Films That Work: Industrial Film and the Productivity of Media*, ed. Vinzenz Hediger and Patrick Vonderau, 19–34. Amsterdam: Amsterdam University Press, 2009.

———. "The New Film History." *Sight and Sound* 55, no. 4 (Autumn 1986): 246–51.

Fairfax, Daniel. *The Red Years of Cahiers du cinéma (1968–1973)*. Vol. 1, *Ideology and Politics*. Amsterdam: Amsterdam University Press, 2021.

Fay, Jennifer. *Inhospitable World: Cinema in the Time of the Anthropocene*. New York: Oxford University Press, 2018.

Field, Allyson Nadia. *Uplift Cinema: The Emergence of African American Film and the Possibility of Black Modernity*. Durham, NC: Duke University Press, 2015.

Field, Allyson Nadia, Jan-Christopher Horak, and Jacqueline Najuma Stewart, eds. *L.A. Rebellion: Creating a New Black Cinema*. Oakland: University of California Press, 2015.

Fielding, Raymond. "Hale's Tours: Ultrarealism in the Pre-1910 Motion Picture." *Cinema Journal* 10, no. 1 (Autumn 1970): 34–47.

Friedberg, Anne. *Window Shopping: Cinema and the Postmodern*. Berkeley: University of California Press, 1993.

Furuhata, Yuriko. *Climatic Media: Transpacific Experiments in Atmospheric Control*. Durham, NC: Duke University Press, 2022.

Gaines, Jane. *Fire and Desire: Mixed-Race Movies in the Silent Era*. Chicago: University of Chicago Press, 2001.

———. *Pink-Slipped: What Happened to the Women in the Silent Film Industries?* Urbana: University of Illinois Press, 2018.

Galili, Doron. *Seeing by Electricity: The Emergence of Television, 1878–1939*. Durham, NC: Duke University Press, 2020.

Galt, Rosalind. *Alluring Monsters: The Pontianak and Cinemas of Decolonization*. New York: Columbia University Press, 2021.

———. *Pretty: Film and the Decorative Image*. New York: Columbia University Press, 2011.

Gaudreault, André. "Narration and Monstration in the Cinema." *Journal of Film and Video* 39, no. 2 (Spring 1987): 29–36.

Gómez-Barris, Macarena. *The Extractive Zone: Social Ecologies and Decolonial Perspectives*. Durham, NC: Duke University Press, 2017.

Gosser, H. Mark. "The Bazar de la charité Fire: The Reality, the Aftermath, the Telling." *Film History* 10, no. 1 (1998): 70–89.

Grieveson, Lee. "Cinema and the (Common) Wealth of Nations." In *Empire and Film*, ed. Lee Grieveson and Colin MacCabe, 73–114. London: BFI, 2011.

———. *Cinema and the Wealth of Nations: Media, Capital, and the Liberal World System*. Berkeley: University of California Press, 2018.

———. "Introduction: Film and the End of Empire." In *Film and the End of Empire*, ed. Lee Grieveson and Colin MacCabe, 1–12. Houndmills, UK: Palgrave Macmillan, 2011.

———. "The Work of Film in the Age of Fordist Mechanization." *Cinema Journal* 51, no. 3 (Spring 2012): 25–51.

Grieveson, Lee, and Colin MacCabe, eds. *Empire and Film*. Cultural Histories of Cinema. London: BFI, 2011.

———, eds. *Film and the End of Empire*. Houndmills, UK: Palgrave Macmillan, 2011.
Grieveson, Lee, and Haidee Wasson. "The Military's Cinema Complex." In *Cinema's Military Industrial Complex*, ed. Haidee Wasson and Lee Grieveson, 1–24. Oakland: University of California Press, 2018.
Griffiths, Alison. *Wondrous Difference: Cinema, Anthropology, and Turn-of-the-Century Visual Culture*. New York: Columbia University Press, 2002.
Guerin, Frances. *A Culture of Light: Cinema and Technology in 1920s Germany*. Minneapolis: University of Minnesota Press, 2005.
Gumbrecht, Hans Ulrich. "A Farewell to Interpretation." In *Materialities of Communication*, ed. Hans Ulrich Gumbrecht and K. Ludwig Pfeiffer, trans. William Whobrey, 389–404. Stanford, CA: Stanford University Press, 1994.
———. *Production of Presence: What Meaning Cannot Convey*. Stanford, CA: Stanford University Press, 2004.
Gumbrecht, Hans Ulrich, and K. Ludwig Pfeiffer, eds. *Materialität der kommunikation*. Frankfurt am Main: Suhrkamp, 1988.
———, eds. *Materialities of Communication*. Trans. William Whobrey. Stanford, CA: Stanford University Press, 1994.
Gunning, Tom. "The Cinema of Attractions: Early Film, Its Spectator and the Avant-Garde." *Wide Angle* 8, nos. 3–4 (1986): 63–70.
———. *D. W. Griffith and the Origins of American Narrative Film*. Urbana: University of Illinois Press, 1991.
———. "Modernity and Cinema: A Culture of Shocks and Flows." In *Cinema and Modernity*, ed. Murray Pomerance, 297–315. New Brunswick, NJ: Rutgers University Press, 2006.
———. "Systematizing the Electric Message: Narrative Form, Gender, and Modernity in *The Lonedale Operator*." In *American Cinema's Transitional Era: Audiences, Institutions, Practices*, ed. Charles Keil and Shelley Stamp, 15–50. Berkeley: University of California Press, 2004.
———. "An Unseen Energy Swallows Space: The Space in Early Film and Its Relation to American Avant-Garde Film." In *Film Before Griffith*, ed. John L. Fell, 355–66. Berkeley: University of California Press, 1983.
———. "The Whole Town Is Gawking: Early Cinema and the Visual Experience of Modernity." *Yale Journal of Criticism* 7, no. 2 (1994): 189–201.
———. "'The Whole World Within Reach': Travel Images Without Borders." In *Cinéma sans frontières, 1896–1918* [*Images Across Borders*], ed. Roland Cosandey, François Albera, and Richard Abel, 21–36. Sciences Humaines; Variation: Sciences Humaines (Lausanne, Switzerland). Québec: Nuit blanche, 1995.

Hallett, Hilary. *Go West, Young Women! The Rise of Early Hollywood*. Oakland: University of California Press, 2013.

Hansen, Miriam. "Benjamin, Cinema and Experience: 'The Blue Flower in the Land of Technology.'" Special issue on Weimar film theory, *New German Critique* 40 (Winter 1987): 179–224.

———. "The Mass Production of the Senses: Classical Cinema as Vernacular Modernism." *Modernism/Modernity* 6, no. 2 (April 1999): 59–77.

Haraway, Donna J. "Tentacular Thinking: Anthropocene, Capitalocene, Chthulucene." *E-Flux* 75 (September 2016). http://www.e-flux.com/journal/tentacular-thinking-anthropocene-capitalocene-chthulucene/.

Harrison, Rebecca. *From Steam to Screen: Cinema, the Railways and Modernity*. London: I.B. Tauris, 2018.

Hastie, Amelie. *Cupboards of Curiosity: Women, Recollection, and Film History*. Durham, NC: Duke University Press, 2007.

Hayes, Christian. "Phantom Carriages: Reconstructing Hale's Tours and the Virtual Travel Experience." *Early Popular Visual Culture* 7, no. 2 (July 2009): 185–98.

Hediger, Vinzenz. "Thermodynamic Kitsch: Computing in German Industrial Films, 1928/1963." In *Films That Work: Industrial Film and the Productivity of Media*, ed. Vinzenz Hediger and Patrick Vonderau, 127–49. Amsterdam: Amsterdam University Press, 2009.

Hediger, Vinzenz, and Patrick Vonderau. Introduction to *Films That Work: Industrial Film and the Productivity of Media*, ed. Vinzenz Hediger and Patrick Vonderau, 9–16. Amsterdam: Amsterdam University Press, 2009.

Hediger, Vinzenz, and Patrick Vonderau, eds. *Films That Work: Industrial Film and the Productivity of Media*. Amsterdam: Amsterdam University Press, 2009.

Hogan, Mel. "The Data Center Industrial Complex." In *Saturation: An Elemental Politics*, 283–305. Durham, NC: Duke University Press, 2021.

———. "Data Flows and Water Woes: The Utah Data Center." *Big Data and Society* 2, no. 2 (2015). https://doi.org/10.1177/2053951715592429.

Holt, Jennifer, and Alisa Perren, eds. *Media Industries: History, Theory, and Method*. Malden, MA: Wiley-Blackwell, 2009.

Horn, Eva. "Editor's Introduction: 'There Are No Media.'" *Grey Room* 29 (2007): 6–13.

Ingram, David. *Green Screen: Environmentalism and Hollywood Cinema*. Exeter: University of Exeter Press, 2000.

Ivakhiv, Adrian J. *Ecologies of the Moving Image: Cinema, Affect, Nature*. Waterloo, Canada: Wilfred Laurier University Press, 2013.

Jacobs, Steven. "A Concise History and Theory of Documentaries on the Visual Arts." In *A Companion to Documentary Film History*, ed. Joshua Malitsky, 291–310. Hoboken, NJ: Wiley-Blackwell, 2021.

Jacobson, Brian R. "Corporate Authorship: French Industrial Culture and the Culture of French Industry." In *A Companion to Documentary Film History*, ed. Joshua Malitsky, 147–64. Hoboken, NJ: Wiley-Blackwell, 2021.

——. "Fantastic Functionality: Studio Architecture and the Visual Rhetoric of Early Hollywood." In "Early Hollywood and the Archive." Special issue, *Film History* 26, no. 2 (2014): 52–81.

——. "Fire and Failure: Studio Technology, Environmental Control, and the Politics of Progress." *Cinema Journal* 57, no. 2 (Winter 2018): 22–43.

——. "Found Memories of Film History: Industry in a Post-Industrial World; Cinema in a Post-Filmic Age." In *New Silent Cinema*, ed. Paul Flaig and Katherine Groo, 243–62. New York: AFI, 2015.

——. "Infrastructural Affinity: Film Technology and the Built Environment in New York circa 1900." *Framework* 57, no. 1 (Spring 2016): 7–31.

——. "Prospecting: Cinema and the Exploration of Extraction." In *Cinema of Exploration: Essays on an Adventurous Film Practice*, ed. James Leo Cahill and Luca Caminati, 280–94. New York: AFI, 2021.

——. "*The Shadow of Progress* and the Cultural Markers of the Anthropocene." *Environmental History* 24, no. 1 (2019): 158–72.

——. *Studios Before the System: Architecture, Technology, and the Emergence of Cinematic Space*. New York: Columbia University Press, 2015.

Jaikumar, Priya. "An 'Accurate Imagination': Place, Map and Archive as Spatial Objects of Film History." In *Empire and Film*, ed. Lee Grieveson and Colin MacCabe, 167–88. Cultural Histories of Cinema. London: BFI, 2011.

——. *Where Histories Reside: India as Filmed Space*. Durham, NC: Duke University Press, 2019.

Jaikumar, Priya, and Lee Grieveson. "Media and Extraction: A Brief Research Manifesto." *Journal of Environmental Media* 3, no. 2 (2022): 197–206.

James, David E. *Allegories of Cinema: American Film in the Sixties*. Princeton, NJ: Princeton University Press, 1989.

Jameson, Fredric. *The Political Unconscious: Narrative as a Socially Symbolic Act*. Ithaca, NY: Cornell University Press, 1981.

Johnson, Martin L. *Main Street Movies: The History of Local Film in the United States*. Cinema and the American Experience. Bloomington: Indiana University Press, 2018.

Kara, Selmin. "Anthropocenema: Cinema in the Age of Mass Extinctions." In *Post-Cinema: Theorizing 21st-Century Film*, ed. Shane Denson and Julia Leyda, 750–84. Falmer, UK: REFRAME Books, 2016.

Kazimzade, Aydin. "Cinema in Azerbaijan: The Pre-Soviet Era." *Azerbaijan International* 5, no. 3 (Autumn 1997): 30–35.

Keil, Charlie. "Transition Through Tension: Stylistic Diversity in the Late Griffith Biographs." *Cinema Journal* 28, no. 3 (Spring 1989): 22–40.

Kessler, Frank, and Eef Masson. "Layers of Cheese: Generic Overlap in Early Non-Fiction Films on Production Processes." In *Films That Work: Industrial Film and the Productivity of Media*, ed. Vinzenz Hediger and Patrick Vonderau, 75–84. Amsterdam: Amsterdam University Press, 2009.

Kirby, Lynne. *Parallel Tracks: The Railroad and Silent Cinema*. Durham, NC: Duke University Press, 1997.

Kittler, Friedrich A. "Afterword to the Second Printing." In *Discourse Networks, 1800/1900*, trans. Michael Metteer, 369–72. Stanford, CA: Stanford University Press, 1990.

———. *Discourse Networks, 1800/1900*. Trans. Michael Metteer. Stanford, CA: Stanford University Press, 1990.

———. *Gramophone, Film, Typewriter*. Trans. Geoffrey Winthrop-Young and Michael Wutz. Stanford, CA: Stanford University Press, 1999.

———. *Optical Media: Berlin Lectures 1999*. Trans. Anthony Enns. Cambridge: Polity, 2010.

Kornbluh, Anna. *The Order of Forms: Realism, Formalism, and Social Space*. Chicago: University of Chicago Press, 2019.

———. *Realizing Capital: Financial and Psychic Economies in Victorian Form*. New York: Fordham University Press, 2014.

Koszarski, Richard. *Fort Lee: The Film Town*. Rome: John Libbey, 2004.

Kracauer, Siegfried. *Theory of Film: The Redemption of Physical Reality*. Pbk. ed. Princeton, NJ: Princeton University Press, 1997.

Larkin, Brian. "Promising Forms: The Political Aesthetics of Infrastructure." In *The Promise of Infrastructure*, ed. Nikhil Anand, Akhil Gupta, and Hannah Appel, 175–202. Durham, NC: Duke University Press, 2018.

———. *Signal and Noise: Media, Infrastructure, and Urban Culture in Nigeria*. Durham, NC: Duke University Press, 2008.

Leblanc, Gérard. "Poussières: Writing the Real vs. the Documentary Real." In *Films That Work: Industrial Film and the Productivity of Media*, ed. Vinzenz Hediger and Patrick Vonderau, 119–26. Amsterdam: Amsterdam University Press, 2009.

LeMenager, Stephanie. *Living Oil: Petroleum Culture in the American Century*. New York: Oxford University Press, 2014.

Levine, Caroline. *Forms: Whole, Rhythm, Hierarchy, Network*. Princeton, NJ: Princeton University Press, 2015.

Lewis, Jon, and Eric Smoodin, eds. *Looking Past the Screen: Case Studies in American Film History and Method*. Durham, NC: Duke University Press, 2007.

Lovejoy, Alice. "Celluloid Geopolitics: Film Stock and the War Economy, 1939–47." *Screen* 60, no. 2 (2019): 224–41.

Majumdar, Rochona. *Art Cinema and India's Forgotten Futures: Film and History in the Postcolony*. New York: Columbia University Press, 2021.

Mallory, Mary. *Hollywoodland*. Images of America. Charleston, SC: Arcadia, 2011.

Mannoni, Laurent. *Le grand art de la lumière et de l'ombre: archéologie du cinéma*. Paris: Nathan Université, 1994.

Marcum, Joni K. Hayward. "Infrastructural Cinema: Seeing Energy on Film in the Long 1930s." PhD diss., University of Wisconsin-Milwaukee, 2023.

Marzola, Luci. *Engineering Hollywood: Technology, Technicians, and the Science of Building the Studio System*. New York: Oxford University Press, 2021.

Maxwell, Richard, and Toby Miller. *Greening the Media*. New York, NY: Oxford University Press, 2012.

Mayer, Vicki, Miranda J. Banks, and John T. Caldwell, eds. *Production Studies: Cultural Studies of Media Industries*. New York: Routledge, 2009.

McNeill, J. R., and Peter Engelke. *The Great Acceleration: An Environmental History of the Anthropocene since 1945*. Cambridge, MA: Harvard University Press, 2016.

Meador, Daryl. "The Cinema of Extractions in Dallas, Texas." *Social Text Online*, June 7, 2018. https://socialtextjournal.org/periscope_article/the-cinema-of-extractions-in-dallas-texas/.

Menne, Jeff. *Post-Fordist Cinema: Hollywood Auteurs and the Corporate Counterculture*. New York: Columbia University Press, 2019.

Metz, Christian. *Film Language: A Semiotics of Cinema*. Trans. Michael Taylor. Chicago: University of Chicago Press, 1991.

———. "Methodological Propositions for the Analysis of Film." Trans. Diana Matias. *Screen* 14, no. 1–2 (1973): 89–101.

Meyers, Cynthia B. "The Best Thing on TV: 1960s US Television Commercials." In *Films That Sell: Moving Pictures and Advertising*, ed. Bo Florin, Nico de Klerk, and Patrick Vonderau, 173–93. Cultural Histories of Cinema. London: BFI, 2016.

Michelson, Annette. "Track Records, Trains of Events: The Limits of Cinematic Representation." In *Junction and Journey: Trains and Film*, ed. Alexandra Bonfante-Warren, 24–31. New York: Museum of Modern Art, 1991.

Mitman, Gregg. *Reel Nature: America's Romance with Wildlife on Film*. Cambridge, MA: Harvard University Press, 1999.

Morgan, Daniel. *The Lure of the Image: Epistemic Fantasies of the Moving Camera*. Oakland: University of California Press, 2021.

Morton, Timothy. *Hyperobjects: Philosophy and Ecology After the End of the World*. Minneapolis: University of Minnesota Press, 2013.

Mukherjee, Debashree. "The Aesthetic and Material Force of Landscape in Cinema: Mediating Meaning from the Scene of Production." *Representations* 157, no. 1 (Winter 2022): 115–41.

——. *Bombay Hustle: Making Movies in a Colonial City*. New York: Columbia University Press, 2020.

Mukherjee, Rahul. *Radiant Infrastructures: Media, Environment, and Cultures of Uncertainty*. Durham, NC: Duke University Press, 2020.

Mumford, Lewis. *Technics and Civilization*. New York: Harcourt, Brace, 1934.

Murray, Robin L., and Joseph K. Heumann, eds. *Ecology and Popular Film: Cinema on the Edge*. Albany: State University of New York Press, 2009.

Musser, Charles. *Before the Nickelodeon: Edwin S. Porter and the Edison Manufacturing Company*. Los Angeles: University of California Press, 1991.

——. "Early Advertising and Promotional Films, 1893–1900: Edison Motion Pictures as a Case Study." In *Films That Sell: Moving Pictures and Advertising*, ed. Bo Florin, Nico de Klerk, and Patrick Vonderau, 83–90. London: BFI, 2016.

——. *The Emergence of Cinema: The American Screen to 1907*. Vol. 1, *History of the American Cinema*. New York: Scribner, 1990.

Nair, Kartik. "Striking Out: Visual Space, Production Design, and Labor History in Joker." *Quarterly Review of Film and Video* 39, no. 8 (2022): 1905–33.

Naremore, James. "The Treasure of the Sierra Madre." In *An Invention without a Future: Essays on Cinema*, 215–30. Oakland: University of California Press, 2014.

Navitski, Rielle. *Public Spectacles of Violence: Sensational Cinema and Journalism in Early Twentieth-Century Mexico and Brazil*. Durham, NC: Duke University Press, 2017.

Neale, Steve. *Cinema and Technology: Image, Sound, Colour*. London: BFI, 1985.

Nixon, Rob. *Slow Violence and the Environmentalism of the Poor*. Cambridge, MA: Harvard University Press, 2011.

Nye, David E. *Image Worlds: Corporate Identities at General Electric, 1890–1930*. Cambridge, MA: MIT Press, 1985.

Orgeron, Devin, Marsha Orgeron, and Dan Streible, eds. *Learning with the Lights Off: Educational Film in the United States*. Oxford: Oxford University Press, 2012.

Page, Max. *The Creative Destruction of Manhattan, 1900–1940*. Historical Studies of Urban America. Chicago: University of Chicago Press, 1999.

Parikka, Jussi. *A Geology of Media*. Minneapolis: University of Minnesota Press, 2015.

Parks, Lisa. "Around the Antenna Tree: The Politics of Infrastructural Visibility." *Flow*, March 6, 2009. http://www.flowjournal.org/2009/03/around-the-antenna-tree-the-politics-of-infrastructural-visibilitylisa-parks-uc-santa-barbara/.

Parks, Lisa, and Nicole Starosielski, eds. *Signal Traffic: Critical Studies of Media Infrastructures*. Urbana-Champaign: University of Illinois Press, 2015.

Peters, John Durham. "Introduction: Friedrich Kittler's Light Shows." In *Optical Media: Berlin Lectures 1999*, by Friedrich Kittler, 1–17. Trans. Anthony Enns. Cambridge: Polity, 2010.

———. *The Marvelous Clouds: Toward a Philosophy of Elemental Media*. Chicago: University of Chicago Press, 2015.

Peterson, Jennifer Lynn. "An Anthropocene Viewing Condition." *Representations* 157, no. 1 (Winter 2022): 17–40.

———. *Education in the School of Dreams: Travelogues and Early Nonfiction Film*. Durham, NC: Duke University Press, 2013.

———. "Workers Leaving the Factory: Witnessing Industry in the Digital Age." In *The Oxford Handbook of Sound and Image in Digital Media*, ed. Carol Vernallis, Amy Herzog, and John Richardson, 598–619. New York: Oxford University Press, 2013.

Pfeiffer, K. Ludwig. "The Materiality of Communication." In *Materialities of Communication*, ed. Hans Ulrich Gumbrecht and K. Ludwig Pfeiffer, trans. William Whobrey, 1–12. Stanford, CA: Stanford University Press, 1994.

Pollmann, Inga. "Invisible Worlds, Visible: Uexküll's Umwelt, Film, and Film Theory." *Critical Inquiry* 39, no. 4 (Summer 2013): 777–816.

Posner, Miriam. "Communicating Disease: Tuberculosis, Narrative, and Social Order in Thomas Edison's Red Cross Seal Films." In *Learning with the Lights Off: Educational Film in the United States*, ed. Devin Orgeron, Marsha Orgeron, and Dan Streible, 90–106. Oxford: Oxford University Press, 2012.

Rabinowitz, Lauren. "From Hale's Tours to Star Tours: Virtual Voyages and the Delirium of the Hyper-Real." *Iris* 25 (1998): 133–52.

Redrobe, Karen, and Jeff Scheible, eds. *Deep Mediations: Thinking Space in Cinema and Digital Cultures*. Minneapolis: University of Minnesota Press, 2020.

Resmini, Mauro. *Italian Political Cinema: Figures of the Long '68*. Minneapolis: University of Minnesota Press, 2022.

Rhodes, John David. *Spectacle of Property: The House in American Film*. Minneapolis: University of Minnesota Press, 2017.

Rice, Tom. *Films for the Colonies: Cinema and the Preservation of the British Empire*. Oakland: University of California Press, 2019.

Richmond, Scott C. *Cinema's Bodily Illusions: Flying, Floating, Hallucinating*. Minneapolis: University of Minnesota Press, 2016.

Rony, Fatimah Tobing. *The Third Eye: Race, Cinema, and Ethnographic Spectacle*. Durham, NC: Duke University Press, 1996.

Ross, Steven J. *Working-Class Hollywood: Silent Film and the Shaping of Class in America*. Princeton, NJ: Princeton University Press, 1998.

Russell, Patrick, and James Piers Taylor. "Sponsorship." In *Shadows of Progress: Documentary Film in Post-War Britain*, ed. Patrick Russell and James Piers Taylor, 60–107. London: BFI, 2010.

Salt, Barry. *Film Style and Technology: History and Analysis*. London: Starword, 1983.

Sammond, Nicholas. *Birth of an Industry: Blackface Minstrelsy and the Rise of American Animation*. Durham, NC: Duke University Press, 2015.

Schivelbusch, Wolfgang. *The Railway Journey: The Industrialization of Time and Space in the 19th Century*. Berkeley: University of California Press, 1986.

Schleier, Merrill. *Skyscraper Cinema: Architecture and Gender in American Film*. Minneapolis: University of Minnesota Press, 2008.

Schoonover, Karl, and Rosalind Galt. *Queer Cinema in the World*. Durham, NC: Duke University Press, 2016.

Schwartz, Vanessa R. *Jet Age Aesthetic: The Glamour of Media in Motion*. New Haven, CT: Yale University Press, 2020.

———. "On the Move: Seeing the World in Early Transport Films." In *City of Cinema: Paris 1850–1907*, ed. Leah Lehmbeck, Britt Salvesen, and Vanessa R. Schwartz, 136–53. Los Angeles: Los Angeles County Museum of Art, 2022.

———. *Spectacular Realities: Early Mass Culture in* Fin-de-Siècle *Paris*. Berkeley: University of California Press, 1998.

Schwartz, Vanessa R., and Jeannene M. Przyblyski. "Visual Culture's History: Twenty-First Century Interdisciplinarity and Its Nineteenth-Century Objects." In *The Nineteenth-Century Visual Culture Reader*, ed. Vanessa R. Schwartz and Jeannene M. Przyblyski, 3–14. New York: Routledge, 2004.

Serna, Laura Isabel. *Making Cinelandia: Americans Films and Mexican Film Culture Before the Golden Age*. Durham, NC: Duke University Press, 2014.

Shiel, Mark. *Hollywood Cinema and the Real Los Angeles*. London: Reaktion, 2012.

Singer, Ben. *Melodrama and Modernity: Early Sensational Cinema and Its Contexts*. New York: Columbia University Press, 2001.

Skvirsky, Salomé Aguilera. *The Process Genre: Cinema and the Aesthetic of Labor*. Durham, NC: Duke University Press, 2020.

Slugan, Mario, and Daniël Biltereyst, eds. *New Perspectives on Early Cinema History: Concepts, Approaches, Audiences*. London: Bloomsbury Academic, 2022.

Smith, Terry. *Making the Modern: Industry, Art, and Design in America*. Chicago: University of Chicago Press, 1993.

Somaini, Antonio. "Walter Benjamin's Media Theory: The Medium and the Apparat." *Grey Room* 62 (Winter 2016): 6–41.

Stamp, Shelley. *Lois Weber in Early Hollywood*. Oakland: University of California Press, 2015.

———. *Movie-Struck Girls: Women and Motion Picture Culture after the Nickelodeon*. Princeton, NJ: Princeton University Press, 2000.

Starosielski, Nicole. *Media Hot and Cold*. Elements. Durham, NC: Duke University Press, 2021.

Starosielski, Nicole, and Janet Walker, eds. *Sustainable Media: Critical Approaches to Media and Environment*. London: Routledge, 2016.

Steffen, Will, Wendy Broadgate, Lisa Deutsch, Owen Gaffney, and Cornelia Ludwig. "The Trajectory of the Anthropocene: The Great Acceleration." *Anthropocene Review* 2, no. 1 (2015): 81–98.

Steinhardt, Daniel. *Runaway Hollywood: Internationalizing Postwar Production and Location Shooting*. Oakland: University of California Press, 2019.

Stewart, Jacqueline Najuma. *Migrating to the Movies: Cinema and Black Urban Modernity*. Berkeley: University of California Press, 2005.

Streible, Dan. "66mm 8k Phantoms." *Orphan Film Symposium* (blog), February 29, 2020. https://wp.nyu.edu/orphanfilm/2020/02/29/haverstrawtunnel/.

Szeman, Imre, and Jennifer Wenzel. "What Do We Talk About When We Talk About Extractivism?" *Textual Practice* 35, no. 3 (2021): 505–23.

Thompson, Kristin. "The Lonedale Operator." In *The Griffith Project*, ed. Paolo Cherchi Usai, vol. 5, *Films Produced in 1911*, 18–22. London: British Film Institute, 2002.

Turner, Fred. "The Family of Man and the Politics of Attention in Cold War America." *Public Culture* 24, no. 1 (2012): 55–84.

Uhlin, Graig. "The Anthropocene's Nonindifferent Nature." *Journal of Cinema and Media Studies* 58, no. 2 (Winter 2019): 157–62.

Uricchio, William, and Roberta Pearson. *Reframing Culture*. Princeton, NJ: Princeton University Press, 1993.

Vaughan, Hunter. *Hollywood's Dirtiest Secret: The Hidden Environmental Costs of the Movies*. New York: Columbia University Press, 2019.

Vonderau, Patrick. "Introduction: On Advertising's Relation to Moving Pictures." In *Films That Sell: Moving Pictures and Advertising*, ed. Bo Florin, Nico de Klerk, and Patrick Vonderau, 1–18. London: BFI, 2016.

——. "Touring as a Cultural Technique: Visitor Films and Autostadt Wolfsburg." In *Films That Work: Industrial Film and the Productivity of Media*, ed. Vinzenz Hediger and Patrick Vonderau, 153–66. Amsterdam: Amsterdam University Press, 2009.

Waller, Gregory A. "Cornering *The Wheat Farmer* (1938)." In *Learning with the Lights Off: Educational Film in the United States*, ed. Devin Orgeron, Marsha Orgeron, and Dan Streible, 249–70. Oxford: Oxford University Press, 2012.

Wasson, Haidee. *Everyday Movies: Portable Film Projectors and the Transformation of American Culture*. Oakland: University of California Press, 2020.

Wasson, Haidee, and Charles R. Acland. "Introduction: Utility and Cinema." In *Useful Cinema*, ed. Charles R. Acland and Haidee Wasson, 1–14. Durham, NC: Duke University Press, 2011.

Weis, Elisabeth, and John Belton, eds. *Film Sound: Theory and Practice*. New York: Columbia University Press, 1985.

Wellbery, David. E. Foreword to *Discourse Networks, 1800/1900*, by Friedrich A. Kittler, vii–xxxiii. Trans. Michael Metteer. Stanford, CA: Stanford University Press, 1990.

Wenzel, Jennifer. *The Disposition of Nature: Environmental Crisis and World Literature*. New York: Fordham University Press, 2020.

Whissel, Kristen. *Picturing American Modernity: Traffic, Technology, and the Silent Cinema*. Durham, NC: Duke University Press, 2008.

White, Hayden. *The Content of the Form: Narrative Discourse and Historical Representation*. Baltimore, MD: Johns Hopkins University Press, 1987.

Wickberg, Adam, and Johan Gärdebo. "Editors' Introduction: What Are Environing Media?" In *Environing Media*, 1–12. London: Routledge, 2023.

Wilson, Sheena, Adam Carlson, and Imre Szeman, eds. *Petrocultures: Oil, Politics, Culture*. Montreal-Kingston: McGill-Queen's University Press, 2016.

Winthrop-Young, Geoffrey. "Implosion and Intoxication: Kittler, a German Classic, and Pink Floyd." *Theory, Culture, and Society* 23, no. 7–8 (2006): 75–91.

———. "Material World: Geoffrey-Winthrop Young Talks with Bernhard Siegert." *Artforum International* 53, no. 10 (Summer 2015): 324–33.

Winthrop-Young, Geoffrey, and Michael Wutz. "Translators' Introduction: Friedrich Kittler and Media Discourse Analysis." In *Gramophone, Film Typewriter*, by Friedrich A. Kittler, xi–xxxviii. Stanford, CA: Stanford University Press, 1999.

Wojcik, Pamela Robertson. *The Apartment Plot: Urban Living in American Culture and Popular Culture, 1945 to 1975*. Durham, NC: Duke University Press, 2010.

Wolfson, Susan J., and Marshall Brown, eds. "Reading for Form." *Modern Language Quarterly* 61, no. 1 (2000): 1–16.

Young, Paul. "Media on Display: A Telegraphic History of Early American Cinema." In *New Media 1740–1915*, ed. Lisa Gitelman and Geoffrey B. Pingree, 229–64. Cambridge, MA: MIT Press, 2003.

Yusoff, Kathryn. *A Billion Black Anthropocenes or None*. Minneapolis: University of Minnesota Press, 2018.

Zimmermann, Yvonne. "'What Hollywood Is to America, the Corporate Film Is to Switzerland': Remarks on Industrial Film as Utility Film." In *Films That Work: Industrial Film and the Productivity of Media*, ed. Vinzenz Hediger and Patrick Vonderau, 101–17. Amsterdam: Amsterdam University Press, 2009.

Zryd, Michael. "Experimental Film as Useless Cinema." In *Useful Cinema*, ed. Charles R. Acland and Haidee Wasson, 315–36. Durham, NC: Duke University Press, 2011.

INDEX

Figures and tables are indicated by *italicized* page numbers.

Accursed Share, The (Bataille) (1949), 118
Acland, Charles, 110–11, 112
actor objects, 30
aeronautics, 1–2
AIOC. *See* Anglo-Iranian Oil Company
Alice Guy tourne une photoscène sur le théâtre de pose des Buttes-Chaumont (Guy, 1905), 39–40
allegorical reading, 12, 13; in cinema studies, 169n44; of *Sunshine Molly*, 61, 67–68, 70
Allegories of Cinema (James), 13, 127, 143
Alpers, Svetlana, 6, 165n16
AMB. *See* American Mutoscope and Biograph
American Manifest Destiny, 134
American Mutoscope and Biograph (AMB), 43, 44, 45, *45*, 46, 47, *47*, 48, 55, 66, *126*, 180n5, 181n11
American Petroleum Institute: *Destination Earth* sponsored by, 108; films produced by, 107, 108

Anglo-Iranian Oil Company (AIOC), 152–53, 155, 156. *See also* British Petroleum
Angus, Siobhan, 179n34
Anthropocene, 31, 38, 141, 175n7, 194n49; Fay on, 105; *Tungsten: A Treasure of the Sierra Nevada* on, 106
apparatus theory, feminist criticisms of, 190n15
Araya (Benacerraf, 1959): Benacerraf directing, 27, 146, 147, *148*, 150, 151; salt-mine laborers in, 146–48, *148*, 149, *149*, 150–51
Araya Peninsula (Venezuela), 146, 148, *148*, 149, 151; closed economy in, 147, *149*; colonial history of, 150
Arbuckle, Fatty, 66
arc lamps: carbon in, 79–80, 81–85, *85*, 86; lighting from, 79–80, 81–83
Armitage, Frederick S., 43
Arsenjuk, Luka, 174n6

de Baecque, Antoine, 115
Baku oil fields, 43, *44*
Balshofer, Fred J., 44–45
Bao, Weihong, 22
Barthes, Roland, 8–9
Bataille, Georges, 118, 131
Baxandall, Michael, 6, 7, 165nn15–16
Beach, Rex, 71
Benacerraf, Margot, 27, 146, 147, *148*, 150, 151
Berger, John, 157–58
Bergman, Ingmar, 90, *91*
Bhopal pesticide factory breakdown (India), 87, 187n19
Biograph Bulletin, 53
Birth of a Nation, The (Griffith, 1915), 181n11
Bison/New York Motion Picture Company (NYMP), 44–45
Bitzer, G. W.: AMB industrial films directed by, 46; *Interior New York Subway* by, 43; *The Lonedale Operator* shot by, 53, 55–56; *Panorama exterior Westinghouse works* directed by, 46, *47*
Black Diamonds: The Collier's Daily Life (1904), 93
Black feminist avant-garde films, DeClue on, 146, 196n14
Black Magic (1949), *82*
Blacksmithing Scene (Dickson, 1893), 42
de Blois, Natalie, 88
Bluebook of Projection (Richardson), 83
Bogart, Humphrey: Fred Dobbs played by, 97, 99, 100, 101–2, *102*, 104; in *High Sierra*, 188n34

Bordwell, David, 117, 163n9; on Baxandall and Alpers, 165n16; *The Classical Hollywood Cinema* by, 23
Bosworth, *Sunshine Molly* produced by, 59, 61
Bozak, Nadia, 177n14
BP. *See* British Petroleum
"Brain Damage," 12
Braun, William T., *84*
Breen, Joseph, 100
Brinkema, Eugenie, 8, 16
British imperial domination, 42
British Petroleum (BP), 34, 35, 152, 154. *See also* Anglo-Iranian Oil Company
Bunshaft, Gordon, 88
Bureau of Mines, 107
Burma (Myanmar), 154, 155
Burnham, Daniel, 87
Burning of the Standard Oil Co's tanks, Bayonne, N.J. (1900), 44
Business Screen, 107, 109, *110*

Cabruja, Jose Ignacio, 147
Cahiers du cinéma: Godard in, 114; Moullet in, 114–15
Cahill, James Leo, 172n64, 194n49; on media, 22; on *Le Monde du silence*, 115; on worlding, 176n10
Caldwell, John, 18, 19
California (U.S.): Los Angeles, 1–2, 44, 59, 65; oil fields, 58–60, 62, *63*, 64, *64*, 65, 68, 69, 70, 71, 72, 73, 182n18; Pine Creek tungsten mine in, 90, 92, 93–94, *94*, 95, 104
California Oil Wells in Operation (1900), 44

Calypso, 34
Canjels, Rudmer, 136–37
capitalism: racial, 178n25; Traven's messages against, 100, 105; Western, 32, 34, 38, 42
carbon, 25, *82*; in arc lamps, 79–80, 81–85, *85*, 86; lighting shaped by, 77, *78*, 79–80, 83–84, *84*, 85, *85*, 86; *Moving Picture World* ads on, *78*; projectionists on, 84, 85–86; rods, 81–87, 88, 90, *91*
Cawston, Richard, 112, 120
chant du styrène, Le (Resnais, 1958), 166n21
Chaplin, Charlie, 1, 2, 30, 31, 59, 141, 161n1
Chaplin Revue, The (Chaplin, 1959), 1, 2
Charney, Leo, 41, 162n5
Chinatown (Polanski, 1974), 65
Chomón, Segundo de, 40
Christensen, Jerome, 18, 19
cinema. *See specific topics*
cinema and media studies, 4, 5, 6, 7, 9
cinema of attractions, 24, 28–31, 40, 48, 49, 51, 56, 57, 58, 62, 68, 70–71, 76, 170n47, 174n6; Gaudreault and Gunning on, 14–15; Méliès, Georges, and Chomón self-presentation through, 40
"Cinema of Attractions, The" (Gunning), 28–29
cinema of extractions. *See specific topics*
cinema of narrative integration, 49, 52, 56, 57
cinema of reparations, 145

cinema of resource integration, 15, 16, 24, 39, 48, 56, 58, 79; *The Lonedale Operator* depicting, 51–53; *Sunshine Molly* and, 59–62, *62*, *63*, 64, *64*, 65–67, *67*, 68–69, *69*, 70, *70*, 71; Universal City exemplifying, 57
cinema studies, 29; allegorical reading in, 169n44; on resource and environmental work, 177n14
cinematic perception, 124–25
City Hall to Harlem in 15 Seconds, via the Subway (Porter, 1904), 43
Clark, E. P., 65
Clark & Sherman Land Company, 65
Classical Hollywood Cinema, The (Bordwell, Staiger and Thompson), 23
climate crisis, 137, 141
coal mines, lighting of, 93
colonial cinema historians, 145
colonial films, 156, 193n47
colonial history, 141; of Araya Peninsula, 150; *Scenes of Extraction* on, 154
colonial labor, *Scenes of Extraction* on, 156
colonial space, Jaikumar on, 154–55
Comolli, Jean-Louis, 163n9
conceptual synchronicity, 21
Connor, J. D., 19, 171n61
Coolidge, William D., 89
counter-cinemas of extraction, 140, 146–48, *148*, 149, *149*, 150; cinema of reparations, 145; *Scenes of Extraction*, 151, 154, 157
Cousteau, Jacques-Yves, 34, 35

crosscutting, Griffith's formal strategy of, 54, 55
culture: *Shellarama* oil, 127, 128–29, *129*, *132*, 137, 152; of Trans-Iranian Railway, 152
Czech Republic, National Film Archive of, 71

Dallas (1978-1991), 184n37
Daney, Serge, 115–16
Dark Side of the Moon, 12
Day in the Life of the Coal Miner, A (1910), 93
DeClue, Jennifer, 146, 196n14
decolonization, 108, 178n25
De Forest Radio Company, G.E. tungsten filament patent lawsuit of, 89
De Grasse, Joseph, 25, 58–59, *75*, 77
Demolishing and Building up the Star Theatre (Armitage, 1901), 43
Demolition d'un mur (Lumière, 1896), 42, 43
Destination Earth: American Petroleum Institute sponsoring, 108; Urbano directing, 108, *109*
Dickson, W. K. L., 39, 42
Dickson Greeting (Dickson, 1891), 39
Dimendberg, Edward, 166n21
directors: Armitage, 43; Balshofer, 44–45; Benacerraf, 27, 146, 147, *148*, 150, 151; Bitzer, 46, *47*; Cawston, 112, 120; De Grasse, 25, 58–59, *75*, 77; Dickson, 39, 42; Griffith, 25, 45, 49, 51, *52*, 53–55, 180n10; John Huston, 26, 97, 100, 101, 102, *102*, 103, 104–5, 107; Michon, 43, *44*, 58; Resnais, 114; Smalley, *63*; Urbano, 108, *109*;

Vertov and Bergman, *91*; Weber, 25, 49, 58, 59, 60–61, 62, *63*, 64, 65, 68–69, 70
discourse network, 11–12
Doheny, Edward L., 73, 184n37
Don Carlos (Schiller), 168n36
Doniol-Valcroze, Jacques, 114

ecomedia studies, 21
Edison Manufacturing Company, 42, 44, 46, 56, 66, 175n8
electricity, carbon rods conducting, 83
elemental screen forms, 90, *91*, 92–94, *94*, 95–97
Elsaesser, Thomas, 5, 111, 189n7
Empire Marketing Board, 107
energy: hydrocarbon, 107–8; material transformation of, 128–29; Mukherjee on, 20; unseen, 125, *125*, 126, *126*, 127, 153
extraction. *See specific topics*
extractive industries, 7, 14, 48, 76, 140; counter-narratives about, 145; externalities of, 141–42; media relationship with, 106; ways of seeing and knowing influenced by, 158; worlding of, 108

Fairbanks, Douglas, 30, 31
"Family of Man, The" (photo exhibition), 133
Fay, Jennifer, 176n12; on film noir, 105; *Inhospitable World* by, 19–20
feminism: on apparatus theory, 190n15; Black feminist avant-garde films, 146, 196n14
feminist film historians, 145
Field, Allyson, 190n12

film analysts, 142
film industry, capital accumulation through, 38
Film Language (Metz), 173n73
film noir: projection of, 105–6; *The Treasure of the Sierra Madre* classified as, 105
films: colonial, 156, 193n47; early nonfiction, 41; experimental, 190n16; feature, 12–13, 15; neoformalist, 4; prestige, 118; transport, 45; western, 101, 104. *See also specific topics*
films, early oil, 44–45, *45*, 58–60, 62, *63*, *64*, *64*, 65. *See also* Shellarama
films, industrial, 4, 9, 12–14, 24, 49, 90; AMB, 46, 47, *47*, 48; Hediger on, 111; James on, 112; poetics of, 25, 26, 117, 128–29, *129*, 136; prosaic poetics of, 80, 113; about railroads, 30, 46; Skvirsky on, 187n24; Vonderau on, 111, 189n6, 192n27; Wolper Productions advertisement for, 109, *110*. *See also* films, useful; industrial cinema
films, useful, 80, 131; formal devices of, 145; uselessness of, 112, 113, 117–18, 139, 190n16, 191n17; Wasson and Acland on, 110–11. *See also* films, industrial
Films That Work (Hediger and Vonderau), 111
Fine Feathers (1912), 60, 61
First National Pictures, *Flowing Gold* released by, 58–59, 72–73
Flowing Gold (De Grasse, 1924): De Grasse directing, 25, 58–59, *75*, *77*; First National Pictures releasing, 58–59, 72–73; marketing for, 73–74, *74*, *75*, *75*, *77*; oil fields in, 71, 72

Ford Motor Company, 48
forgerons, Les (Lumière, 1895), 42
form, 18, 21–22, 108, 112, 117, 166n22; building mechanism of, 167n23; of contents, 22, 23, 24, 142–43, 144–45; elemental screen, 90, *91*, 92–94, *94*, 95–97; of expression, 22, 23, 24; James on, 138; of production, 143–45; salt-mine laborers' gestural, 147–48, *148*, *149*; in *The Wire*, 50
formal devices: in *Shellerama*, 119; of useful films, 145
formalism, 9, 19, 21, 158; Brinkema on, 8, 16; Metz on, 173n73
formal language, of films, 144
formal systems: in *The Lonedale Operator*, 52–53, 54–56, 76; of oil field, 66
formation, 9–10, 50
Forms (Levine), 9. *See* Levine, Caroline
Fort Lee, New Jersey, 180n10
France, 35; Montreuil-sous-bois in, 31–32, *33*; public relations in, 190n13
Friedberg, Anne, 122
"From Forest to Film," 37
Fuller, Samuel, 114–15

Galt, Rosalind, 16–17, 170n51
Gance, Abel, 28, 30
Gaudreault, André, 14–15, 30
Gaumont, 46, 66
General Electric (G.E.), 89, 185n5
geological survey work, *Scenes of Extraction* on, 154
George Westinghouse, 46
German chemical companies, 81
German media theory, 5, 21
gestural forms, of salt-mine laborers, 147–48, *148*, *149*

Getty Oil Company, 65
Giant (Stevens, 1956), 184n37
Godard, Jean-Luc: in *Cahiers du cinéma*, 114; on tracking shots, 114, 115, 137
Goethe, Johann Wolfgang von, 12
Gone with the Wind (Fleming, 1939), 177n14
Good Neighbor policy, of U.S., 100
Great Acceleration, 108, 113
greenhouse (Montreuil-sous-bois, France), 31–32, *33*
Greening the Media (Miller and Maxwell), 177n14
Grieveson, Lee, 7, 39, 42, 56, 107, 144, 191n17, 195n7; *Cinema and the Wealth of Nations* by, 38; on Hollywood reinvestment, 112–13; on media, 159
Griffith, D. W.: class injustice criticisms of, 181n11; *Lonedale Operator, The* directed by, 25, 49, 51, 52, 53–55; *Lonely Villa, The* directed by, 180n10; *A Rich Revenge* directed by, 45
"Guaranty Oil Company of Oregon," 184n43
Gumbrecht, Hans Ulrich, 10, 22, 173n72
Gunning, Tom, 51, 58, 122, 180n8; on cinema of attractions, 14–15; on early film history, 28–29; on Léger, 28, 30; on *The Lonedale Operator*, 53

Hallelujah Trail, The (Sturges, 1965), 134–35
Hallett, Hilary, 68
Handbook of Projection for Theater Managers and Projectionists (Richardson) (1922), *85*

Hansen, Mark, 124
Harding administration, Teapot Dome scandal of, 73
Hartman, Saidiya, 196n14
Haverstraw Tunnel, The (1897), 125, *126*, 127
Hawks Nest Tunnel Disaster, 187n19
Hediger, Vinzenz, 111, 117
High Sierra (Walsh, 1941), 188n34
Hiroshima mon amour (Resnais, 1959), 114
historicism, 8, 19
history, early film: Gunning on, 28–29; worlding and, 31–32, *33*, 34, *34*, 35, *35*, 36, *37*, 38–43
Hjelmslev, Louis, 22, 23–24, 173nn71–72, 180n8
Hollywood, 76, 144; distribution system of, 75; material crisis impacting, 80–81; narrative resolutions of, 102; oil in, 65–66, 70; reinvestment, 112–13; *Sunshine Molly* allegory about, 61, 67–68, 70; women in, 68
Horn, Eva, 173n67
How to Make Movies, 2, 161n1
human-built world, 38
Huston, John: *High Sierra* scripted by, 188n34; *The Treasure of the Sierra Madre* directed by, 26, 97, 100, 101, 102, *102*, 103, 104–5, 107
Huston, Walter, 99, 100, 101, 102
hydrocarbon energy, 107–8

ideological illusion, of *Shellerama*, 124
implosion reading method, of Kittler, 12
incandescent lights, 79
India, Bhopal, 87, 187n19
indigenous subjects: Native Americans, 135; *Scenes of Extraction* on, 152

industrial cinema, 76, 90, 107–8, 127;
    materiality of, 140; poetics of, 25, 26.
    See also films, industrial
infrastructural aesthetics, Schwartz and
    Larkin on, 128
Inhospitable World (Fay), 19–20
instrumentalization, 96
Interior New York Subway (Bitzer,
    1905), 43
Iran, 152, 155–56

Jaikumar, Priya, 7, 17, 195n7; on
    colonial films, 156; on colonial
    space, 154–55; on media, 159; on
    place-images, 18
James, David, 24; *Allegories of Cinema*
    by, 13, 127, 143; on form, 138; on
    industrial films, 112
Jameson, Fredric, 169n44
Jam Handy company, 109
Japanese Idyll, A (Weber, 1912), 60–61
Jet Age Aesthetic (Schwartz), 2
jet age aesthetics, Schwartz on,
    128, 141

Kapo (Pontecorvo, 1960), 115
Keaton, Buster, 20, 66, 73
Kiel, Charlie, 55
Kiewert, George, 81
Kittler, Friedrich: *Don Carlos*
    interpretation of, 168n36; implosion
    reading method of, 12; materialist
    approach of, 5, 10, 164n12; on media,
    11; Winthrop-Young on, 11, 12,
    167n29, 168nn38–39
knowing, ways of seeing relationship
    with, 157–58
Kodak, 35–36

Kornbluh, Anna, 167n23
Kracauer, Siegfried, 40–41
Kunzmann, W. C., 86–87

labor: colonial, 156; in *The Treasure
    of the Sierra Madre*, 100; Union
    Carbide valorizing, 99
laborers: salt-mine, 146–48, *148*, 149, *149*,
    150–51; unseen energy of, 153
Langlois, Henri, 31–32
Larkin, Brian, 128
Lee, Harper, 17
Léger, Fernand, 28, 30, 40
LeMenager, Stephanie, 184n37
Levine, Caroline, 166n22; *Forms* by,
    9; neoformalist literary criticism
    of, 23, 50, 53, 54, 166n22, 167n23,
    180n8
lighting: from arc lamp, 79–80, 81–83;
    carbon shaping, 77, *78*, 79–80, 83–84,
    84, 85, *85*, 86; of coal mines, 93; film
    noir projection of, 105–6; tungsten
    shaping, 77, 79
Lonedale Operator, The (1911): Bitzer
    shooting, 53, 55–56; cinema of
    resource integration shown in,
    51–53; formal systems in, 52–53,
    54–56, 76; Griffith directing, 25, 49,
    51, *52*, 53–55; telegraphs in, 52, *52*,
    53, 55
Lonely Villa, The (Griffith, 1909),
    180n10
Los Angeles (California), 1–2; early oil
    films in, 44, 59; real estate, 65; Salt
    Lake Oil Field, 64, *64*, 65, 68, 69, 70
Lumière, Auguste: Lumière company
    of, 41–42, 43, 45, 46, 56; worlding of,
    39–42, 43

Lumière, Louis: Lumière company of, 41–42, 43, 45, 46, 56; *La sortie de l'usine Lumière à Lyon* by, 40–41, 42, 47–48; worlding of, 39–42, 43

Lumière company, 41–42, 43, 45, 46, 56; *La sortie de l'usine Lumière à Lyon* released by, 40–41, 42, 47–48; *Puits de pétrole à Bakou* released by, 43, *44*, 58

Lupino, Ida, 188n34

Lure of the Image, The (Morgan), 115–16

Majumdar, Rochona, 18

Malle, Louis, 34

Man with a Movie Camera (Vertov, 1929), *91*

match-cut universalism, in *Shellerama*, 132, *133*, *134*

material crisis, 80–81, 85

materialism, Marxist historical, 169n44

materialist method, historical, 143

materialist theory, Comolli on, 163n9

Materialität der kommunikation (Materialities of Communication) (Gumbrecht and Pfeiffer), 10

materiality, 3; cinema and media studies approach of, 4, 5, 6, 7; of industrial cinema, 140; Kittler on, 5, 10, 164n12; Rhodes on, 17

Maxwell, Richard, 177n14

Meador, Daryl, 15

media, 3, 4, 31, 86–89; Cahill, Bao, and Jacobson on, 22; extractive industries' relationship with, 106; German media theory, 21; industry studies, 143; Jaikumar and Grieveson on, 159; Kittler on, 11; material basis of, 106n11; Peters on, 80; scholarship, 18

media-extraction relations, 25–26

media studies: cinema and, 4, 5, 6, 7, 9; Horn on, 173n67

Méliès, Georges, 32, 33, 35, 40

Méliès, Jean-Louis Stanislas, 31–32

Menne, Jeff, 18–19

methodology, 142

Metz, Christian, 22, 173n71, 173n73, 180n8

Mexico: *The Treasure of the Sierra Madre* shot in, 100–101, 105, 188n30; U.S. mine operations in, 97, 100, 101

Meyerhold, Vsevolod, 174n6

Michon, Alexandre, 43, *44*, 58; *Puits de pétrole à Bakou* by, 43, *44*, 58

military, U.S., 191n17

Miller, Toby, 177n14

mines, 143; coal, 93; in Mexico, 97, 100, 101; Pine Creek tungsten, 90, 92, 93–94, *94*, 95, 104; salt, 146–48, *148*, 149, *149*, 150–51

Mitchell and Kenyon, *Black Diamonds* produced by, 93

modernity, Schwartz and Charney on, 41, 162n5

Monde du silence, Le (Cousteau and Malle, 1956), 115

Moneyball (Miller, 2011), 171n61

monstration, 30

Montreuil-sous-bois (Paris, France), 31–32, *33*

Morgan, Daniel, 115–16

Motion Picture News, 81, 86

Motography (1911), *84*

Moullet, Luc, 114–15

Moving Picture World, 44–45, 74–75; carbon ads in, *78*; on *Sunshine Molly*, 61–62, *62*

Mukherjee, Debashree, 20
Mulligan, Robert, 17
Mumford, Lewis, 41, 48
Musser, Charles, 23–24, 175n8, 177n18
Myanmar (Burma), 154, 155

Nair, Kartik, 170n54
Naremore, James, 101, 104
National Carbon Company (NCC), 86–87
National Film Archive, of Czech Republic, 71
National Film Preservation Foundation, 71
Native Americans, racism against, 135
NCC. *See* National Carbon Company
neoformalist literary criticism, 9, 50, 54, 142
New Film History, 23, 26, 28, 111, 175n8, 189n7
New Jersey, Fort Lee, 180n10
Nisoli, Giuseppe, 146, 147
Nye, David, 41, 42, 48, 185n5
NYMP. *See* Bison/New York Motion Picture Company

object-oriented ontology, 30
oil, 1–2, 36, 190n13; BP, 34, 35, 152, 154; culture, 127, 128–29, *129*, *132*, 137, 152; *Destination Earth* on, 108, *109*; Doheny's propaganda about, 184n37; in Hollywood, 65–66, 70; in Iran, 152; *Shellarama* about, 114, 116, 119, *119*, 120–22, 127, 128–29, *129*, *132*, 137, 152; Shell Oil, 26, 35, 112, 136–37, 138; well burnings, 58, 72, *72*, 183n32, 183n34
oil fields: Baku, 43, *44*; California, 58–60, 62, *63*, 64, *64*, 65, 68, 69, 70, 71, 72, 73, 182n18; in *Flowing Gold*, 71, 72; formal systems of, 66; in *Sunshine Molly*, 58, 59–60, 62, *63*, 64, *64*, 65, 182n18
oil industry, 59, 118; distribution system of, 75–76; forms of, 142–43; *Sunshine Molly* about, 61, 66–67, *67*, 69, *69*, 70, *70*, 71

Painlevé, Jean, 172n64
Panama Canal, 45–46
Panorama exterior Westinghouse works (Bitzer, 1904), 46, *47*
Paramount, forests bought by, 36
Pathé, 46, 66
pays des mines, Au (Zecca, 1905), 93
pêche aux poissons rouges, La (Lumière, 1895), 39
Persian Gulf, 34
Persona (Bergman, 1966), *91*
Peters, John Durham, 10–11, 21, 80
Pfeiffer, Karl Ludwig, 10
phantom rides: in *The Haverstraw Tunnel*, 125, *126*, 127; in *Shellarama*, 127, *134*, 135; in *The Trans-Persian Railway*, 153; unseen energy of, 125, *125*, 126, *126*, 127
Photoplay, 37, 66
Picture-Play Magazine, *Flowing Gold* marketed in, *74*
Pine Creek tungsten mine (California, U.S.), 90, 92, 93–94, *94*, 95, 104
Pink Floyd, 12
place-images, 18
poetics, of industrial films, 25, 26, 117, 128–29, *129*, 136
Political Unconscious, The (Jameson), 169n44

Pontecorvo, Gillo, 115
Porter, Edwin S.: *City Hall to Harlem in 15 Seconds, via the Subway* by, 43; Musser on, 175n8
Pretty (Galt), 170n51
"Problems of the Operating Room" (Braun), *84*
producers: American Petroleum Institute, 107, 108; Bosworth, 59, 61; Bureau of Mines and American Petroleum Institute, 107; Mitchell and Kenyon, 93; Union Carbide, 25–26, 90, 92, 95, 96, 99, 104, 108, 109; Warner Brothers, 97, 100, 101, 105
production, forms of, 143–45
production studies, 4, 10, 19, 23, 143
projection, 105–6. *See also* carbon
projectionists, on carbons, 84, 85–86
projectors, Wasson on, 109–10
property relations: Fort Lee, 180n10; race-driven, 17
proprioception, Richmond on, 122, 124
prosaic poetics, of industrial films, 80, 113
Przyblyski, Jeannene, 8, 14
public relations: in France, 190n13; of Shell Oil, 138
Puits de pétrole à Bakou (Oil Wells of Baku) (Michon, 1897–1899), 43, *44*, 58
Push Button Go, of *Shellarama* alternate release title of, 130–31, *131*

Queer Cinema in the World (Galt and Schoonover), 17

racial capitalism, 178n25
racial hierarchies, *Scenes of Extraction* analyzing, 154, 156
racism, against Native Americans, 135
railroads, 125; industrial films about, 30, 46; laborers for, 153; in *The Lonedale Operator*, 54; *The Trans-Persian Railway* on, 152–53, *153*, 155
rare earths, 79, 82, 186n11
Redrobe, Karen, 5–6, 192n35
repas de bébé, Le (Lumière, 1895), 39
repetition, in *Shellarama*, 131–32, *132*
Resnais, Alain, 114
Rex Theatre, 75, *75*
Rhodes, John David: on Fort Lee property relations, 180n10; *Spectacle of Property* by, 17
Richardson, F. H., 86; *Bluebook of Projection* by, 83; *Handbook of Projection for Theater Managers and Projectionists* by, *85*
Richmond, Scott, 122, 124
Rich Revenge, A (Griffith, 1910), 45
Rivalry in the Oil Fields (Balshofer, 1910), 44–45
Rivette, Jacques, 115
Rockefeller, John, 36
Rohmer, Eric, 114
Rose, Polly, 183n27
Ross, Steve, 181n11
roue, La (Gance, 1923), 28, 30, 40

Salt Lake Oil Field (Los Angeles, California), 64, *64*, 65, 68, 69, 70
salt-mine laborers, 146–48, *148*, 149, *149*, 150–51
San Francisco Silent Film Festival, 71
Saussure, Ferdinand de, 22
Scenes of Extraction (Sohrabi, 2023), *153*, 155, *155*; on BP, 152, 154; on colonial labor, 156; counter-cinemas

of extraction, 151, 154, 157; on indigenous subjects, 152; by Sohrabi, 27, 146, 152, 153, 156, 157; *The Trans-Persian Railway* used in, 152–53

Schiller, Friedrich, 168n36

Schoonover, Karl, 17

Schwartz, Vanessa, 2, 8, 14; on decolonization, 178n25; on jet age aesthetics, 128, 141; on modernity, 41, 162n5; on transport films, 45

Searchers, The (Ford, 1956), 69

seeing, ways of, 159; extractive industries influencing, 158; knowing relationship with, 157–58

Seghers, Pierre, 146

Selig Polyscope, *Shooting an Oil Well* by, 44

sexual violence, in workplace, 60

Shell Aramare, 129–30, 137

Shellarama (Cawston, 1965): Cawston directing, 112, 120; colonial film, 192; consumption in, 122; formal devices in, 119; human stories in, 150; ideological illusion in, 124; match-cut universalism in, 132, *133*, *134*; about oil, 114, 116, 119, *119*, 120–22, 127, 128–29, *129*, *132*, 137, 152; opening scene of, 119, *119*, 120; phantom rides in, 127, *134*, 135; *Push Button Go* alternate release title of, 130–31, *131*; repetition in, 131–32, *132*; Shell Oil sponsoring, 26, 112, 136–37; in Super Technirama, 118, 137; tracking shots in, 114, 116, 123, 127, 129, 130, 132, 135, *136*; unseen energy in, 127; worlding of, 139

Shell Oil, 35; public relations of, 138; *Shellarama* sponsored by, 26, 112, 136–37

Sherman, Moses Hazeltine, 65

Shoes (Weber, 1916), 60

Shooting an Oil Well, 44

Sierra Nevada mountains, 94, 95, 96, 97, *98*

signifier-signified model, 22

silver, 36

Singin' in the Rain (Kelly and Donen, 1952), 177n14

Skidmore, Owings, and Merrill, 88

Skvirsky, Salomé Aguilera, 166n21, 187n24

Smalley, Phillips, *63*

social history, of art, 6

Sohrabi, Sanaz, 27, 146, 152, 153, 156, 157

sortie de l'usine Lumière à Lyon, La (1895), 40–41, 42, 47–48

Spectacle of Property (Rhodes), 17

Speer Carbon Company, 81, *82*

Staiger, Janet, 23, 163n9

Station 307 (Malle, 1955), 34, *34*

Steichen, Edward, 133

studio-built world, 38

Sturges, John, 134

substance, of content and expression, 22, 23, 24

Suez Canal, 45

Sunshine Molly (Weber, 1915), 76; Bosworth producing, 59, 61; cinema of resource integration and, 59–62, 62, *63*, 64, *64*, 65–67, *67*, 68–69, *69*, 70, 70, 71; derricks in, *67*; Hollywood allegory of, 61, 67–68, 70; Molly in, 60, 64, 67, 68–69; oil fields in, 58, 59–60, 62, *63*, 64, *64*, 65, 182n18; about oil industry, 61, 66–67, *67*, 69, 69, 70, 70, 71; opening panorama of, 62, *63*, 64; Weber directing, 25, 49, 58, 59, 60–61, 62, *63*, 64, 65, 68–69, 70

Super-Mazda Lamps, *35*
Super Technirama, 114, 118, 125, 137
Survey of Anglo-Iranian Oil Company Operations in Iran (1938), 154
Sutherland, John, 108
Sweet, Blanche, 51, 52

Teapot Dome scandal, of Harding administration, 73
technology firms, 181n15
telegraph: in *The Lonedale Operator*, 52, *52*, 53, 55; Young on, 180n9
theater fires, 83, 105–6, 188n38
This Is Cinerama! (1952), 121, 125
Thompson, Kristin, 23, 51, 163n9
Todd, Mike, 121
To Kill a Mockingbird (Lee), 17
Total, 35
tracking shots, 24, 144; Godard on, 114, 115, 137; morality of, 114–16, 138; Morgan on, 115–16; of Pontecorvo, 115; in *Shellarama*, 114, 116, 123, 127, 129, 130, 132, 135, *136*; in *Scenes of Extraction*, 153
train, in *La roue*, 30
Trans-Iranian Railway, 152
Trans-Persian Railway, The (1930), *153*; by Anglo-Iranian Oil Company, 152–53, 155; phantom rides in, 153
Traven, B., 100, 105
Treasure of the Sierra Madre, The (Huston, 1948), *103*; Bill Curtin in, 99, 101, 102; Fred Dobbs in, 97, 99, 100, 101–2, *102*, 104; genre of, 101, 104–5; Howard in, 99, 100, 101, 102; John Huston directing, 26, 97, 100, 101, 102, *102*, 103, 104–5, 107; in Mexico, 100–101, 105, 188n30;

Tungsten: A Treasure of the Sierra Nevada compared to, 99–100, 103–4; Warner Brothers producing, 97, 100, 101, 105; western film classification of, 101, 104
Tully, Richard Walton, 72
tungsten, 25, 80; Coolidge's filament from, 89; drills made from, 93–94, *94*; lighting shaped by, 77, 79; Pine Creek mine of, 90, 92, 93–94, *94*, 95, 104; from Union Carbide, 88, 90
Tungsten: A Treasure of the Sierra Nevada (1960s): on Anthropocene, 106; *High Sierra* counterpart to, 188n34; human stories in, 150; Pine Creek tungsten mine setting of, 90, 92, 93–94, *94*, 95, 104; Sierra Nevada mountains in, 94, 95, 96, 97, *98*; *The Treasure of the Sierra Madre* compared to, 99–100, 103–4; Union Carbide producing, 25–26, 90, 92, 95, 96, 99, 104, 108, 109; worlding of, 139
Turner, Fred, 133

Union Carbide, 80; Bhopal pesticide factory breakdown of, 87, 187n19; headquarters of, 87–88; *Tungsten: A Treasure of the Sierra Nevada* produced by, 25–26, 90, 92, 95, 96, 99, 104, 108, 109; tungsten from, 88, 90
Union Oil of California, 65
United Kingdom, 190n13
United States (U.S.): military, 191n17; mine operations of, 97, 100, 101. *See also* California
United Studios, 73

Universal City, cinema of resource integration exemplified by, 57
unseen energy: of phantom rides, 125, *125*, 126, *126*, 127; of railroad laborers, 153; in *Shellarama*, 127
Urban, Charles, 93
Urbano, Carl, 108, *109*
U.S. *See* United States
uselessness, of useful films, 112, 113, 117–18, 139, 190n16, 191n17
U.S. Vanadium Company, 88

Variety, 65–66
Vaughan, Hunter, 177n14
Venezuela, Araya Peninsula, 146–48, *148*, 149, *149*, 150, 151
vertical resource integration, 71–72, 72, 73–74, *74*, 75, *75*, 76
Vertov, Dziga, 90, *91*
vibrant materialism, 30
visual objectivity, 154
Vonderau, Patrick, 111, 117, 189n6, 192n27

Walsh, Raoul, 188n34
"Wanderer's Nightsong" (Wandrers Nachtlied) (Goethe), 12
Warner Brothers, 73, 97, 100, 101, 105
Wasson, Haidee, 112, 191n17; persuasive techniques described by, 190n11; on projectors, 109–10; on useful film, 110–11
weather comedy, 20
Weber, Lois: *Fine Feathers* directed by, 60, 61; *A Japanese Idyll* directed by, 60–61; Molly played by, 60, 64, 67, 68–69; *Sunshine Molly* directed by,

25, 49, 58, 59, 60–61, 62, *63*, 64, 65, 68–69, 70
Wellbery, David, 11
Wenzel, Jennifer, 167n23
western film, *The Treasure of the Sierra Madre* classified as, 101, 104
Westinghouse Works, AMB industrial film series on, 46, 47, *47*, 48
whiskey, in *The Hallelujah Trail*, 134–35
White, Hayden, 13, 166n22
Who Framed Roger Rabbit? (Zemeckis, 1988), 65
Winthrop-Young, Geoffrey, 11, 12, 167n29, 168nn38–39
Wire, The, 50
Wolper Productions, industrial film advertisement for, 109, *110*
women, in Hollywood, 68
worlding, 140, 144–45; Berger on, 157; Cahill on, 176n10; early film history and, 31–32, *33*, 34, *34*, 35, *35*, 36, *37*, 38–43; of early oil films, 59; of extractive industries, 108; of Lumière, Auguste, and Lumière, Louis, 39–42, 43; of *Shellarama* and *Tungsten: A Treasure of the Sierra Nevada*, 139
World War I, 85, 86
World War II, 107, 193n47
Wutz, Michael, 11, 167n29

Young, Paul, 180n9

Zecca, Ferdinand, 93
Zryd, Mike, 190n16

GPSR Authorized Representative: Easy Access System Europe, Mustamäe tee 50, 10621 Tallinn, Estonia, gpsr.requests@easproject.com

www.ingramcontent.com/pod-product-compliance
Lightning Source LLC
Chambersburg PA
CBHW032336300426
44109CB00041B/1064